D0065663

CAMBRIDGE STUDIES IN PHILOSOPHY

Rational decision and causality

CAMBRIDGE STUDIES IN PHILOSOPHY

General editor D. H. MELLOR

Advisory editors J. E. J. ALTHAM, SIMON BLACKBURN,
DANIEL DENNETT, MARTIN HOLLIS, FRANK JACKSON,
JONATHAN LEAR, T. J. SMILEY, BARRY STROUD

Rational decision and causality

Ellery Eells

Assistant Professor of Philosophy
University of Wisconsin at Madison

Cambridge University Press

CAMBRIDGE

LONDON NEW YORK NEW ROCHELLE

MELBOURNE SYDNEY

Published by the Press Syndicate of the University of Cambridge
The Pitt Building, Trumpington Street, Cambridge CB2 1RP
32 East 57th Street, New York, NY 10022, USA
296 Beaconsfield Parade, Middle Park, Melbourne 3206, Australia

First published 1982

Printed in Great Britain by
J. W. Arrowsmith Ltd., Bristol

Library of Congress catalogue card number: 81-18001

British Library cataloguing in publication data
Eells, Ellery
Rational decision and causality. –
(Cambridge studies in philosophy)
1. Statistical decision   2. Philosophy
I. Title
519.5'42'01   QA279.4

ISBN 0-521-24213-4

To my parents

Contents

Preface

This book deals mainly with the decision-theoretic paradox known as 'Newcomb's paradox', with related examples of decision problems and with the current philosophical controversy surrounding the principle of maximizing expected utility, "causal decision theory" and such decision problems. I have taken care, in two ways, to make the book self-contained and generally accessible. First, two appendixes review the elementary logic and probability theory occasionally used; and second, the first three chapters present, somewhat in the way of a review, the more general "Bayesian" philosophical ideas and theories in relation to which the issues dealt with in the bulk of the book are philosophically significant. Also, the bibliography, though incomplete in relation to all the published work in the area, should be helpful to those interested in further pursuing the questions dealt with here.

I first became interested in these issues as a graduate student at the University of California at Berkeley. I am especially grateful to Charles Chihara, who supervised my Ph.D. dissertation, for all of his help and advice in all aspects and stages of the development of that project, out of which this book has arisen, and for his continued interest and advice. I have also benefited from discussions with Ernest Adams. Discussions with Brian Skyrms inspired many and corrected many of my views on his theory of K-expectation. I have had the benefit of discussing the ideas of Chapter 6 at talks given at the University of Chicago, North Carolina State University at Raleigh, the University of Wisconsin at Milwaukee, the University of Illinois at Chicago Circle, State University of New York at Buffalo and the University of Wisconsin at Madison. Richard Jeffrey and David Lewis have offered helpful comments and supplied me with useful pre-publication manuscripts dealing with the relevant issues. I am also indebted to N. A. Blue, James H. Fetzer, Morry Lipson and especially D. H. Mellor, editor of the series, for many helpful and strategic suggestions in connection with the introductory chapters. In addition, I am pleased to acknowledge the Department of Philosophy and Religion at North Carolina State University at Raleigh, where I visited in the 1980–81 academic year, for secretarial service that extended well into the summer of 1981; Ann P. Rives' excellent and heroic typing made that time infinitely less hectic for me than it would otherwise have been. Finally, for other kinds of help, I thank my parents and Joanne.

Introduction

Imagine yourself in the following situation. There are two boxes before you: one transparent and one opaque. You can see that there is $1,000 in the transparent box, and you know that there is either $1,000,000 or nothing in the opaque box. You must choose between the following two acts: take the contents only of the opaque box or take the contents of both boxes. Furthermore, there is a being in whose predictive powers you have enormous confidence, and you know that he has already determined the contents of the opaque box according to the following rules: If he predicted that you would take the contents only of the opaque box, he put the $1,000,000 in the opaque box, and if he predicted that you would take the contents of both boxes, he put nothing in the opaque box. What would you do?

A paradox, known as 'Newcomb's paradox', seems to arise. Robert Nozick (1969) discusses the paradox in detail. It appears that two principles of decision – both of which are well-respected and intuitively attractive – prescribe different courses of action in the decision situation described above. Consider this version of the *principle of dominance*: If (i) you must perform either act A or act B, (ii) which act you perform does not causally affect which of two states of affairs, S and $-S$, obtains, and (iii) no matter which of S and $-S$ obtains, you are better off doing A than doing B, then do A. In the decision situation described above, (i) you must either take the contents only of the opaque box or take the contents of both boxes, (ii) which act you perform does not affect whether or not the $1,000,000 is in the opaque box, and (iii) whether the $1,000,000 is in the opaque box or not, you get $1,000 more by taking the contents of both boxes than you get by taking the contents only of the opaque box. So the principle of dominance recommends taking the contents of both boxes.

Now consider this rough statement of the *principle of maximizing conditional expected utility* (hereafter, *PMCEU*): perform the act that

1

makes the most desirable outcomes the most probable. In the decision situation described above, if you take the contents only of the opaque box, then, since the predictor is so accurate, the predictor probably predicted you would do that, in which case he would have put the $1,000,000 in the opaque box and you would walk away with $1,000,000. If you take the contents of both boxes, then, since the predictor is so accurate, the predictor probably predicted you would do *that*, in which case he would have left the opaque box empty and you would walk away with only $1,000. *PMCEU* seems to prescribe taking only the contents of the opaque box.

Several philosophers who believe, as I do, that the correct act is to take the contents of both boxes believe, as I do not, that *PMCEU* should be given up. Recently a number of other *prima facie* counter-examples to *PMCEU*, all inspired by Newcomb's paradox, have been constructed. These involve decision situations that are less fantastic than that of Newcomb's paradox and in which almost everyone would agree that the correct act is the counterpart of the two-box act in Newcomb's paradox. Central to the alleged counter-examples is the observation that *PMCEU* seems not to be sensitive to causal beliefs of a certain kind that an agent might have, which suggests that some causal notions need to be introduced into the calculation of expected utility. Thus, various "causal decision theories" have recently emerged as rivals to *PMCEU*.

The first three chapters of this book provide an exposition of the more general philosophical ideas and theories in terms of which the controversy surrounding Newcomb's paradox, *PMCEU* and causal decision theory is philosophically significant. Chapter 1 is an introduction, from the decision-theoretic point of view, to the philosophical view known as 'Bayesianism'. In Chapter 2, the philosophical significance and empirical adequacy of Bayesian decision theory are explored. And Chapter 3 presents, in more detail, several versions of traditional ('noncausal") Bayesian decision theory, of which *PMCEU* is one.

In Chapter 4, I present a number of *prima facie* counterexamples to *PMCEU* of the kind inspired by Newcomb's paradox, and I try to clarify their causal structure. Chapter 5 deals with some of the new causal decision theories. In it, I argue that a successful *PMCEU* approach to the problem would have important advantages over the causal approach. And in Chapters 6 and 7, I argue that *PMCEU* really gives the correct prescriptions in the decision situations of the alleged counterexamples and in general – indeed, the same prescriptions given by the principle of dominance and by causal decision theory. Chapter 8 deals with Newcomb's paradox itself in detail.

1

Bayesianism

Bayesianism is usually characterized as the philosophical view that, for many philosophically important purposes, probability can usefully be interpreted subjectively, as an individual's "rational degree of belief," and that the rational way to assimilate new information into one's structure of beliefs is by a process called 'conditionalization'. The subjective interpretation of probability is connected, however, in very important ways with a mathematically precise and intuitively plausible theory of rational decision, called the 'subjective expected utility maximization theory'. Because of this connection, and the nature of it, Bayesianism can alternatively be characterized as the view that (i) rational decision and rational preference go by subjective expected utility, (ii) subjective probabilities (and numerical subjective utilities) are more or less theoretical entities that "lie behind," explain and are given partial empirical interpretation by, an individual's choices and preferences and (iii) learning goes by conditionalization. In this chapter and the next two, I will describe these three aspects of Bayesianism, discuss their plausibility and indicate various ways in which they are philosophically significant. The subsequent chapters will deal with a formidable challenge to this potentially very powerful philosophical theory.

SUBJECTIVE EXPECTED UTILITY

Deliberation is the process of *envisaging* the possible consequences of pursuing various possible courses of action and *evaluating* the merits of the possible courses of action in terms of their possible consequences. Roughly, the Bayesian model says that a course of action has merit to the extent that it makes good consequences probable and that a rational person pursues a course of action that makes the best consequences the most probable, where the goodnesses and probabilities of the consequences are the agent's subjective assessments thereof: how true, reasonable or otherwise

4

objectively or morally sound these assessments are is regarded as a separate question.

This last point is quite important; it indicates an essential feature of Bayesianism and Bayesian decision theory which is worth fully noting at the outset. It is implicit in the theory that whether or not a given course of action in a given decision making situation is rational is not an absolute kind of thing: a course of action is rational only relative to a possessed body of information (beliefs and desires) in terms of which the merits of the available courses of action can be rationally evaluated. Properly conceived, therefore, decision making involves two processes: (i) obtaining a body of relevant information (the process of information-acquisition) and (ii) evaluating the available courses of action in terms of the information at hand (the process of deliberation, or of information-use). We may say that an action is *rational* to the extent to which process (ii) is successfully carried out. And we may say that an action is *prudential* (or rational *and* well-informed) to the extent to which *both* processes are successfully carried out and, therefore, to the extent to which the action is truly, objectively in the agent's best interest to perform. Bayesian decision theory is primarily concerned with part (ii) of the decision making process. (Since the activity of information-gathering itself involves decisions, however, it is not surprising that the theory has also been applied (e.g., by Adams & Rosenkrantz 1980) to part (i) of the decision making process.) It is a theory about how one's actions, preferences, values and beliefs must be related *to each other* – not how they should be related to the objective world – for them to be rationally so related. Thus, Bayesian decision theory is as applicable to the deliberation of the ignorant and inexperienced as it is to that of the knowledgeable expert; and it is as applicable to the deliberation of a monster as it is to that of a saint.

Before considering a precise general statement of the theory, consider this concrete example, adapted from Richard Jeffrey's *The Logic of Decision* (1965b). You are to be the dinner guest of some acquaintances tonight, and you are to provide the wine. You remember that they plan to serve either chicken or beef, but you have forgotten which, although you know that they typically serve chicken. You have a bottle of white and a bottle of red, no telephone and can bring only one bottle, as you are going by bicycle. Associated with this decision situation are three matrices: the *outcome* (or *consequence*) *matrix*, the *desirability matrix* and the *probability matrix*. The consequence matrix for this decision problem may be:

	Chicken	Beef
White	⌈White wine with chicken	White wine with beef⌉
Red	⌊Red wine with chicken	Red wine with beef ⌋.

It indicates the possible outcomes, or consequences, of each possible course of action. The two row-headings indicate the available *acts*, the column-headings the possible *states* and the entries the *outcomes* that result from performing a given act under a given state. The desirability matrix, plausibly

	Chicken	Beef
White	⌈10	−10⌉
Red	⌊ 0	10⌋,

indicates the numerical *desirabilities*, or *utilities*, that correspond to the entries in the outcome matrix. These desirabilities are subjective in the sense that they represent the agent's assessments of the desirabilities of the outcomes. Finally, the probability matrix, say

	Chicken	Beef
White	⌈0.6	0.4 ⌉
Red	⌊0.6	0.4 ⌋,

indicates subjective assessments of the probabilities of the outcomes, assuming that the act which the entry-row represents is performed. Note that the entries in each row add to 1.

The subjective expected utility of the acts is calculated as follows. First, multiply corresponding entries of the desirability and probability matrices. The result in this case, dropping the column headings, is:

White	⌈6	−4 ⌉
Red	⌊0	4 ⌋.

6

Then add the entries in each row to get:

White: 2

Red: 4.

Thus, the subjective expected utility of bringing the bottle of white is 2; that of bringing the red is 4. In symbols, $SEU(\text{White}) = 2$ and $SEU(\text{Red}) = 4$. The subjective expected utility maximization theory (SEU theory, for short) recommends bringing the red wine.

Note that in the above example, the two rows in the probability matrix are identical. This is only a special case. For suppose that even though your hosts prefer chicken and typically serve chicken to guests, they may be influenced by (among other things) your choice of wine. In this case, the probability matrix might be:

	Chicken	Beef
White	$\begin{bmatrix} 0.9 \end{bmatrix}$	0.1
Red	0.3	0.7

Relative to this probability matrix and the old desirability matrix, $SEU(\text{White}) = 8$ and $SEU(\text{Red}) = 7$ so that SEU theory recommends bringing the white wine. In this case, because of your hosts' cooperation, the SEUs of both acts are higher than those in the previous case.

Thus, to apply SEU theory to a decision problem, the decision situation must first be represented in terms of outcome, desirability and probability matrices. The possible outcomes of an act A can be denoted by 'O_{Ai}'; the desirability of O_{Ai} can be denoted by 'd_{Ai}'; and the probability of getting the outcome O_{Ai} when act A is performed can be denoted by 'p_{Ai}'. Note that the outcomes have act-subscripts. This is reasonable because the ultimate carriers of desirability are not just the things you get, independently of the act: they involve also *how* you get them (Adams & Rosenkrantz 1980). This was suppressed in the example given above; but, if the example were worked out in more detail, one might wish to distinguish between the outcome of bringing white wine and drinking it with chicken and the outcome of bringing red wine and drinking (perhaps your hosts') white wine with chicken. Of course, the ultimate carriers of desirability could alternatively be symbolized by expressions like 'O_i & A', which symbolizes the "act-specific" outcome of doing A and getting the non-act-specific O_i.

7

An alternative way of denoting probabilities and desirabilities is by using function, or assignment, symbols: say 'P' and 'D', respectively. Thus, instead of writing 'd_{Ai}', we could write '$D(O_{Ai})$' (or '$D(O_i \& A)$'). As to the p_{Ai}s, various suggestions have been made as to what precisely they should be the probabilities of. On one suggestion, p_{Ai} is the probability of O_{Ai} conditional on A, i.e., $P(O_{Ai}|A) = P(O_{Ai} \& A)/P(A)$ (or the probability of O_i conditional on A, $P(O_i|A)$); on another, it is the unconditional probability of the *state* under which performing A results in the outcome O_{Ai} (or O_i); and on a third, it is the probability of the counterfactual conditional 'If A were performed, then O_{Ai} (or O_i) would result'. In Chapters 3 and 5, we will look at a number of suggestions. Here, I just want to present the basic idea which is common to all the ways in which Bayesian decision theory has been developed.

Given the entries of the desirability and probability matrices, we can calculate the subjective expected utility of an act A as follows:

$$SEU(A) = \sum_i p_{Ai} d_{Ai}.$$

The *SEU* theory asserts that rational preference goes by *SEU* – i.e., that an act A is rationally preferred to an act B if, and only if, $SEU(A) > SEU(B)$ – and that a rational person chooses a course of action that has the greatest *SEU*. The *SEU* theory can be interpreted normatively, descriptively, or both. In the next chapter, the normative and descriptive adequacy and significance of the theory will be discussed.

It should be borne in mind that the present statement of *SEU* theory is rough and sidesteps some important issues, such as the nature of the distinction between states and outcomes and the possibility that an act and state together do not determine a unique outcome but rather may result in different outcomes with different probabilities. Such issues as these will be dealt with in Chapter 3, which discusses various detailed ways in which Bayesian decision theory has been developed.

FOUNDATIONS OF SUBJECTIVE PROBABILITY

Subjective probabilities, or degrees of belief, are, on the decision-theoretic analysis, more or less theoretical entities which, together with subjective desirabilities, "lie behind" and explain the more or less observable phenomena of preference and choice. In this respect, subjective probability theory stands in the same relation to preference and choice as, for example, the kinetic theory of gases (about the behavior of the molecules) stands to the behavior of gases. The philosophical foundations of the view that belief is just that which is so related to preference and choice is to be found in the dispositional theory of belief, which will be discussed in the next chapter. But something more is needed for foundations of a theory of *degrees* of belief, when those degrees are, on the theory, *probabilities*. That something more is provided by various "representation theorems" (Savage 1954, Bolker 1967, Domotor 1978, Jeffrey 1978). These theorems relate preference data to a pair of functions: a probability function, which is, plausibly, the relevant agent's subjective probability assignment, and another, which is, plausibly, the agent's subjective desirability assignment. I will give the general idea of the theorems without fully stating them or discussing them in detail.

The theorems are all to the effect that if a preference relation (i.e., 'is preferred to') satisfies certain axioms (which in general are intuitively plausible), then there exists a probability function P and another function D such that, when SEU is calculated in terms of them, an item X will be preferred to an item Y if, and only if, $SEU(X) > SEU(Y)$. The nature of the entities over which the preference relation is defined depends on the detailed way in which SEU theory is developed. On Ramsey's (1926) and Savage's (1954) theories (discussed in Chapter 3), they are gambles, i.e., options of the form: you get consequence O_1 if proposition p is true and consequence O_2 otherwise. And on Jeffrey's (1965*b*) theory (also discussed in Chapter 3), they are propositions. It should also be noted that the preference data do not determine *unique* functions P and D. On Ramsey's and Savage's theories, P is uniquely determined, but D is unique only up to linear transformations, i.e., if D and D' are both derivable from the preference data, then there exist real numbers a and b such that for any item X over which the preference relation is defined, $D'(X) = aD(X) + b$. On Jeffrey's theory, neither P nor D is uniquely determined – a family of pairs of functions is determined.

Also, it might be useful to point out the basic insight as to how probability data can be derived just from preference data. If an

9

agent prefers O_1 to O_2 and he prefers the gamble in which he gets O_1 if p, O_2 otherwise, to the gamble in which he gets O_1 if q, O_2 otherwise, then this must be because he thinks that p is more probable than q; clearly one prefers to stake one's chances of getting the more desirable outcome on the most probable proposition. (Note that if preference is defined only on gambles, we can still think of an outcome O as the "gamble" in which you get O if $p \vee -p$ is true and O' otherwise, or as the "gamble" in which you get O if p, O otherwise.)

There are two kinds of axioms that the representation theorems assume a preference relation to satisfy, sometimes called 'the *necessary* axioms' and 'the *nonnecessary* axioms'. The necessary axioms are consequences of the conclusion of the theorems: conditions that must be satisfied for the conclusion of the theorems to be true. It is obvious, for example, that the conclusion of the theorems implies that the preference relation must be *transitive*. Letting '$>$' denote the relation of preference (i.e.,'$X > Y$' means 'X is preferred to Y'), the conclusion of the theorems is that there exists a probability function P and a (desirability) function D such that, when SEU is calculated in terms of these assignments, then $X > Y$ if, and only if, $SEU(X) > SEU(Y)$, for all X and Y. Thus, since $>$ is transitive, $>$ must be as well. Also, since $>$ is *trichotomous*, it is obvious that $>$ must be as well, i.e., for every X and Y, either $X > Y$ or $Y > X$ or $X \sim Y$ (where '$X \sim Y$' indicates indifference, i.e., not $X > Y$ and not $Y > X$, and the 'or's are "exclusive").

Another important and, as we shall see later, somewhat controversial necessary postulate is what Savage calls 'the sure-thing principle': If two acts have the same outcome in a particular state of nature, then which act one prefers should be independent of what that outcome is. More precisely, if, for example, the relevant outcome matrix is as in Table 1, then, according to the sure-thing principle, $A_1 > A_2$ if, and only if, $B_1 > B_2$. Assuming that the decision problem is formulated in such a way that the acts do not affect the probabilities of the states (Chapter 3 indicates a way in which this can be done), it is easy to see that the conclusion of the representation theorems implies the sure-thing principle.

Most empirical research on the descriptive adequacy of Bayesian decision theory consists of experimentally testing subjects' conformity to one or more of the necessary postulates. In the next chapter, some of this research will be described.

Table 1

	S	$-S$
A_1	O_1	O_3
A_2	O_2	O_3
B_1	O_1	O_4
B_2	O_2	O_4

The nonnecessary axioms of a representation theorem are of a technical nature and assert that the set of acts, states and outcomes satisfy certain formal, structural conditions, not all of which involve the preference relation. The nonnecessary axioms are sometimes called 'structural axioms'. I shall not discuss these until, in Chapter 3, we look at some of the detailed ways in which *SEU* theory has been developed. Meanwhile, two examples might help to clarify their nature. Bolker (1967) assumes that the set of propositions involved in Jeffrey's decision model is an atomless Boolean algebra (see Appendix 1), the main effect of which is that for any proposition X, there is a nonequivalent proposition Y which implies X. And Savage (1954) assumes that for every outcome, there is an act which invariably results in that outcome.

The main significance of the representation theorems for our purposes is that, by indicating how subjective probabilities can be measured, they, together with the *SEU* theory and a dispositional theory of belief, provide foundations for the theory of subjective probability. Assuming a dispositional theory of belief and the correctness of the *SEU* theory, the representation theorems give partial empirical interpretation to subjective probabilities, since preference and choice are observable phenomena. In the next chapter, I will delineate this idea in more detail, contrast it with other approaches and indicate the potential power and importance of a well-founded theory of subjective probability.

LEARNING

Bayesianism has a static part and a dynamic part. The static part asserts that rational degrees of belief can be represented by a probability assignment over propositions (or events, gambles, etc.). One way of justifying this static part is along the lines sketched just above, relying on the intuitive attractiveness of the preference axioms and on a dispositional theory of belief; other suggested justifications will be considered later. The dynamic part of the theory asserts that rational change of (degrees of) belief takes place in a certain way.

Now, just as Bayesian *decision* theory tells you what course of action it is rational to pursue *relative* to your beliefs and desires, irrespective of how factually or morally justified they may be, so Bayesian *learning* theory tells you what new degree of belief assignment it is rational to adopt when new evidence comes in *relative* to what your prior degrees of belief are. Just as decision making involves both past information-acquisition and present deliberation, so changing your degrees of belief involves both (i) having already adopted a prior degree of belief assignment and (ii) changing it to accommodate the new evidence. The adoption of a particular posterior assignment which accommodates new evidence may be said to be a *rational* move to the extent to which process (ii) is successfully (i.e., favorably, validly, correctly) carried out; the move may be said to be *well-grounded* to the extent to which *both* processes are successfully (favorably, validly, correctly) carried out and, thus, to the extent to which the posterior assignment accommodates not only the recently acquired evidence, but also previous experiences of the agent. Bayesian learning theory is concerned with part (ii) of the process of belief change. It is a theory about how the new assignment must be related *to the old one* – and not how it must be related to the objective world – for it to be rationally so related just in virtue of the acquisition of the new evidence. Thus, the learning theory is as applicable to the learning undergone by the ignorant and inexperienced as it is to that undergone by the knowledgeable expert.

The dynamic part of Bayesian theory asserts that *rational change of belief goes by conditionalization*: i.e., that if one learns that some proposition E is true, then one's new degree of belief in any proposition X should equal his old degree of belief in X conditional on E:

$$P_n(X) = P_o(X \mid E) = P_o(X \ \& \ E)/P_o(E),$$

where 'P_o' denotes the old (prior) subjective probability assignment and 'P_n' denotes the new (posterior) assignment, the one the rational person adopts after having learned that E is true. Let us call this belief change rule 'the *rule of conditionalization*' ('*ROC*' for short).

It is sometimes convenient to express this rule in a different form. Suppose the agent (perhaps a scientist) is considering m mutually exclusive and collectively exhaustive hypotheses H_i and has just acquired evidence E. Note that:

$$P_o(H_i \mid E) = \frac{P_o(H_i \,\&\, E)}{P_o(E)} = \frac{P_o(E \mid H_i)P_o(H_i)}{\sum_{j=1}^{m} P_o(E \mid H_j)P_o(H_j)}.$$

This is known as 'Bayes' theorem'; and the rule, which is equivalent to ROC, that asserts that $P_n(H_i)$ is equal to the term on the right above is known as 'Bayes' rule'. $P(E \mid H_i)$ is called 'the *likelihood of H_i on E*' (which, of course, is quite different from the *probability of H_i conditional on E*, i.e., $P(H_i \mid E)$). Thus, Bayes' rule tells you how to get the posterior probability of a hypothesis from the prior probabilities of each of the competing hypotheses and their likelihoods on the evidence. Note that if the degree of confirmation of a hypothesis H_i is construed as the difference between $P_n(H_i)$ and $P_o(H_i)$, then Bayes' rule shows that likely hypotheses are confirmed more (or disconfirmed less) than unlikely ones: taking the ratio of Bayes' rule with respect to two hypotheses H_i and H_j yields:

$$\frac{P_n(H_i)}{P_n(H_j)} = \frac{P_o(E \mid H_i)P_o(H_i)}{P_o(E \mid H_j)P_o(H_j)}.$$

So we may think of the likelihoods as measures of the *impacts* of the evidence on the hypotheses. (More on confirmation later.)

Why should learning go by conditionalization? And does it in fact? The next chapter focuses on the normative, descriptive and what I call 'explanatory' adequacy and significance of Bayesian *decision* theory. Some of the discussion there will presuppose, in an idealized setting, the plausibility of ROC. So, for the remainder of this chapter, I will discuss some of the considerations that have been brought to bear on the normative and descriptive plausibility of Bayesian *learning* theory.

There are basically four ways (that I know of) in which attempts have been made to justify ROC as a normative principle of belief change. First, it follows readily from the basic decision-theoretic postulate of Jeffrey's (1965*b*) decision model plus one additional plausible assumption. Jeffrey's main postulate is his *desirability axiom*: If $P(X \,\&\, Y) = 0$, then $P(X \vee Y)D(X \vee Y) = P(X)D(X) + P(Y)D(Y)$. (I will discuss this axiom in detail in Chapter 3.

Plausibly, it is equivalent to the principle that rational preference and choice go by *SEU*.) Let 'D_o' denote the "old" desirability assignment, and let 'D_n' denote the "new" one, the one adopted after evidence E is learned. Then the second assumption is that for any proposition X, $D_n(X) = D_o(E \ \& \ X)$. Actually, we really need only to assume this for such propositions X that $E \ \& \ X$ is *maximally specific* relative to the Boolean closed set of propositions the agent considers, i.e., for such propositions X that any proposition considered by the agent which implies $E \ \& \ X$ is equivalent to $E \ \& \ X$. See Appendix 1 for more on maximally specific propositions.) The first assumption makes the second one plausible, for the desirability axiom implies that

$$D(X) = P(E \mid X)D(E \ \& \ X) + P(-E \mid X)D(-E \ \& \ X),$$

so that if $P(E)$ becomes 1, $D(X)$ becomes $D(E \ \& \ X)$. Given these assumptions, it is easy to see that for any proposition X (where T is the necessary proposition),

$$P_n(X) = \frac{D_n(T) - D_n(-X)}{D_n(X) - D_n(-X)} = \frac{D_o(E) - D_o(E \ \& \ -X)}{D_o(E \ \& \ X) - D_o(E \ \& \ -X)}$$

$$= \frac{P_o(E \ \& \ X)}{P_o(E)} = P_o(X \mid E)$$

(Jeffrey 1965*b*: 80). Of course the force of this justification of *ROC* depends on the plausibility of Bayesian decision theory as developed by Jeffrey.

In another attempt to justify *ROC*, Peter Brown (1976) argues that adopting *ROC* has subjective expected utility at least as great as that of adopting any other rule of belief change. Brown makes two assumptions: (i) the choice of a belief change rule does not affect the probabilities of the relevant states of the world and (ii) one always acts in such a way as to maximize *SEU*. Let 'A_R' denote the act of adopting belief change rule R. More specifically, A_R is the act of adopting the policy of maximizing *SEU* in future decisions where *SEU* will be calculated in terms of a probability assignment derived from one's current assignment by assimilating new information using rule R. Then Brown provides a proof that for any belief change rule R, $SEU(A_{ROC}) \geqslant SEU(A_R)$.

Without going into the details of Brown's proof, two things may still be fairly pointed out. first, the force of this justification of *ROC* relies on the adequacy of *SEU* theory as *descriptive*. Many empirical tests of descriptive *SEU* theory have been conducted, and, as we shall see later, most researchers have interpreted the results of the tests as indicating that *SEU* is a poor descriptive theory. But a weaker conclusion for Brown's argument may seem more plausible: If one adopts the *SEU* theory to live by, then one is best off changing one's beliefs according to *ROC*.

Secondly, however, as Charles Chihara has remarked in discussion, Brown's proof assumes that the desirabilities of maximally specific propositions will remain constant over time. More specifically, A_R is the act of adopting the policy of maximizing *SEU* in one's future decisions where *SEU* will be calculated in terms of future probabilities derived from one's current probabilities by rule R and one's *current* desirabilities for the maximally specific cases. Now Bayesian decision theories typically assume that desirabilities for maximally specific cases remain constant in very short intervals of time just before decisions take place (unless the probability of such a case becomes 0). And the justification of *ROC* sketched previously assumes that maximally specific propositions of the form $E \& X$ have constant desirability around the time of the belief change. But Brown's proof assumes that the desirability of each maximally specific case will remain constant throughout the time the chosen belief change rule is to be applied (unless, of course, its probability becomes 0). This does not seem to me to be a plausible assumption, for it seems that one's basic desires (desirabilities for maximally specific cases) *can* and *do* change, consistently with one's remaining rational.

A quite different kind of attempted justification of *ROC* assumes that degrees of belief correspond to betting odds in the natural way: $P(X) = a$ if, and only if, the highest betting odds for X the agent would be willing to offer are $a : (1 - a)$. It is argued that if one's changes of belief do not obey *ROC*, then it is possible to construct a "Dutch book" against the agent, i.e., one can find a series of bets, each acceptable to the agent, such that if the agent accepts all of the bets, then – no matter what happens – a loss to the agent is certain. It was long thought that such an argument could not successfully be carried out (Hacking 1967), but Teller (1976) reports an argument of this type devised by David Lewis. Assume:

> (i) the domains of the old and the new subjective probability assignments P_o and P_n contain mutually exclusive and

15

collectively exhaustive propositions $E_1, \ldots, E_m$ that describe, in full detail, all the alternative bodies of information the agent and his betting opponent might get between time o and time n;

(ii) $E'_1, \ldots E'_{m'}$ are the E_is with positive prior probability;

(iii) at time o, both the agent and his betting opponent know what the agent's new degree of belief assignment (P_n) will be if E'_i should turn out to be true, for *some* i, say i^*;

(iv) if E'_{i*} should turn out to be true, P_n would not be derived from P_o by conditionalization on E'_{i*};

and

(v) at time o, the agent is indifferent between buying and selling the gamble '$\$x$ if X, $\$0$ if $-X$' for $\$xP_o(X)$; and at time n, he is indifferent between buying and selling that gamble for $\$xP_n(X)$, for any amount x and any proposition X.

Then the betting opponent can induce the agent to buy and sell such bets that the agent will suffer a loss no matter which E'_i turns out to be true.

This is a theorem and, thus, it is uncontroversial. What is controversial is what can validly be inferred from the theorem. Perhaps it is not always irrational to leave oneself open to a Dutch book. Perhaps betting quotients do not always correspond to subjective probabilities in the natural way. Unfortunately, there are many objections to Dutch book type arguments whose conclusions assert that one's degrees of belief must have certain properties if they are rational. Dutch book arguments have been used in attempts to show that rational degrees of belief must conform to the probability axioms if the agent is rational, and they suggest a method of measuring degrees of belief. These arguments will be discussed in the next chapter; it will be seen that the argument outlined above suffers from many of the shortcomings that will be pointed out there.

In yet a different kind of argument for *ROC*, which seems quite promising, Paul Teller (1976) formulates a qualitative condition that is equivalent to *ROC* in the presence of a certain structural condition, and he argues intuitively for the plausibility of that qualitative condition. I will not state the qualitative condition in qualitative form, but it will be easy to see that it can be stated using just the relations 'is more probable$_o$ than' and 'is more probable$_n$

than', where the subscripts 'o' and 'n' indicate prior and posterior probability, respectively. The formal part of Teller's justification of *ROC* shows that if the necessary condition:

For all propositions X and Y, if:
 (i) $0 < P_o(E) < 1$;
 (ii) $P_n(E) = 1$;
 (iii) X implies E;
 (iv) Y implies E;
 (v) $P_o(X) = P_o(Y)$;
then: $P_n(X) = P_n(Y)$;

and the nonnecessary condition:

For every X, q and r, if $P_o(X) = r$ and $q \leq r$, then there is a Y such that Y implies X and $P_o(Y) = q$;

are satisfied, then $P_n(X) = P_o(X | E)$, for every proposition X in the agent's domain of belief. The agent's domain of belief is said to be *full* if the nonnecessary condition is met. Teller shows that the proof will go through with a weaker, more complicated and more plausible nonnecessary constraint to the effect that the agent's domain of belief is "*full enough.*" But the really important condition is the necessary condition which, in the presence of the stronger or the weaker nonnecessary condition, is equivalent to *ROC*. Is this qualitative necessary condition plausible? Should one's old and new subjective probabilities satisfy the necessary condition when E is learned?

Teller advances a qualitative principle of inductive reasoning, $\mathscr{P}$, which says, roughly:

Interpreting P_o (P_n) as an agent's degree of belief assignment just before (after) having learned that E is true, then the necessary condition accurately characterizes reasonable belief change if we add two premises: (vi) P_o is a reasonable degree of belief assignment and (vii) after learning that E is true, any good reasons the agent might have, as a result of this learning experience, for changing degrees of belief in other propositions are already implicit in E.

The additional premises indicated in $\mathscr{P}$ are supposed to characterize those situations in which *ROC* is reasonably applicable. If P_o is not reasonable in the first place, perhaps because earlier information was not reasonably assimilated into the agent's beliefs, then it would perhaps be reasonable to assimilate them in a reasonable way at the time of the move from P_o to a new assignment – at the time E is learned – and this may very well not be possible just by conditionalization on E. And premise (vii) is really just a form of the principle of total evidence for belief change, which states that in any application of ROC, the proposition conditionalized on should capture the totality of the new evidence and not just a part of it. I should point out that principle $\mathscr{P}$ as stated here is not the same as stated by Teller but does, I think, capture the basic idea and intuitive content of Teller's formulation.

But how can $\mathscr{P}$ be justified? Teller states that the principle is, to him, intuitively plausible, and he offers some examples and considers some possible general objections to it. But perhaps the following can enhance its intuitive plausibility. Suppose premises (i)–(vii) are satisfied relative to degree of belief assignments P_o and P_n and propositions E, X and Y. Why would the new probability of X be different from (say less than) the new probability of Y? Intuitively, this would be because the evidence, E, rules out more "ways" in which X would be true than "ways" in which Y would be true. By premise (vii), that E does this must be implicit in E. A natural way to think of this is as follows: E implies $-w$ for more ways w that imply X than imply Y. But this is impossible, since, by hypothesis, both X and Y imply E. Suppose w implies X and that E implies $-w$. Since X implies E, w must imply $-w$, and, thus, w cannot be a "way", or possible case, at all.

The situation can be characterized graphically. (See Figure 1.) The rectangle has area 1, corresponding to probability 1. The areas of the regions labeled 'X', 'Y' and 'E' correspond to the prior probabilities of the propositions. The points inside the regions labeled 'X', 'Y' and 'E' correspond to the ways in which the propositions X, Y and E can be true, respectively. The regions labeled 'X' and 'Y' are both inside the region labeled 'E', corresponding to the hypotheses, (iii) and (iv), that both X and Y imply E. The regions labeled 'X' and 'Y' have the same area, corresponding to the hypothesis, (v), that X and Y have the same prior probability. The points in the shaded region correspond to ways or possible cases that are ruled out by E. The situation is such that there is no point that is both inside X and outside E. Thus, there is no way in which X could be true that is ruled out by E.

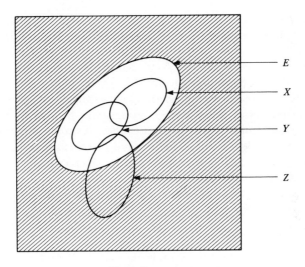

Figure 1.

Thus, it is not the case that E rules out more ways in which X would be true than ways in which Y would be true: it rules out ways of neither kind.

Note that ROC has a natural graphic representation. The prior probability of Z is equal to the area of the region labeled 'Z'. Its posterior probability, i.e., its probability after learning E, is equal to the ratio of the area of the unshaded portion of the region labeled Z to the area of the region labeled E. Since none of the region labeled X is shaded, the posterior probability of X is equal to the ratio of the area of region X to the area of the region labeled E, according to ROC.

ROC requires that the precise content of what is learned can be formulated in some proposition E in the agent's language; that is, it requires that what is learned is the truth of some such proposition E. But there are learning experiences that are not plausibly the learning of some such proposition and in which probability change is clearly called for. For example, suppose you own two tablecloths, one green and the other blue, and, for some reason, you are interested in which is on your table. Having completely forgotten, your degrees of belief are such that $P_o(G) = P_o(B) = 0.5$. You look across the dimly lit room at the tablecloth and become more confident

19

that it is green, but, due to the darkness of the room, you are not completely certain: $P_n(G) = 0.9$ and $P_n(B) = 0.1$. In this case, plausibly, there is no proposition E in the agent's language such that $P_n(G) = P_o(G \mid E)$ and $P_n(B) = P_o(B \mid E)$. Assuming that G and B are the only propositions the agent's degrees of belief in which were directly affected by this learning experience – i.e., that changes in his degrees of belief in *other* propositions will not be a result *only* of his learning experience, but of that plus some antecedent beliefs – the problem is this: How should the changes in his degrees of belief in G and B be reflected in his degrees of belief in the rest of the propositions he entertains?

Jeffrey (1965*b*: 157–63) suggests that, given this assumption, for any proposition X,

$$P_n(X) = P_n(G)P_o(X \mid G) + P_n(B)P_o(X \mid B).$$

For instance, in our example the agent's degree of belief in the proposition (S) that the tablecloth on the table has a stain on the far edge might not be *directly* affected by his learning experience; the visual observation *alone* does not provide any information about whether or not the cloth has a stain on the far edge, which, say, is not within his view. Then his probabilities of S conditional on G and B should not change as a result of the observation. If the agent is pretty sure that his green tablecloth has a stain on it and is pretty sure that his blue one does not, then perhaps $P_n(S \mid G) = P_o(S \mid G) = 0.8$ and $P_n(S \mid B) = P_o(S \mid B) = 0.3$. Then,

$$P_n(S) = P_n(G)P_n(S \mid G) + P_n(B)P_n(S \mid B)$$

$$= P_n(G)P_o(S \mid G) + P_n(B)P_o(S \mid B)$$

$$= (0.9)(0.8) + (0.1)(0.3) = 0.75;$$

whereas,

$$P_o(S) = P_o(G)P_o(S \mid G) + P_o(B)P_o(S \mid B)$$

$$= (0.5)(0.8) + (0.5)(0.3) = 0.55.$$

In general, where $E_1, \ldots E_m$ are the (mutually exclusive and collectively exhaustive) propositions the agent's degrees of belief in which are directly affected by a learning experience, the *generalized rule of conditionalization* says: For any proposition X,

$$P_n(X) = \sum_{i=1}^{m} P_n(E_i)P_o(X \mid E_i).$$

20

Teller (1976) attempts a justification of the generalized rule of conditionalization along the same lines as his justification of *ROC*. And Skyrms (1980*a*: 162–8) shows that given some not unreasonable constraints on the relation between first- and second-order probabilities, generalized conditionalization is equivalent to conditionalization at the second level on a proposition specifying the new probabilities of the E_is.

Despite the intuitive plausibility of *ROC*, empirical research shows that, in fact, we are not Bayesian in our movement from prior to posterior degrees of belief. Some earlier studies relied on Bayes' rule as roughly correctly descriptive and sought to adjust it in certain ways to make it more accurate. The general, but not universal, finding was "conservatism." That is, when revising probability estimates in light of evidence, subjects tended to be conservative in that their estimates did not move as much as the Bayes norm prescribes: the posterior probabilities tended to be too evenly distributed. Recall that taking the ratio of Bayes' theorem with respect to two hypotheses, H_i and H_j, yields what might be called another form of Bayes' theorem:

$$\frac{P(H_i|E)}{P(H_j|E)} = \frac{P(E|H_i)}{P(E|H_j)} \frac{P(H_i)}{P(H_j)}.$$

Typically, new symbols are introduced:

$$\Omega_n = L\Omega_o,$$

where Ω_n is called 'the *posterior odds*', L is called 'the *likelihood ratio*' and Ω_o is called 'the *prior odds*'. Recall that the likelihoods measure the impact of the evidence on the hypotheses. Thus, given conservatism, to change the above to a more descriptively accurate rule of belief change, the likelihood ratio may be raised to some power b, $0 < b < 1$:

$$\Omega_n = L^b \Omega_o.$$

A large part of empirical Bayesian research can be characterized as attempts to explain why $b < 1$. For reviews, see Slovic & Lichtenstein (1971) and Rapoport & Wallsten (1972).

More recent studies (notably, Tversky & Kahneman 1971, 1973, 1974, Kahneman & Tversky 1972, 1973) indicate, however, that subjects' deviance from the Bayes norm is not best explained in terms of conservatism: "In his evaluation of evidence, man is apparently not a conservative Bayesian: he is not Bayesian at all" (Kahneman & Tversky 1972: 450). In these studies, Kahneman and Tversky describe three commonly used heuristics for probabilistic reasoning which, though efficient and at times accurate, often result in large biases, not always of a conservative nature, that have serious implications for practical decision making. These heuristics, described below, not only infect probability movement in learning, but also indicate the need for normative guidelines for the establishment of prior probabilities. Kahneman and Tversky's three heuristics are called 'representativeness', 'availability' and 'anchoring and adjustment'.

Using the heuristic of representativeness, people will sometimes, in some circumstances, judge the probability that an object B belongs to a class A, or the probability that a process A will generate an event B, according to how "representative" A is of B. For example, people judge the probability that a person under some description is an engineer or a lawyer according to how strongly the description matches their stereotype of an engineer or a lawyer, respectively. This heuristic can lead to serious errors because it is insensitive to factors that should influence the probability judgment. Information about the proportion of lawyers and engineers in the population, for instance, should influence the judgment, but it does not affect the degree to which a description resembles one's stereotype of an engineer or lawyer. In one experiment, subjects were given a description of Dick – married, no children, high ability and motivation, well liked – that was meant to give no information relevant to whether Dick was an engineer or lawyer. The subjects judged the probability that Dick was an engineer to be 0.5 regardless of whether they were given the information that the ratio of engineers to lawyers was 0.7 : 0.3 or 0.3 : 0.7 (Kahneman & Tversky 1973). It was also reported that people expect even very short sequences of randomly generated events to represent some essential properties of the generating mechanism. For example, in fair coin tossing, "people regard the sequence H-T-H-T-T-H to be more likely than the sequence H-H-H-T-T-T, which does not appear random, and also more likely than the sequence H-H-H-H-T-H, which does not represent the fairness of the coin" (Tversky & Kahneman 1974: 1125). Of course a short sequence is more likely than not *not* to be representative of the entire sequence. This fallacy is similar to the gambler's fallacy.

Another commonly used heuristic that leads to biases is availability. People judge the probability of an event by how easy it is to recall or bring to mind similar events. For example, one may base the probability that the person knocking on his door is such and such an acquaintance according to how easy it is to recall instances of that acquaintance visiting. This heuristic is efficient, but there are many probability judgment problems in which it leads to significant biases. To give just one example, it is easier to bring to mind English words that begin with the letter 'k' (e.g., 'key') than it is to bring to mind those that have 'k' in the third position; and in fact most subjects judge it to be more probable that a randomly chosen English word of at least three letters begins with a 'k' than that it has a 'k' in the third position. Actually, there are three times as many words with 'k' in the third position than there are that begin with a 'k' (Tversky & Kahneman 1973).

In using the third heuristic, anchoring and adjustment, people fix on some probability and adjust this value in order to take account of some new information or certain factors given in the formulation of the problem. The adjustment tends to be insufficient. This heuristic can explain the finding (Bar-Hillel 1973) that people tend to overestimate the probabilities of conjunctive events (they anchor on the probability of a conjunct and adjust insufficiently downwards) and underestimate the probabilities of disjunctive events (they anchor on the probability of a disjunct and adjust insufficiently upwards) (Tversky & Kahneman 1974).

Of course evidence disconfirming the hypothesis that *ROC* correctly describes actual probabilistic reasoning need not shake one's confidence in *ROC* as a normative principle. And even the descriptive significance of this kind of research has been questioned. L. J. Cohen (1981) argues that experimenters in this area either trick subjects into local "performance-malfunctions" or test their intelligence or education or are themselves guilty of some kind of normative error. In any case, as a normative rule, *ROC* is intuitively plausible, has been impressively defended and can, I think, be regarded as a roughly accurate descriptive rule at least of idealized rational behavior. An aspect of the philosophical significance of *ROC* that lends it further support – its tie-in with a Bayesian theory of confirmation that is able to explicate and justify a wide variety of kinds of accepted inductive practices – will be explored in the last section of the next chapter.

2

The philosophical and psychological significance of Bayesian decision theory

Decision theory and other theories, maxims and principles about human behavior often have both normative and descriptive interpretations. Such is the case with *SEU* theory. As normative, it is a theory about how we should make decisions; as descriptive, it is a theory about how we do make decisions. Both as a normative and as a descriptive theory, it is a model of human rationality. As normative, the theory is an outline of part of a philosophical account of the concept of rationality: it is a theory about how one's actions, preferences, values and beliefs must be related to each other for them to be rationally so related. Thus, it is not surprising that the theory has been applied to philosophical problems in areas where the concept of rationality is central: epistemology and moral theory. In this chapter, I will explore some ways in which *SEU* theory can be applied in the theories of induction and value. As descriptive, *SEU* theory is an outline of a psychological account of human behavior. Thus, it is not surprising that the theory has been put to much empirical test. In this chapter, I will also describe some of this empirical research and discuss its descriptive and normative implications for *SEU* theory.

Finally, there is an aspect of *SEU* theory which, perhaps, is properly a part of the descriptive aspect but which, because of its special and detachable philosophical importance, I will distinguish as 'the explanatory aspect'. According to this part of the theory, preference and choice phenomena are explainable in terms of theoretical degrees of belief and degrees of desire: one makes certain choices and has certain preferences because of the existence of certain theoretical entities: certain degrees of belief and desire. Thus, preference and choice are the observable manifestations of degrees of belief and desire. This suggests the possibility that these degrees can be measured from their observational manifestations.

And, indeed, the representation theorems, described earlier, show that this can, in principle, be done. Of course it must be argued that the theoretical entities lying behind choice and preference are actually degrees of *belief* and degrees of *desire*. And a dispositional theory of belief and desire – what might be called the philosophical foundations of this explanatory aspect of *SEU* theory and this measurement technique – makes this plausible. Roughly, according to the dispositional theory, beliefs and desires are just dispositions to action. After the two sections discussing the prescriptive and descriptive aspects of Bayesian decision theory, the remainder of the chapter will focus on the explanatory aspect: primarily, the decision-theoretic foundations of subjective probability, its advantages over other approaches and the significance of a well-founded theory of subjective probability.

A THEORY OF HUMAN RATIONALITY

The two main problems in the theory of induction are: (i) that of *characterizing* our inductive practices (our rational inference patterns when they are not of a deductive nature) and (ii) that of *justifying* them. In this section I will show a way in which *SEU* theory can be applied to the first problem. In the last section of this chapter, I will discuss a different Bayesian approach that addresses both problems. Also in this section, some applications of *SEU* theory to moral philosophy will emerge.

According to one kind of conception of scientific inductive practice, scientists sometimes *accept* hypotheses. Thus, on such a conception, a part of the first problem is specifying criteria for the rational acceptance of a hypothesis. Hempel (1960) outlines an analysis of acceptance on which the acceptance of a hypothesis is interpreted decision-theoretically as one among several available acts. Suppose a scientist is presented with n mutually exclusive and collectively exhaustive hypotheses h_i, somehow obtained, and that he must choose among the following $n + 1$ courses of action:

A_1:   accept h_1 and add it to the body of accepted scientific theory;

A_2:   accept h_2 and add it to the body of accepted scientific theory;

$\vdots$

A_n: accept h_n and add it to the body of accepted scientific theory;

25

A_{n+1}: accept none of the h_is and leave the body of accepted scientific theory unchanged.

The possible outcomes are:

O_1: enlarge the body of accepted scientific theory by h_1 where h_1 is true;

O_2: enlarge the body of accepted scientific theory by h_1 where h_1 is false;

$\vdots$

O_{2n-1}: enlarge the body of accepted scientific theory by h_n where h_n is true;

O_{2n}: enlarge the body of accepted scientific theory by h_n where h_n is false;

O_{2n+1}: the accepted body of scientific theory remains unchanged.

Hempel considers the following rule of acceptance: Choose the A_i that has the highest expected utility, i.e. the highest value of the form

$$\sum_{j=1}^{2n+1} P(O_j|A_i)D(O_j \text{ \& } A_i),$$

where $P(O_j|A_i)$ is the probability of O_j conditional on A_i and $D(O_j \text{ \& } A_i)$ is the desirability, or utility, of $O_j \text{ \& } A_i$. Of course the application of this rule requires specification of the relevant conditional probabilities and of the desirabilities of the outcomes. I will put off until later a discussion of the problems involved in coming up with a probability assignment except to note two points. First, the probabilities must reflect the current state of scientific knowledge. Thus, all the probabilities can be thought of as conditional on a complicated sentence e that expresses everything accepted by science at that time. Second, it should be mentioned that Hempel's inspiration for the rule was Carnap's "rule of maximizing the estimated utility" (Carnap 1950: 269), where the probability assignment is determined by some given system of inductive logic, in which case the expected utility is not necessarily *subjective* expected utility. Let us turn to the problem of specifying the desirabilities of the possible outcomes.

26

There are two important problems in connection with the desirabilities. First, what values are these desirabilities supposed to reflect? That is, in virtue of what features of the outcomes should their desirabilities be high or low? Second, how can the desirabilities be determined? I shall discuss the second question later. As to the first question, it is clear that the kind of good that is to be maximized is not to include such things as fame or research grants that might accrue to the scientist who decides to accept a hypothesis. Otherwise, a scientist might, following the proposed rule, accept a comprehensive and plausible hypothesis that he believes is false in hopes of deceiving other researchers and acquiring riches and fame.

While it is clear that such *personal* practical features of the outcomes should not figure in the evaluation of their desirabilities, some philosophers (Churchman 1948, 1956, Braithwaite 1953, Rudner 1953) have argued that *other* kinds of practical and ethical judgments are essentially involved in deciding which scientific hypothesis to accept. Rudner, for example, argues that whether or not the evidence is "strong enough" to warrant the acceptance of a hypothesis will typically depend on what the practical, moral consequences would be if the hypothesis were accepted, but false; thus, he argues, decisions as to whether or not to accept a hypothesis will involve moral evaluations of the importance of avoiding such bad consequences.

To illustrate his point, Rudner considers two hypotheses, the first to the effect that a toxic component of a drug is not present in a lethal quantity and the second to the effect that a certain lot of machine stamped belt buckles does not contain defective buckles. Given that the two hypotheses have the same probability – that one has the same degree of confidence in each – it is still possible that the first hypothesis rationally be not accepted and the second rationally be accepted: we require a higher degree of confidence to accept the first hypothesis than we do to accept the second. And this is because, by our moral standards, the outcomes of accepting the first hypothesis, if false, are much graver than those of accepting the second, if false. Though this particular example is from factory quality control, Rudner believes the point is quite general.

Rudner's point is that acceptance essentially involves ethical judgments. My point here is just that insofar as it does – *if* it does – Bayesian decision theory models the involvement *via* the desirability assignment. But it should be pointed out that there are serious objections to Rudner's view. For instance, one may object that it is not part of the role of the scientist *qua* scientist to consider the moral consequences of accepting certain hypotheses, though this may be part of the role of the scientist *qua* member of his society. Indeed, the objection goes, the role of the scientist *qua* scientist does not even include accepting or rejecting hypotheses; the scientist *qua* scientist just determines probabilities of hypotheses. Rudner responds to this objection by equating "the determination that the degree of confirmation is say, *p*" with "*the acceptance by the scientist of the hypothesis that the degree of confidence is p*" (1953: 4). However, following Jeffrey (1956), one may respond that just as the scientist *qua* scientist does not accept or reject hypotheses of other sorts, he does not accept or reject hypotheses about degrees of confidence. Rudner's response does raise a problem for the "probabilistic theory of science": it presupposes a satisfactory theory of degree of confirmation of hypotheses on given evidence. But, as Jeffrey says, "[This and other] difficulties may be fatal for that [probabilistic] theory; but they cannot save the view that the scientist, *qua* scientist, accepts hypotheses" (1956: 246).

The following considerations bring into sharper focus the problems inherent in Rudner's view. Consider again the hypothesis to the effect that the drug does not contain a lethal amount of the toxic ingredient. It is possible that the scientist does not know whether the drug would be used on human patients or pet monkeys if it proved to be acceptable. And certainly different degrees of confidence in the hypothesis are required for the acceptability of the drug's use on the different species of patients, according to our moral standards. Given some degree of confidence in the hypothesis *between* the degrees required for the acceptibility of the drug's use on men and monkeys, and given our moral standards, it seems that the scientist should not simply accept or reject the hypothesis: simply accepting it would lead to unacceptable practice on the part of the physician; simply rejecting it would result in unacceptable practice on the part of the veterinarian. As Jeffrey (1956) points out, the dilemma will be resolved if the scientist *either* provides a single probability for the hypothesis in question (so that each can then make separate decisions as to whether or not to act on the hypothesis) *or* makes separate decisions as to the acceptability of the hypothesis for the veterinarian and for the physician. But, in either of these two cases, the scientist does not simply accept or reject the hypothesis.

There is, however, another approach to characterizing the relevant desirabilities which would make the decision-theoretic approach to acceptance immune to the problems Jeffrey raises. According to this approach, the desirabilities should not reflect values involved in scientists' personal goals or those involved in the goals of the society of which they are members. Rather, they should reflect only values inherent in the goals of scientific research – such goals as arriving at the truth, comprehensive truth, nothing but the truth, simplicity of description of the truth, and so on. Hempel (1960) called such desirabilities 'epistemic utilities', and Levi (1961) called this decision-theoretic approach to inductive inference 'a nonbehavioral approach' to distinguish it from the "behaviorist" approaches of Jeffrey's (the "guidance-counselor" conception according to which scientists assign probabilities for the use of the practical decision maker) and of Rudner's, Churchman's and Braithwaite's (the scientist as decision maker conception according to which the acceptability of a hypothesis is, roughly, the acceptability of acting as if the hypothesis were true). Of course there are very difficult problems that must be overcome if this nonbehavioral decision-theoretic approach is to prove satisfactory. The relevant epistemic goals must be identified and appropriately weighed in importance, and it must be shown that scientists can and should have these goals, that they are separable from practical goals and that the relevant outcomes can be assigned epistemic utilities, utilities that reflect value only relative to the epistemic goals. Much work has recently been done in this area. For defenses and criticisms of the program, and references to other work in the area, see the collection *Local Induction*, edited by R. J. Bogdan (1976).

In the *SEU*-theoretic formulation of Rudner's view of acceptance, we saw one way in which moral deliberation can be modeled *SEU*-theoretically. However, I have at times heard the charge that the theory is unethical because it only takes into consideration the values of the possible *outcomes* of courses of action and leaves out of consideration whatever value or disvalue that may attach to the *means* (acts) that bring them about. This charge, however, is mistaken. For the propositions (or events, etc., depending on how decision theory is developed) whose desirabilities enter into the calculation of expected utility are always "act-specific" in the sense that they always specify some act. This was pointed out earlier. The symbols used to stand for desirabilities ($'d_{Ai}'$) always have act-subscripts, and the outcomes can be thought of as really of the form O_i & A.

More accurately, *SEU* theory can be characterized as ethically neutral. That is, it does not tell one how to arrive at basic values (modeled decision-theoretically by desirabilities for the maximally specific cases); it only tells you how your values for less specific cases, e.g., those that are acts, should be related to your basic values, given your degree of belief assignment. One's basic values are taken to be subjective in *SEU* theory in that they merely reflect an agent's preferences. As pointed out previously, *SEU* theory is as applicable to the deliberation of a monster as it is to that of a saint.

Jeffrey, however, suggests that a thesis of "radical optimism" about human nature might be correct. According to the thesis, human nature is such that our basic values – modeled decision-theoretically by desirabilities for maximally specific cases – are, basically, morally good. If this is true, then perhaps if we knew what our basic values were, Bayesian decision theory would be adequate as a guide and model for moral deliberation: "One might envisage a totally bad Bayesian robot; but perhaps for human beings, coherence [i.e., having one's preferences ranked according to *SEU*] is incompatible with moral evil" (Jeffrey 1965a: 535–6).

But if radical optimism is correct, how do we explain our failures? Of course, if *SEU* theory really *is* adequate for moral deliberation, our failures may result from incoherence, from preferences not going by *SEU*. But suppose *SEU* theory is descriptively correct. Jeffrey suggests that the failures may really be "failures of intelligence or of honesty or, generally, of understanding what we are really like" (p. 536). They may be failures to understand what we are really like if we do not know our true desirabilities; and they may be failures of intelligence if our degrees of belief are not factually – or, at some level epistemologically deeper than Bayesian decision theory, rationally – justified. Thus, they may not really be moral failures at all.

These considerations point out again that *SEU* theory is not only ethically neutral, but also "intellectually neutral" in the sense that it is as applicable to the deliberation of the ignorant (one with inaccurate, perhaps even foolish, probabilities) as it is to that of the knowledgeable (one who has fairly accurate and rational degrees of belief). But, of course, what the rational man wants is a method of selecting (or discovering) an appropriate (or true) desirability assignment and a degree of belief distribution that makes best use of available information.

In connection with the problem of selecting P, Bayesian theory has been criticized both as a prescriptive and as a descriptive theory. As indicated earlier, according to Bayesian theory rational *change* of belief goes by conditionalization. We have already seen that, as a descriptive thesis, this is very questionable. But there is also this (normative) problem: How should the agent choose an *original* probability assignment, original in the sense that it is not itself a posterior assignment gotten from some prior assignment by conditionalization? Of course it should be selected in a way that makes good use of available information. But, as Suppes remarks with reference to decision theory as developed by Savage and himself,

The present theory or Savage's offers little help on this point... Given certain prior information is one *a priori* distribution as reasonable as any other? As far as I can see, there is nothing in my or Savage's axioms which prevents an affirmative answer to this question. Yet if a man bought grapes at [a certain] store on fifteen previous occasions and had always got green or ripe, but never rotten grapes, and if he had no other information prior to sampling the grapes I for one would regard as unreasonable an *a priori* distribution which assigned a probability 2/3 to the rotten state. Unfortunately, though I am prepared to reject this one distribution as unreasonable, I am not prepared to say what I think is optimal. (1956: 72)

In connection with this it is perhaps helpful to note three alternatives to *SEU*: (i) *OEU* (where the probabilities in terms of which the expectation is calculated are *objective*, e.g., relative frequencies or propensities), (ii) *SEV* (where, instead of calculating expectation in terms of subjective utility, or desirability, we calculate it in terms of *objective value* somehow characterized, e.g., in terms of monetary values or some other physical quantity) and (iii) *OEV* (calculated in terms of objective probability and objective value). None of the three theories corresponding to the three alternative notions of expectation is considered to be even roughly accurate descriptively (Edwards 1961: 474–5). What of the prescriptive theories corresponding to the three alternative notions of expectation? Perhaps what is meant by 'optimal assignments' is 'true, objective assignments'. But clearly it is an unrealistic prescriptive

31

theory that recommends using these, for an agent generally does not know them (if such things even exist). Clearly, he can at best use his subjective estimates of the objective assignments. But these are just his subjective assignments, it has been suggested (Jeffrey 1965*b*: 190–6, Skyrms 1980*a*: 19–20); subjective probability, for example, is the subjective expectation of the true objective probability. Then the demand for a method of arriving at optimal assignments may be interpreted as a demand for a method of getting optimal estimates of the objective assignments.

Bayesians have a partial answer to the problem, which is based on a theorem (Savage 1954: 46–50) that is interpreted as showing that if learning goes by conditionalization, then, as evidence comes in, one will almost certainly eventually become convinced of the true hypothesis. (The hypotheses considered could be about what the true, objective probability assignment is.) Roughly, the theorem states that if posterior probabilities are gotten from priors by conditionalization on the evidence (and the priors satisfy some mild restrictions), then, as the evidence comes in, the probability that the probability of the true hypothesis will get greater than α approaches 1, for all $\alpha < 1$. Thus, it is claimed, in the long run, it does not matter what prior assignment (e.g., prior probabilities for what the true, objective probability assignment is) one starts out with. However, this Bayesian interpretation of the theorem has been criticized on several grounds. For instance, the rate at which the probability of the true hypothesis approaches 1 depends on the nature of the prior assignment. For *some* prior assignments, the convergence might be too slow to benefit mortals (Hesse 1974: 117). Also, the theorem invokes second-order probabilities. If these are also interpreted subjectively, then "the theorem does not tell us that in the limit any rational Bayesian will assign probability 1 to the true hypothesis and probability 0 to the rest; it only tells us that rational Bayesians are certain that he will. It may assure those that are already Bayesians, but it is hardly grounds for conversion" (Glymour 1980: 73). Of course, we might try interpreting the second-order probabilities objectively – say as relative frequencies – in which case the theorem tells us that virtually all rational Bayesians become convinced of the truth – eventually.

In any case, I think it is appropriate to conclude that prescriptive *SEU* theory is a weak normative theory in the sense that it does not tell you how to get *optimal* probability and desirability assignments. However, I do not think this is a really serious shortcoming. At least one natural way to think of the rationality of acts is as *relative to a set of beliefs and desires, where the quality of the beliefs and desires is irrelevant.* Even if an agent does not have optimal beliefs and desires, in some realistic sense of 'optimal', it is still plausible that if he *has* beliefs and desires and knows what they are, *SEU* theory will prescribe the correct act relative to them: the correct act for him given what he does in fact want and what he does in fact believe.

Various other weaknesses of *SEU* theory depend on the detailed way in which it is developed. Recall that deliberation consists in evaluating the available courses of action in terms of the possible consequences *after* the consequences have been *envisaged.* (See page 4.) That is, the decision problem must also be structured in a particular way. The precise way in which the problem must be structured on the *SEU* theory depends on how *SEU* theory is developed in detail. Some versions of the theory are more demanding than others on the ability of the agent to appropriately set up his decision problem. In Chapters 3 and 5, we will be in a position to evaluate the relative merits of the various detailed developments of *SEU* theory in connection with weaknesses of this kind.

A THEORY OF HUMAN BEHAVIOR

In investigations of the theory that people act in such a way as to maximize their subjective expected utility, both descriptive and prescriptive doubts about *SEU* theory have been raised. Chapter 4 and the subsequent chapters will focus on what is probably the most important kind of *prima facie* counterexample to *normative SEU* theory. In this section I will focus primarily on research concerning the *descriptive* adequacy of the theory.

Of course in investigating the descriptive adequacy of *SEU* theory, the question is not whether people actually consciously manipulate a particular formal decision-theoretic apparatus when making decisions. Just as an unconscious, intuitive grasp of the laws of mechanics underlies the skill of a cyclist or a tight-rope walker, so, in the same way an unconscious, intuitive grasp of some principles of decision theory may underlie human decision making (Jeffrey 1965a). To say that a decision rule is descriptively adequate is, however, at least to say that people generally behave and rank their preferences "as though" they used the rule, i.e., in the same way as they would if they actually did consciously manipulate the formal apparatus.

Most research concerning the descriptive aspect of the theory has concentrated on experimentally testing one or more of the necessary preference postulates. The approach involves attempting to construct counterexamples to the postulates. The most famous are the *prima facie* counterexamples to Savage's sure-thing principle constructed by Allais (1953) and Ellsberg (1961).

In the Allais paradox, one is asked to express a preference between gamble A and gamble B in situation 1 and between gamble C and gamble D in situation 2:

Situation 1
> Gamble A: probability 1 of receiving \$1,000,000;
> Gamble B: probability 0.1 of receiving \$5,000,000,
> probability 0.89 of receiving \$1,000,000,
> probability 0.01 of receiving nothing.

Situation 2
> Gamble C: probability 0.11 of receiving \$1,000,000,
> probability 0.89 of receiving nothing;
> Gamble D: probability 0.1 of receiving \$5,000,000,
> probability 0.9 of receiving nothing.

Interpreting the situations as lotteries (see Table 2), as Savage (1954: 103) suggests, it is easy to see that the sure-thing principle implies that one prefers A to B if, and only if, one prefers C to D. Recall that the sure-thing principle states that if two acts have the same outcome in a particular state, then one's preference between the two acts should be independent of what the outcome in that state is. Since A and B have the same outcome given that a ticket numbered between 12 and 100 is drawn, as do C and D, and since the only difference between situation 1 and situation 2 is the difference in outcome in that state, the sure-thing principle implies that A is preferred to B if, and only if C is preferred to D. (Also, it is easy to see that $SEU(A) > SEU(B)$ if, and only if, $SEU(C) > SEU(D)$.) However, in testing business executives, MacCrimmon (1968) found that 40% preferred A to B and D to C, and in testing students, Slovic and Tversky (1974) found that 17 out of 29 preferred A to B and D to C. The suggested rationale (Allais 1953,

34

Table 2

		Ticket Number		
		1	.2–11	12–100
Situation 1	Gamble A	$1,000,000	$1,000,000	$1,000,000
	Gamble B	0	$5,000,000	$1,000,000
Situation 2	Gamble C	$1,000,000	$1,000,000	0
	Gamble D	0	$5,000,000	0

MacCrimmon 1968, Slovic & Tversky 1974) is that in situation 1, the small probability of missing the chance in a lifetime to become a millionaire is very unattractive and in situation 2, both gambles involve a high – almost indistinguishable – probability of receiving nothing, so one might as well try for the $5,000,000.

In connection with examples of a different kind, Ellsberg (1961) suggests that Savage's postulate is insensitive to the difference between risk and uncertainty. In a risk (or "measurable uncertainty") type gamble, one knows the probabilities for the possible states. In an uncertainty type gamble, one does not. Ellsberg asks us to imagine an urn containing 90 balls: 30 red balls and 60 black and yellow balls in unknown proportion. One ball is to be drawn at random from the urn. Again, we are asked to imagine two situations, in each of which there is a choice between two gambles. The payoffs for each gamble are shown in Table 3. Very frequently, A is preferred to B and D to C; the sure-thing principle implies that A is preferred to B if, and only if, C is preferred to D. This suggests that people prefer betting on risky gambles over uncertain gambles, a distinction to which the sure-thing principle seems insensitive.

Other experimental tests of the necessary postulates have been made. Tversky (1969) found systematic and predictable intransitivities of preference under certain experimental conditions. MacCrimmon (1968) reports violations of most of Savage's postulates. In tests of quite different kinds, Coombs, et al (1967) found the theory inadequate to predict preference in less than 10% of cases in one experiment and 5% in another. And in experiments using "additivity analysis," which do not focus on any particular

Table 3

		30	60	
		Red	Black	Yellow
Situation 1	Gamble A	$100	$0	$0
	Gamble B	$0	$100	$0
Situation 2	Gamble C	$100	$0	$100
	Gamble D	$0	$100	$100

implication of the theory, Tversky (1967a, 1967b) found some implications confirmed and others disconfirmed.

It is not clear, however, how the violations should be interpreted. Not only possible descriptive implications but also possible normative implications of the violations have been debated in the literature. As to the descriptive implications of the experiments, MacCrimmon points out that the decision problems he used were highly unordinary and designed specifically to elicit violations of particular postulates. He suggests that the postulates might better describe behavior in more ordinary situations. However, the decision problems involved in other tests of the theory, e.g., those described in Coombs *et al* (1967) and Tversky (1967a, 1967b, 1969), are quite ordinary. Today, the *SEU* maximization theory is generally regarded by psychologists as a poor descriptive theory. Below, however, I will point out a way in which the descriptive theory may be defended from the results of the empirical tests.

In addition to the empirical evidence described above, there is another reason for the behavioral scientist's dissatisfaction with the *SEU* theory as descriptive: the static character of its central concepts of subjective probability and desirability. As Suppes points out, "Ideally, what he desires is a dynamic theory of the inherent or environmental factors determining the acquisition of a particular set of beliefs or values" (1961: 614). But, of course, this just indicates that *SEU* theory is *incomplete*, that it deals only with the process of deliberation and not with the process of information-acquisition, a fact that has already been acknowledged in Chapter 1.

As to the normative implications of the experiments, it is perhaps significant that when MacCrimmon's subjects – these "successful, practicing decision makers" – were interviewed after they had made their choices "under a neutral form of questioning, there were large shifts towards conforming with the postulates" (1968: 21). Slovic and Tversky suggest, however, that "despite the intent to keep the discussion neutral, subtle pressures, in combination with the cooperativeness of the subjects participating in a training course for a prestigious job, may have influenced the subjects to conform to the axioms" (1974: 369). And Ellsberg reports that for the decision problems he constructed, the violating choices were carefully made, deliberate and persistent. Indeed, Ellsberg suggests that the behavior of the subjects strongly indicates "the operation of definite normative criteria, different from and conflicting with the familiar ones, to which these people are trying to conform" (1961: 656–7). In fact, he (and, independently, Fellner 1961) has attempted to construct a decision model that is sensitive to these other normative criteria. Allais' paradox, too, raises questions not only about the descriptive adequacy of the Savage postulates, but also questions about their normative adequacy. Some researchers believe that the preferences of the violators in Allais' example are correct (Allais 1953) or at least consistent and reasonable (Morrison 1967).

Before leaving the topic of experimental tests of *SEU* theory, I would like to point out some lines along which the sure-thing principle can be defended from charges that it is descriptively or normatively incorrect. I will not discuss here experiments other than those involving the Allais and Ellsberg decision problems in connection with the sure-thing principle. But some of what I say here will be relevant to other experiments designed to test other parts of the *SEU* maximization theory.

Given a preference of A over B and D over C – in either the Allais example or the Ellsberg example – one may defend the sure-thing principle by arguing either that (i) it is an *irrational* violation of the principle or that (ii) it is *not a violation* of the principle at all. An argument for (i) is a defense of the sure-thing principle as normative; an argument for (ii) could constitute a defense of the principle both as normative and as descriptive.

In arguing for (i), one tries to make the conforming preferences look very intuitively correct and the unconforming preferences very intuitively incorrect. Thus, Savage reformulates the Allais example as a lottery (see Table 2) and points out that, "if one of the tickets numbered from 12 to 100 is drawn, it will not matter, in either situation, which gamble I choose. I therefore focus on the possibility that one of the tickets numbered from 1 to 11 will be drawn, in which case Situations 1 and 2 are exactly parallel" (1954: 103); so one's preferences should be exactly parallel. Interestingly, Borch (1968: 489) points out that most people, if they got the $1 000 000 by choosing A, would probably spend only a small amount of it and invest the rest with an eye for good growth potential and small risk. That is, they would exchange A for something very like B. Borch's suggestion seems to be that the *considered* opinion of most violators is that B is better than A and D is better than C, in conformity with the sure-thing principle. (Note that with monetary utilities, $SEU(B) > SEU(A)$ and $SEU(D) > SEU(C)$.)

As to the Ellsberg example, Raiffa (1961) points out a seemingly unacceptable consequence of the preference for A over B and D over C. He defines two new gambles whose consequences depend on the toss of a fair coin:

	Heads	Tails
Gamble E	A	D
Gamble F	B	C

That is, if you choose E and the coin lands heads, gamble A is in effect; if you choose E and the coin lands tails, gamble D is in effect, etc. Suppose you prefer A to B and D to C. Since which gamble – E or F – you choose does not affect whether the coin lands heads or tails and since no matter how the coin lands you prefer the consequence of E to that of F, you must prefer E to F. (The principle that justifies the reasoning of the preceding sentence is called 'the principle of dominance', which will be formally presented and discussed later.) Raiffa then presents a table which indicates the possible outcomes of the gambles E and F (which depend both on the toss of the coin and on the selection of a ball) in a different way:

	Red	Black	Yellow
Gamble E	An "objective" 50–50 chance of \$100 and \$0	same	same
Gamble F	same	same	same

So it seems that you should be indifferent between E and F. Since the above reasoning shows that if you prefer A to B and D to C, then you should prefer E to F, you must have been wrong in preferring A to B and D to C.

In arguing for (ii), one tries to show that the decision situations are not accurately characterized by Allais' and Ellsberg's descriptions. For example, as Joel Rubin has suggested in discussion, in the Allais paradox, the consequence of the ticket numbered 1 coming up when one has chosen gamble B is not just getting no money: the person may also suffer intense regret for letting the chance of a lifetime to become a millionaire slip away just for the chance of becoming a multimillionaire. The suggestion is that the correct way of representing the decision situation is by Table 4, and not by Table 2, where 'R' represents intense regret.

If Table 4 accurately represents the decision situation as it is conceived by the subjects of the experiments, then it is obvious that they could prefer A to B and D to C without violating the sure-thing principle. Also, the Ellsberg risk-uncertainty type "violations" can be explained in the same way. If one feels more regret and feels more foolish in losing an uncertainty type bet than upon losing a risk type bet (and believes this), then Ellsberg's decision problem would be better represented by Table 5 than by Table 3.

The idea of thus redefining the consequences is plausible and seems to render the sure-thing principle both descriptively and normatively adequate in the Allais and Ellsberg decision problems. And Tversky (1967a) points out that, using this kind of device, some apparent violations of *SEU* theory that he discovered could also be rendered consistent with the theory. However, he also remarks that on this kind of approach, experimental identification of the consequences becomes practically unfeasible and the *SEU* model becomes virtually invulnerable: "Thus, although it is

Table 4

		Ticket Number		
		1	2–11	12–100
Situation 1	Gamble A	$1,000,000	$1,000,000	$1,000,000
	Gamble B	$0 + R	$5,000,000	$1,000,000
Situation 2	Gamble C	$1,000,000	$1,000,000	$0
	Gamble D	$0	$5,000,000	$0

possible to argue that the experimental identification, rather than the *SEU* model is in error, the fruitfulness of such an approach is questionable'' (1967*a*: 198).

But surely *if* a person would feel extra regret at getting nothing as a result of choosing gamble *B* in the Allais example and especially foolish at getting nothing as a result of choosing one of the uncertain gambles in the Ellsberg example, then the experimental identification of the consequences as sums of money is *not* entirely adequate. At the end of the last section it was indicated that some versions of a detailed development of *SEU* theory suffer from the weakness, to be described later, that they make exacting demands on the agent's ability to envisage consequences and appropriately set up the decision problem. Here, however, it seems that the violating subjects in the experiments are, perhaps unconsciously, doing a better job of this than the experimenters. In a similar vein, D. H. Mellor (1980) points out (specifically in relation to betting behavior, but the point can be taken quite generally) that our actions are affected by many factors (beliefs and desires) and that the appearance of nonconformity with Bayesian theory in some experimental tests may really be a result of a failure to eliminate or experimentally identify some of the factors. My own view is that *both* the experimental identification of consequences *and* descriptive *SEU* theory are crude, though roughly accurate, and that, given adequate identification of consequences and an appropriate set-up of the decision situation by the agent, prescriptive *SEU* theory, though weak in the innocuous sense that it does not say how to get *optimal* probability and desirability assignments, is still a very credible and promising model of rational deliberation.

Table 5

		30	60	
		Red	Black	Yellow
Situation 1	{ Gamble *A*	$100	$0	$0
	{ Gamble *B*	$0	$100	$0 + *R*
Situation 2	{ Gamble *C*	$100	$0 + *R*	$100
	{ Gamble *D*	$0	$100	$100

Bayesian decision theory as explanatory is a theory that (i) degrees of belief and desirabilities: action = *explanans* : *explanandum* and (ii) degrees of belief and desirabilities have empirical interpretation and can be measured. Thesis (i) relies on a dispositional theory of belief and desire. The main significance of (i), for our purposes, is that, plausibly, it, together with the representation theorems, implies (ii). Recall that the representation theorems involve assumptions of two kinds: the "necessary axioms" and the "nonnecessary axioms". I have already discussed some of the constraints of the first kind, both as normative and as descriptive principles, and I will put off discussion of the other constraints until, in the next chapter, we look in more detail at some ways in which *SEU* theory has been developed, for the nature of the constraints depends on the way in which the theory is developed in detail. In this section on the explanatory aspect of *SEU* theory, I will discuss: first, a dispositional theory of belief and desire; second, how (i) together with the representation theorems makes (ii) plausible; third, alternative methods of measuring subjective probabilities and desirabilities; and finally, a way in which (ii) is philosophically significant.

Without going much into detail or at all into survey, I would like to distinguish three broad kinds of analysis of '*x* has belief *p*' (or '*x* believes *p*'). Generally, such analyses can take one of the following three forms:

(a) x has a conscious feeling of conviction or confidence in p;

(b) x has a disposition to act as if p were true (in situations where whether or not p is true is thought to be relevant to the outcomes of x's act);

(c) x has a disposition to have a conscious feeling of conviction or confidence in p (when the issue of whether or not p is true is raised).

Note that (c) is a kind of hybrid of (a) and (b). Note also that, at first glance, each of the three kinds of analysis seems plausible. But suppose now that 'degree of belief', or 'partial belief', makes sense. For example, one may not have *full belief* in the proposition that it will rain tomorrow, but, given the forecast, a rather *strong belief*, or a *high degree of belief*, in the proposition. While each of (a), (b) and (c) may be at least initially plausible as analyses of *full* belief, it will emerge that only (b) can plausibly characterize belief when belief is thought of as coming in degrees.

Along the lines of analysis (a), it seems that the way in which a belief in p would vary in degree is by variance of the intensity of the feeling of conviction or confidence in p. But, as Ramsey points out, "the beliefs which we hold most strongly are often accompanied by no feeling at all; no one feels strongly about things he takes for granted" (1926: 169). Thus, (a) is inadequate to deal with degrees of belief. Not only, it seems, can one have a strong belief without having strong feelings of confidence, one can also have a strong belief without *any feeling* of confidence in the proposition believed: one can have beliefs of which one is, at times, unconscious. For example, I believe that Jupiter has at least a dozen moons, but I am not always conscious of that. An advantage of (c) over (a) is that it allows that one may have beliefs the contents of which are not always before one's mind. But (c), too, seems inadequate to deal with degrees of belief. Along the lines of analysis (c), it seems that the only ways in which a belief in p can come in degrees is by variance of the intensity of the feeling of confidence to which one who believes p is disposed or by variance of the strength of the disposition to have some feeling of confidence in p when the issue of whether or not p is true is raised, or both. We have already seen that the intensity of the feeling one has toward p is irrelevant to the degree of belief in p. But it follows from this that the strength of the disposition to have feelings of confidence in p is also irrelevant. One may have no disposition to have any feeling of conviction in p even if one believes quite strongly that p is true. Braithwaite, who believes that belief involves both "entertainment" (which happens, for instance, when the issue is raised) and disposition to act in certain ways, states, "I believe quite thoroughly that the sun will rise tomorrow, but experience no particular feeling attached to the proposition believed (1933: 37).

It seems, however, that a plausible analysis of the notion of degree of belief is possible along the lines of (b). Thus, one's degree of belief in p is the strength of one's disposition to act as if p were true, or, as Ramsey admittedly vaguely puts it, "the extent to which we are prepared to act on it" (1926: 169). One way to make this vague analysis clear is to show how the strength of such a disposition can be measured. Surely strengths of dispositions of other kinds can be measured. For example, degree of fragility – strength of disposition to break when dropped – can, plausibly, be measured by the minimum *height* above a standard floor from which the relevant object must be dropped for it to break on impact. Degree of solubility – strength of disposition to dissolve when placed in an appropriate solvent – can, plausibly, be measured by the *speed* of dissolution of a standard amount of the relevant solute in a standard amount of the appropriate solvent, under some standard conditions. How can the strength of one's disposition to act as if p were true be measured? One intuitively plausible way (which will be discussed more thoroughly later) is by experimentally determining the maximum *price*, maximum number $P(p)$ (≤ 1) of hundreds of dollars, one would be willing to pay to receive \$100 if p is true and \$0 if p is false. That maximum number, $P(p)$, then, is, intuitively plausibly, the relevant person's degree of belief in p.

Leaving aside for the moment the question of how adequate this method is on levels deeper than initial intuitive plausibility, consider this question: Would the method work if, instead of the prize being \$100, it was a cat, or a collector's stamp valued at \$100, or a drink? The answer, of course, is that it depends on how much the person values or desires the prize and how much he values or desires \$100$P(p)$. Let p be the proposition that a certain fair coin will turn up heads on its next fair toss, and suppose the person's degree of belief in p is 0.5. Surely he would not pay \$50 to get \$100 (a cat, a collector's stamp, a drink) if the coin lands heads and nothing if the coin lands tails *unless the* \$100 (*cat, collector's stamp, drink*) *is worth*

43

twice as much to him as the $50 *is.* The point is that particular beliefs dispose one to particular acts in particular situations *only in the presence of particular desires.* Similarly, particular desires dispose one to particular actions only in the presence of particular beliefs. As Mellor puts it,

Believing the pub is open will only take me there if I want a drink. Likewise, wanting a drink will only take me to a pub that I believe to be open. If belief is a disposition to action, so is desire; and what each disposes to can only be stated in terms of the other. Neither can be characterized just in terms of the actions to which together they give rise. Neither on its own disposes me to act at all. (1978: 88–9)

Thus, neither degrees of belief nor desirabilities alone are more or less strong dispositions to act in particular ways. However, attributing to a person *both* a degree of belief assignment *and* a desirability assignment is attributing to him a disposition to act in particular ways. Here is one way in which this can be seen. Suppose the degree of belief and desirability assignments yield the following preferences when *SEU* is calculated in terms of them (for a two-act – A and $-A$ – two-state – S and $-S$ – decision situation):

$$S \& A > S \& -A,$$

$$-S \& -A > -S \& A,$$

$$A > -A.$$

That is, the agent prefers act A to $-A$ given that S obtains, $-A$ to A given that $-S$ obtains and A to $-A$ overall (possibly because he thinks that S is more probable than $-S$). Then attributing to an agent the relevant degree of belief and desirability assignments is attributing to him the dispositional property that can be expressed as follows:

If x were to learn S before the time of decision, x would do A; if x were to learn $-S$ before the time of decision, x would do $-A$; and if x were to learn nothing new before the time of decision, x would do A.

Note four things. First, I have made the Bayesian assumption that preference goes by *SEU*. Second, I have assumed, what is natural, that an agent always behaves preferentially, i.e., he performs the most preferred act under the circumstances. Third, it is natural

44

to characterize dispositional properties using counterfactual (or subjunctive) conditionals. For example, x is flexible if, and only if, if x were bent under suitable pressure, then x would not break; x is soluble if, and only if, if x were immersed in a suitable solvent, x would dissolve. And finally, note that the attribution of degree of belief and desirability assignments was *not* characterized as the attribution of a dispositional property *where the relevant disposition has such and such a strength*. (Although it could be thought of as such: the disposition is strong or weak according to the degree to which the agent is rational or – what might come to much the same thing – the degree to which the agent is inclined to act preferentially and rank his preferences according to *SEU*.) But it should be emphasized that the point is *not* that degrees of belief and desirabilities are not dispositions of certain strengths. Holding the desirabilities fixed, as it were, degrees of belief are dispositions of certain degrees of strength. For example, if an agent's desirabilities are known to an experimenter and measured in units, say of "utiles," then if the maximum number of utiles x would pay to get one utile if p is true and none if p is false is $P(p)$ (≤ 1) utiles, then x has the dispositional property that can be characterized by:

> If x were in a decision situation where the truth of p is relevant, then x would behave as if p were true

to the measurable degree of strength $P(p)$. Also, if degrees of belief are, as it were, held fixed, then desirabilities can be thought of as dispositions of certain degrees of strength to act in ways believed to bring about the objects of desire. If an agent's degrees of belief are known, then his desirability for something ("the prize") can be measured from the odds he would be willing to accept and offer on a bet in which, if he wins he gets the prize and if he loses, he gets nothing, where his stake is arbitrarily defined to be worth 1 utile. (More on these measurements techniques later.)

Assume, with respect to an ideally rational decision maker, *DM*, that (1) action is preferential, (2) the axioms of a representation theorem are satisfied and (3) the dispositional theory of belief and desire – i.e., the theory that degrees of belief and desirabilities are just the things that jointly dispose one to actions – is true. By (1), *DM*'s preferences are empirically detectable. An experimenter can, in principle, give *DM* a choice between any two things: which

DM chooses is the one he prefers. By (2) and the appropriate representation theorem, one can derive functions P (a probability – plausibly, *DM*'s degree of belief assignment) and D (plausibly, *DM*'s desirability assignment) which are unique up to transformations of a particular kind and which "represent" *DM*'s preferences. But how do we know that P and D represent *DM*'s degrees of *belief* and *desir*abilities rather than just being functions whose only significance is that they represent *DM*'s preferences? Recall that the first characteristic of Bayesianism mentioned earlier is the view that preference goes by subjective expected utility. Thus, *DM* prefers one thing over another in virtue of its subjective expected utility's being higher. So at least it seems that P and D are properties of some kind, of *DM*, since they are the *unique* (up to some transformation) functions that represent his preferences by *SEU*. But still, we do not know that they are his degrees of *belief* and *desir*abilities. By (3), however, we know that degrees of belief and desirabilities are what dispose one to particular actions. Since action is preferential and preference goes by *SEU* (and since degrees of belief and desire are what dispose us to particular actions), it is now plausible that P and D are *DM*'s degrees of belief and desirabilities.

Thus, Bayesian decision theory as explanatory not only seeks to *explain* rational action but also to *give empirical interpretation to*, and *measure*, rational degrees of belief and desirabilities. Both the explanatory account of action and the measurement technique for subjective degrees of belief and desire rest on the following theses: an agent performs particular actions because he has certain (rationally related) preferences; he has certain preferences because his *SEU*s are such and such; and (of course) his *SEU*s are such and such in virtue of his degrees of belief and desire being such and such.

It should be pointed out that this decision-theoretic method of measuring a rational agent's subjective probabilities and desirabilities is not the only method that has been proposed. Several philosophers (e.g., Mellor 1971, 1980, Jackson & Pargetter 1976, Skyrms 1980*b*) have recently defended "Dutch book" methods, and deFinetti (1937) described how quantitative subjective probabilities can be inferred from qualitative probability comparisons (desirabilities could then be measured using the derived probabilities together with comparative preference data). I will briefly describe these methods and discuss their merits.

Recall the situation described earlier where one is asked how much he would pay to get $100 if p is true and nothing if p is false. According to the Dutch book method, roughly, if the maximum one would pay for this is $100P(p)$, then one's degree of belief in p is $P(p)$. In general, if the maximum one would pay to get n *utiles* if a proposition p is true and 0 utiles if p is false is m utiles, then his degree of belief in p is m/n. Another way of putting it is: If the highest odds one is willing to offer for a bet on p is $a:b$, then his degree of belief in p is $a/(a+b)$. For example, if one would bet on p at maximum odds of 3 to 1, then his degree of belief in p is 0.75.

Of course more has to be said to *justify* this method. As in the method of measuring degrees of belief from preferences, a move is first made from a normative 'One should ϕ' to a descriptive 'Rational agents ϕ'. (In the previous case, it was from 'One's preferences should satisfy the axioms' to 'DM's preferences satisfy the axioms'.) And then a probability assignment is derived from empirical data about a rational (ϕ-ing) agent's behavior in situations of a certain kind. In this case, ϕ is: '... when forced to set betting odds – and one is informed that he may be forced to take bets at these odds – for all propositions in a set of propositions that is closed under the usual logical (sentential) connectives, set them in such a way that the resulting betting quotients of the propositions satisfy the probability axioms', where, if the odds one sets for p are $a:b$, then his *betting quotient* of p is $a/(a+b)$. Then, it is claimed by proponents of the Dutch book method, one can empirically determine what a person's subjective probabilities over a set of propositions are by forcing him to set betting odds, at which odds he is informed he may be forced to take bets; the resulting betting quotients are his subjective probabilities.

But why should we think that the betting quotients *are* the agent's rational *degrees of belief*, rather than just descriptive of his betting behavior? The argument is in basically two steps. Proponents of the Dutch book method argue for the following two propositions:

(I) Rational people ϕ. (i.e., one's betting quotients are rational only if they satisfy the probability axioms.)

(II) Rational degrees of belief *are* one's (rational) betting quotients.

Proposition (I) is argued for in two steps. It follows from:

(IA) An agent's betting quotients are rational only if it is impossible for an opponent to choose certain propositions for which the agent has set betting odds and bet for or against them (against the agent) at the odds chosen by the agent in such a way that the opponent wins money (or utiles) from the agent *no matter which propositions turn out to be true.*

and

(IB) It is impossible for an opponent to choose certain propositions for which the agent has set betting odds and bet for or against them (against the agent) at the odds chosen by the agent in such a way that the opponent wins money (or utiles) from the agent no matter which propositions turn out to be true if, and only if, the betting quotients corresponding to the odds set by the agent satisfy the probability axioms.

Proposition (IB) is uncontroversial, as it is a theorem, called 'the Dutch book theorem'. The theorem is so-called because a system of propositions, odds and sides that guarantees a sure-win, as described in (IA) and (IB), is called 'a Dutch book'.

However, (IA) and (II) are far from uncontroversial. Proposition (IA) has been challenged on the ground that it may sometimes be rational to leave oneself open to a Dutch book if it is very uneconomical in terms of the agent's time and effort to guarantee against one – especially if the agent thinks it would be very uneconomical in terms of time and effort for an opponent to *detect* an "inconsistency" and construct a Dutch book. And there are certainly situations where it would be irrational for an opponent to bet Dutch book style to insure a small gain: situations in which the opponent thinks that the agent's odds are way off and, thus, where the opponent thinks he can likely make a large gain by betting on a proposition for which the agent has set poor odds. That an opponent *could*, theoretically, detect an inconsistency, construct a Dutch book and use it does not imply that he *would*.

Proposition (II) has been challenged on the ground that an agent may make some bets at unrealistically high odds – odds that do not conform to his rational degrees of belief – if he gets excitement from highly risky situations or likes to impress people – himself included – as being a high roller or just likes to place high odds on, say, the home team's winning. None of these motives themselves seems irrational. Defenders of the Dutch book measurement technique agree that factors such as the ones mentioned in this and the previous paragraph will sometimes influence the agent's setting of odds; so they try to identify and eliminate such factors from the betting situation so that only the agent's degrees of belief will play a role in the choice of odds. (See especially Mellor (1971, 1980) and the "competitive betting situation" approach of Jackson & Pargetter (1976) in this connection.) It would seem, however, that we can never be certain that all of the factors, other than the agent's degrees of belief, that may strongly affect the choice of odds have been eliminated or otherwise taken into account.

Also, (II) has been challenged on the ground that if the stakes are sums of money, then utility must be linear in the amounts involved. The problem, then, is to find this "interval of linearity." If the stakes are "utiles," then the problem is to give a clear analysis of 'utile'. It seems to me that the *unified* decision-theoretic method of measuring subjective probabilities and desirabilities *jointly* from preference data is more promising than the Dutch book method of measuring subjective probabilities from betting behavior and *antecedently* somehow determined desirabilities. (For defenses of the Dutch book approach, see the references cited; for other criticisms, see Kyburg (1978: 159–64), Kennedy & Chihara (1979) and Glymour (1980: 71–2); the criticisms given above were suggested in seminar discussion with Ernest Adams, Charles Chihara and Roger Rosenkrantz.)

Like measurement from preference data alone, deFinetti's (1937) suggestion for measuring subjective probabilities also involves assuming axioms of two kinds: necessary and nonnecessary. Let '$\succ$' stand for the relation 'is more probable than' and let '$\sim$' stand for the relation 'is exactly as probable as'. Then the four necessary axioms are:

(A1) For any propositions E_1 and E_2, either $E_1 \succ E_2$ or $E_2 \succ E_1$ or $E_1 \sim E_2$;

(A2) If E is any proposition that is neither necessarily true nor necessarily false, then $E \vee -E \succ E \succ E \ \& \ -E$;

(A3) For any propositions E_1, E_2 and E_3, if $E_1 \succ E_2$ and $E_2 \succ E_3$, then $E_1 \succ E_3$;

(A4) For any four propositions E_1, E_2, E_3 and E_4, if:

(i) $E_1 \succ E_3$,
(ii) $E_2 \succ E_4$,
(iii) E_1 is incompatible with E_2,
(iv) E_3 is incompatible with E_4;

then: $E_1 \vee E_2 \succ E_3 \vee E_4$.

The one nonnecessary axiom is:

(A5) There exists a set of mutually exclusive, collectively exhaustive and equiprobable ($\sim$) propositions $E_1^*, \ldots, E_n^*$ such that for every proposition E the agent considers, E is equivalent to a disjunction of some of the E_i^* s.

From these axioms, one can infer a unique probability function P on the set of propositions involved such that for any propositions E_1 and E_2, $E_1 \succ E_2$ if, and only if, $P(E_1) > P(E_2)$. The function P is defined as follows: For any proposition E, $P(E) = k/n$ if E is equivalent to a disjunction of k, and of no fewer, of the E_i^* s. (It should be mentioned that deFinetti (1937) also develops an approach involving betting behavior.)

Thus, by getting comparative subjective probability data on a person, one can, if (A1)–(A5) are satisfied by the individual in question, derive quantitative subjective probabilities. These, together with preference data on the individual, will determine numerical desirabilities – assuming that certain axioms of preference are satisfied. Without going into detail, I will intuitively describe how this goes, following, basically, the account of deFinetti (1970: 77–9). The procedure will result in numerical desirabilities being assigned to gains and losses of amounts of money, though it also applies where the outcomes are of other sorts. First, arbitrarily assign desirability 0 to the status quo (or the current fortune of the individual), and pick some arbitrary proposition preferred to the status quo, say one to the effect that the agent gains \$100, and assign to it desirability 1. Desirabilities are assigned to gains between \$0 and \$100 as follows: If a proposition

50

E has probability p and one is indifferent between (i) getting \$100 if E and \$0 if $-E$ and (ii) getting \$$m$, then assign desirability p to a gain of \$$m$. For example, if $P(E) = 0.5$, then m might be 49 so that the desirability of a gain of \$49 would be 0.5. If $P(E) = \frac{1}{3}$, then m might be 32.5 so that the desirability of a gain of \$32.50 would be $\frac{1}{3}$. Desirabilities are assigned to gains of more than \$100 as follows: If a proposition E has probability p and one is indifferent between (i) getting \$0 if $-E$ and \$$m$ ($>$\$100) if E and (ii) getting \$100, then the desirability of a gain of \$$m$ is $1/p$. For example, if $P(E) = 0.5$, one may be indifferent between (i) getting \$0 if $-E$ and \$201.50 if E and (ii) getting \$100, so that the desirability of \$201.50 would be 2. Note that for measuring desirabilities of amounts of gain between \$0 and \$100, we have been solving the equation

$$D(\text{Gaining } \$m) = (1-p) \cdot 0 + p \cdot 1$$

for $D(\text{Gaining } \$m)$ and for measuring desirabilities of gaining amounts greater than \$100, we have been solving the equation

$$1 = (1-p) \cdot 0 + p \cdot D(\text{Gaining } \$m)$$

for $D(\text{Gaining } \$m)$. Thus, this method of measurement assumes that one wants to maximize subjective expected utility. Negative desirabilities are assigned to losses of sums of money in a precisely analogous way.

In summary, we have seen three approaches to the problem of measuring subjective probabilities. The decision-theoretic approach relies on the satisfaction of intuitively plausible axioms of preference and, philosophically, on a dispositional theory of beliefs and desires. This is an integrated approach in which subjective probabilities and desirabilities are measured simultaneously from preference data alone. In the Dutch book approach, subjective probabilities are measured from betting behavior and antecedently somehow determined utilities. And on deFinetti's approach, quantitative probabilities are measured from qualitative probability comparison judgments that are assumed to satisfy a nonnecessary and some necessary axioms; desirabilities can then be measured using the derived probability assignment together with preference data. I have given reasons for doubting the adequacy of Dutch book methods. As to the other two approaches, various reasons in favor of each have been brought to bear. Savage: "It is one of my fundamental tenets that any satisfactory account of probability must deal with the problem of action in the face of uncertainty ... [On deFinetti's approach,] the notion 'more probable than' is supposed to be intuitively evident to the person, without reference to any problem of decision" (1954: 60). DeFinetti: "However, there are also reasons for preferring the opposite approach: the one which we attempt here. This consists in setting aside, until it is expressly required, the notion of utility, in order to develop in a more manageable way the study of probability" (1970: 79–80). However, if, as urged earlier, degrees of belief and desire are, jointly, dispositions to action and, severally, dispositions to nothing in particular, not even probability comparison judgments (or, for that matter, the setting of odds), then neither subjective probability nor subjective desirability can be measured independently. Given this, an integrated, decision-theoretic approach would seem to be conceptually superior both to the probability comparison approach and to the Dutch book approach.

In any case, adequate foundations for the theory of subjective probability are extremely significant philosophically – especially for the theory of confirmation and induction. Confirmation is the relation that obtains between a bit of evidence (or a sentence reporting it) and a hypothesis when learning the evidence makes one rationally more confident in the hypothesis than one was before. The term 'induction' is often used in this connection because the relation of confirmation is generally not that of deductive implication. Thus, we are concerned with the nature of "inductive inference." The core of the Bayesian analysis of confirmation is in two parts. First, according to the analysis, evidence *e confirms, is irrelevant to* or *disconfirms* a hypothesis h according to whether $P(h|e)$ is greater than, equal to or less than $P(h)$ (alternatively, according to whether $P(h|e)/P(h)$ is greater than, equal to or less than 1). And second, the *degree to which e confirms h* is equal to $P(h|e) - P(h)$ (sometimes $P(h|e)/P(h)$ is used instead). Note that this analysis is a natural application of the Bayesian thesis that the learning of a proposition e should change the rest of one's beliefs by conditionalization on e.

Two desirable features of this approach to confirmation can immediately be noted. First (and it should be pointed out that this is not unique to the Bayesian approach), it provides a precise analysis not only of the qualitative notions of confirmation, irrelevance and disconfirmation, but also of the quantitative notion of *degree* of confirmation, Second, and most importantly, how our rational degrees of confidence in hypotheses ought to change, given some new evidence, will typically depend on what background information we possess. To take a rather crude example, the observation of a large number of black ravens makes us more confident that all ravens are black, but the observation of a large number of wooden chairs does not increase our confidence in the hypothesis that all chairs are wooden; for we already have the background information that there are nonwooden chairs. In *this* case, it is *perhaps* crystal clear precisely what the relevant background beliefs *are* and how to *formulate* them. However, this is not always the case. As Suppes puts it,

it is impossible to express in explicit form all the evidence relevant to even our simplest beliefs. There is no canonical set of elementary propositions to be approached as an ideal for expressing exactly what evidence supports a given belief, whether it be a belief about ravens, gods, electrons or patches of red. (1966: 202–3)

Bayesian confirmation theory deals with this problem in a plausible way. As Chihara puts it,

To take account of heterogenous information and evidence obtained from a variety of sources, all of differing degrees of reliability and relevance, as well as of intuitive hunches and even vague memories, the Bayesian theory provides us with a subjective "prior probability distribution," which functions as a sort of systematic summary of such items. (1981: 433)

We shall see later how significant these two advantages are when we look at some of the difficulties with which other approaches to confirmation are confronted and how they can plausibly be dealt with on this Bayesian approach.

To the extent that a theory implies and explains what is already known or believed about its subject matter, the theory is confirmed. And this should hold true for theories about confirmation. Thus, the Bayesian theory of confirmation will be confirmed if it can be shown that it is able to explain and justify accepted forms of inductive inference. Also, a theory is confirmed if it has un- expected or unaccepted consequences that are later borne out. Thus, the Bayesian theory of confirmation should also get confirmation if, on the basis of considerations inspired by the approach, some other accepted forms of inductive inference could be exposed as

53

invalid, rejected and replaced by new, more acceptable ones that are implications of the theory. Finally, it would be important and supportive of the theory if it could be shown that it can deal with some traditionally troublesome cases of confirmation in a promising way. The Bayesian theory is, I think, supported in all three of these ways. Let us first look at how the theory can justify some accepted forms of inductive inference. (For a somewhat different Bayesian point of view on some of what follows, see Hesse (1974: especially 133–62). For criticisms, see Glymour (1980: especially 75–93). And for a non-Bayesian discussion of most of the conditions, see Hempel (1945).)

Entailment condition. This is one of the conditions stated by Hempel in his 'Studies in the logic of confirmation' (1945): If e logically implies h, then e confirms h. The condition is, of course, completely plausible, and, assuming only that $P(h) < 1$, we have

$$P(h|e) = 1 > P(h).$$

Converse entailment condition. It is widely accepted, especially on the hypothetico–deductive model of science, that a theory or hypothesis is confirmed when deductive consequences of the theory or hypothesis are established: If h logically implies e, then e confirms h. The Bayesian criterion implies this, assuming only that $P(h) \neq 0$ (so that also $P(e) \neq 0$) and that $P(e) \neq 1$:

$$P(h|e) > P(h)$$

if, and only if,

$$\frac{P(e|h)P(h)}{P(e)} > P(h) \qquad \text{(applying Bayes' theorem)}$$

if, and only if,

$$\frac{1}{P(e)} > 1 \qquad (P(e|h) = 1 \text{ and dividing by } P(h))$$

if, and only if,

$$P(e) < 1.$$

Initially unexpected evidence. It has often been pointed out that, given two deductive consequences e_1 and e_2, of a hypothesis or theory h, if e_1 is *a priori* (before h is considered) more surprising (unexpected, unlikely) than e_2, then e_1 confirms h more than e_2 does.

54

(For example, let h be Einstein's theory of gravitation, e_1 be a report of a – not perfect but sufficiently accurate – measurement of the movement of Mercury's perihelion and e_2 be a report of an observation of a small pendulum.) Interpreting "degree of *a priori* expectedness" as unconditional ("*a priori*") probability and assuming, as above that $P(h) \neq 0$ and $P(e_1) \neq 1 \neq P(e_2)$, this condition follows from the Bayesian criterion for degree of confirmation:

$$P(h|e_1) - P(h) > P(h|e_2) - P(h)$$

if, and only if,

$$P(h|e_1) > P(h|e_2)$$

if, and only if,

$$\frac{P(e_1|h)P(h)}{P(e_1)} > \frac{P(e_2|h)P(h)}{P(e_2)} \qquad \text{(applying Bayes' theorem)}$$

if, and only if,

$$\frac{1}{P(e_1)} > \frac{1}{P(e_2)} \qquad (P(e_1|h) = P(e_2|h) = 1 \text{ and dividing by } P(h))$$

if, and only if,

$$P(e_2) > P(e_1).$$

A generalized form of another of Hempel's conditions, the *equivalence condition*, is also easily justified by the Bayesian criterion: If e confirms h and h is logically equivalent to h', then e confirms h' to exactly the same degree as it confirms h. But a stronger criterion, endorsed by Hempel, which, as Hempel points out, implies the equivalence condition, is not satisfied by the Bayesian criterion. It is the *special consequence condition*: If e confirms h and h logically implies h', then e also confirms h'. Initially it seems very plausible that if e confirms h, then e must confirm anything else that *must* be true if h is. But, in fact, the special consequence condition is false (at least if the converse entailment condition is true), so it is a virtue of the Bayesian analysis that it does not satisfy the special consequence condition. To see why special consequence is false, if converse entailment is true, consider a hypothesis $f \& g$ and evidence f. Then, by converse entailment, f confirms $f \& g$. Since $f \& g$ logically implies g, f would confirm g

if the special consequence condition were true. But f and g could be any propositions whatsoever. As Hesse describes the situation,

A relation of confirmation which allows any proposition to confirm any proposition is obviously trivial and unacceptable, for it contradicts the tacit condition that confirmation must be a selective relation among propositions. A paradox has arisen by taking together a set of adequacy conditions, all of which seem to be demanded by intuition; hence it is appropriate to call it the *transitivity paradox*. (1974: 143)

My view is that the situation is not a paradox, for I do not believe that the special consequence condition is "demanded by intuition." I would describe the situation as a counterexample to the special consequence condition. To see more intuitively why the special consequence condition should not be expected to hold in general, consider this schema of a situation where the Bayesian criterion violates the condition. Let e, h and h' be such that

   (i) h logically implies h'
  (ii) $P(h') = 0.8$
 (iii) $P(h) = 0.2$
 (iv) $P(e \,\&\, h) = 0.05$
  (v) $P(e \,\&\, -h') = 0.05$
 (vi) $P(e) = 0.1$

The situation can be represented by the Venn diagram of Figure 2. Here we have

$$P(h|e) = 0.5 > P(h) = 0.2,$$

and

$$P(h'|e) = 0.5 < P(h') = 0.8.$$

So it is possible for evidence e to raise the probability of a hypothesis h and lower the probability of a hypothesis h' that is implied by h.

To make the example more concrete, consider a subscriber to a morning newpaper, and suppose his deliverer is so unreliable that on only 0.8 of all days is the paper delivered and on only 0.25 of *these* days does the paper arrive before eight a.m. Thus, h is the hypothesis that the paper will arrive before eight a.m. today and h' is the hypothesis that it will arrive today. Suppose that the deliverer every day takes a different route through the area for which he is responsible, that the subscriber knows this and that

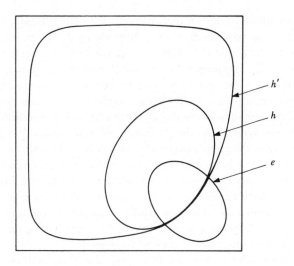

Figure 2.

the subscriber somehow, very early in the morning, obtains the
evidence e: There is a paper shortage for today's morning edition,
so that only about half of the required number of newspapers
could be printed and that the deliverer, with a lighter load and
fewer newspapers to deliver, will surely deliver all the papers he
has – about half the usual number – before eight a.m. Given e,
then, he will get the paper before eight a.m. if he gets it at
all. Thus, $P(h'|e) = P(h|e) =$ about 0.5. Plausibly, e confirms h and
disconfirms h'.

Before leaving the topic of the special consequence condition,
it should perhaps be pointed out that the Bayesian criterion is, as
it should be, about the movement of the probability of a hypothesis
from where it was before to where it is after the evidence comes
in; it is not, as it should not be, about where this probability ends
up relative to any other number. As Hesse (1974: 147) points out,
if we use a different criterion, e.g., what she calls a k-criterion:

e confirms h if, and only if, $P(h|e) > k \geqslant 0.5$,

then the special consequence condition would be satisfied. But, on
a k-criterion, an e can confirm an h even if the result of learning
e is that the probability of h does down. But this seems contrary

to our intuitive notion of confirmation. After all, the general *point* of seeking confirmation of a hypothesis h is (on one view of acceptance) to get $P(h)$ *high* enough for it to be accepted; and even if k is the acceptance "threshold," still it seems that if $P(h) > P(h|e) > k$, then, qualitatively, e renders h less acceptable; and this seems incompatible with e's also confirming h. (Also note that the converse entailment condition is not satisfied by k-criteria.)

As to diagnosing the "paradox of transitivity," it is perhaps sometimes thought, mistakenly, that a hypothesis h' is confirmed by evidence e if its posterior probability is at least as great as that of some other hypothesis h that is definitely confirmed by e. (Note that if h logically implies h', then the probability of h' is necessarily at least as great as that of h.) But, for such h, h' and e, even though $P(h'|e) > P(h|e)$, the probability of h' might have gone down as a result of having learned e, as we have seen.

Positive instance criterion. It is plausible that, at least in a wide variety of cases, a hypothesis that is of the logical form of a universalized conditional is confirmed by positive instances of the hypothesis. That is, a hypothesis of the form *All Fs are Gs* is confirmed by *Fa & Ga*, by *Fb & Gb*, and so on. For example, 'All emeralds are green' is confirmed by the observation of green emeralds (or by sentences describing this evidence). However, there are cases – "the paradoxical cases of confirmation" – where this principle seems not to apply. The Bayesian criterion of confirmation can help isolate precisely where the principle is valid. Let h be the hypothesis *All Fs are Gs* and let e describe a positive instance, e.g., e is *Fa & Ga*. Then, according to the Bayesian criterion, e confirms h if, and only if,

$$P(h|Fa \ \& \ Ga) > P(h)$$

if, and only if,

$$\frac{P(Fa \ \& \ Ga|h)P(h)}{P(Fa \ \& \ Ga)} > P(h) \qquad \text{(applying Bayes' theorem)}$$

if, and only if,

$$\frac{P(Fa|h)P(Ga|Fa \ \& \ h)}{P(Fa \ \& \ Ga)} > 1 \qquad \text{(dividing by } P(h) \text{ and applying the multiplication rule)}$$

58

if, and only if,

$$\frac{P(Fa|h)}{P(Fa \& Ga)} > 1 \qquad \text{(since } Fa \& h \text{ logically implies } Ga\text{)}.$$

Now, let us make the assumption that Fa and h are probabilistically independent. Then, e confirms h if, and only if,

$$\frac{P(Fa)}{P(Fa)P(Ga|Fa)} > 1 \qquad \begin{array}{l} (P(Fa|h) = P(Fa) \text{ and applying} \\ \text{the multiplication rule to} \\ \text{the denominator)} \end{array}$$

if, and only if,

$$P(Ga|Fa) < 1,$$

i.e., if, and only if, one was not already certain that, given that something is an F, it is a G. Thus, the Bayesian criterion of confirmation implies a restricted version of the positive instance criterion: If (i) Fa is independent of h (*All Fs are Gs*) and (ii) $P(Ga|Fa) < 1$, then $Fa \& Ga$ confirms h. Note also that the degree to which $Fa \& Ga$ confirms h is equal to

$$P(h)\left(\frac{1}{P(Ga|Fa)} - 1\right),$$

so that the higher $P(Ga|Fa)$, the lower the degree of confirmation.

Is the positive instance criterion true? Or is only a restricted version, such as the one described above which is implied by the Bayesian criterion, true? I. J. Good (1967) has made a convincing case that the answer to the first question is "no." Interestingly, the examples on which his case is based are ones in which restriction (i) of the Bayesian version of the positive instance criterion is violated. Consider this artificial example, based on one given by Chihara (1981), which in turn was inspired by an example of Good's. There are two urns, each containing 100 marbles. Urn I contains 50 glass black marbles and 50 glass white marbles; urn II contains 5 glass black marbles and 95 plastic white marbles. Suppose you know this, and suppose that one of the two urns is before you, which one it is you do not know. Now consider the hypothesis, 'All the glass marbles in the urn before you are black'. You are allowed to reach in and (randomly) pick one marble. It turns out to be glass and black. Thus, you have evidence $e = Ga \& Ba$ which is (or describes) a positive instance of the hypothesis $h =$ 'All the glass marbles in this urn are black'. Intuitively, given the background information you have, e should actually disconfirm h. And in fact, according to the Bayesian criterion, e does disconfirm h. Supposing that your initial probability for 'Urn I is before me' = your initial probability for 'Urn II is before me' = $\frac{1}{2}$ ($= P(h)$), then $P(h|e) = \frac{1}{11} < \frac{1}{2} = P(h)$ and $P(h|e) - P(h) = -\frac{9}{22}$. Also note that h is not probabilistically independent of Ga, as $P(Ga|h) = \frac{1}{20} < \frac{21}{40} = P(Ga)$, violating restriction (i) of the Bayesian version of the positive instance criterion.

We have seen that the simple Bayesian criterion of confirmation implies and constitutes a justification of the entailment condition, the converse entailment condition, the maxim of initially unexpected evidence and the equivalence condition. On considerations inspired by the Bayesian approach it was seen that the special consequence condition is not universally valid. And we have seen that modifying the positive instance criterion in such a way that it becomes a consequence of the Bayesian criterion makes it immune to one kind of counterexample. All of these considerations support the Bayesian approach to confirmation. (And it should be pointed out that some other, less formal, maxims of inductive reasoning have been given Bayesian explications – such as the maxim that the *simplest* theory for which the evidence provides support should be preferred (e.g. Hesse 1974, Rosenkrantz 1976) and the maxim that the greater the *variety* of supporting evidence, the greater the degree of confirmation (Hesse 1974).) But the approach becomes even more creditable when it is seen that it can resolve some well-known paradoxes and puzzles of confirmation. In what immediately follows, I will briefly indicate how the approach can deal with two of these, known as 'the raven paradox' and 'the grue puzzle'.

The raven paradox is based on the positive instance criterion (one can use the weaker Bayesian criterion) and the equivalence condition. Consider the following logically equivalent hypotheses (where 'Rx' stands for 'x is a raven' and 'Bx' stands for 'x is black'):

h_1: All ravens are black,
h_2: All nonblack things are nonravens,

and the following piece of evidence:

$$e: -Ba \ \& \ -Ra.$$

Plausibly, h_2 is probabilistically independent of $-Ba$, so, since e is a positive instance of h_2, e confirms h_2. Since h_1 is logically equivalent to h_2, it follows, by the equivalence condition, that e also confirms h_1. It has been thought paradoxical that non-black, non-ravens, such as white shoes, confirm the hypothesis that all ravens are black.

Central to the Bayesian resolution of the paradox is its precise explication of 'degree of confirmation'. It will be seen that e indeed confirms h_1, but to a degree so small it is negligible. And we shall see that, compared to the degree to which e confirms h_1, the degree to which

$$e': Rb \ \& \ Bb$$

confirms h_1 (and thus h_2) is quite high. Using the formula given earlier, the degree to which e confirms the hypotheses is

$$P(h_1)\left(\frac{1}{P(-Ra|-Ba)} - 1\right),$$

and the degree to which e' confirms the hypotheses is

$$P(h_1)\left(\frac{1}{P(Ba|Ra)} - 1\right).$$

Given our background information, which is supposed to be systematically summarized in the probability distribution P, $P(-Ra|-Ba)$ should be very, very close to 1. (It is very, very unlikely that a "randomly chosen" nonblack thing would be a raven.) Thus, the degree to which e confirms h_1 should be practically 0. However, the probability that a "randomly chosen" raven would be black may be quite a bit smaller than 1 – especially if we are initially quite uncertain about whether or not h_1 is true. Thus, assuming, reasonably, that $P(-Ra|-Ba)$ is very close to 1 and that $P(Ba|Ra)$ is not, the degree to which e' confirms the hypothesis is quite high compared to the degree to which e does, which is quite low. This is just a bare outline of a Bayesian resolution. The approach has been criticized (e.g., Hempel 1945: 20–1, Scheffler 1963: 284–5, Black 1966: 195–7) and formulated in different ways (e.g., Hosiasson-Lindenbaum 1940, Pears 1950, Alexander 1958, Mackie 1963, Suppes 1966, Swinburne 1973: 156–71, Hesse 1974: 155–62, Chihara 1981) by many philosophers.

The other puzzle to which Bayesian analysis has been applied, the grue puzzle, is also concerned with the relation between hypotheses which are universalized conditionals and their positive instances. But while the raven paradox raises the question of which of two instances confirms one given hypothesis (more) and why, the grue puzzle raises the question of which of two hypotheses a given positive instance (or accumulation of positive instances) confirms (more) and why. The predicate 'grue' is defined as follows:

x is *grue* if, and only if, either (i) x is observed prior to time t_0 and x is green or (ii) x is not observed prior to time t_0 and x is blue

(Goodman 1955: 74). Consider t_0 to be now, and consider the following pieces of evidence and hypotheses:

e_1: A large number of emeralds have been observed (before t_0) and they are all green;
e_2: A large number of emeralds have been observed (before t_0) and they are all grue;
h_1: All emeralds are green;
h_2: All emeralds are grue.

Clearly, e_1 confirms h_1. Does e_2 support h_2 as much as e_1 supports h_1? Intuitively, the answer is "no," especially when it is noticed that e_1 is logically equivalent to e_2. (Since e_1 and e_2 are equivalent, I will henceforth use 'e' and not distinguish between the two pieces of evidence.) The grue puzzle asks: Why does the observation of a large number of green emeralds confirm the hypothesis that all emeralds are green while the observation of a large number of grue emeralds does not confirm the hypothesis that all emeralds are grue?

In 'Quine and the confirmational paradoxes', Charles Chihara (1981) gives a Bayesian analysis of the grue puzzle. What follows is a slightly different analysis that is patterned after and inspired by Chihara's analysis. It should perhaps be pointed out that the problem Chihara addresses is not the same as Goodman's "new riddle of induction" (1955). Chihara: "My problem is the one posed by Quine [(1969: 115)] which I have called the Grue puzzle: that of trying to see why *we, who always come to our experiences with an encompassing complex web of beliefs*, take [e] as giving us confidence in h_1 rather than in h_2" (1981: 437, my italics).

What is to be shown is that $P(h_1|e) - P(h_1) > P(h_2|e) - P(h_2)$, given almost anybody's (reasonable) degrees of belief, and why. Let us first consider the relation between $P(h_1|e)$ and $P(h_2|e)$. It seems that for almost any reasonable person, $P(h_2|e)$ would be very, very low. For, given e, the only way in which h_2 could be true is if we were so fantastically "lucky" that, from among the vast number of emeralds on earth, *all and only* those that are green have been examined and *all and only* the unexamined ones are *blue* (as opposed to red or yellow or clear, and so on). That is extremely improbable. Thus, it is a reasonable assumption that $P(h_1|e) > P(h_2|e)$. It follows that $p(h_1 \& e) > P(h_2 \& e)$. So let α, $\beta > 0$ be such that $\alpha = P(h_2 \& e)$ and $\alpha + \beta = P(h_1 \& e)$. Now consider the relation between $P(h_1|-e)$ and $P(h_2|-e)$. It seems to me that these two probabilities should be about equal. Perhaps, though, $P(h_1|-e)$ should be a bit higher than $P(h_2|-e)$, for $-e$ is compatible with only a few emeralds having been examined, all of which were green; but in all other cases, the two should be about equal. It follows that $P(h_1 \& -e)$ is about equal to $P(h_2 \& -e)$. Thus, let $\gamma > 0$ and δ be such that $\gamma = P(h_2 \& -e)$ and $\gamma + \delta = P(h_1 \& -e)$.

Now,

$$P(h_1|e) - P(h_1) > P(h_2|e) - P(h_2)$$

if, and only if,

$$(P(h_1 \& e)/P(e)) - (P(h_1 \& e) + P(h_1 \& -e))$$
$$> (P(h_2 \& e)/P(e)) - (P(h_2 \& e) + P(h_2 \& -e))$$

if, and only if,

$$\frac{\alpha + \beta}{P(e)} - \alpha - \beta - \gamma - \delta > \frac{\alpha}{P(e)} - \alpha - \gamma$$

if, and only if,

$$\frac{\beta}{P(e)} - \beta > \delta$$

if, and only if,

$$\beta\left(\frac{1 - P(e)}{P(e)}\right) > \delta.$$

And it seems clear that this last inequality should hold. Clearly it holds if $\delta \leq 0$. And if $\delta > 0$, it should also hold. First, δ should be quite a bit smaller than β; and second, initially, before any evidence about the color of emeralds has come in, $P(e)$ should be quite small, say less than 0.5.

In this chapter, I have outlined some of the ways in which Bayesian decision theory is important. As a descriptive theory, *SEU* is not in good repute among psychologists; but we have seen a general way in which it can be defended. We have seen how the normative theory can be applied to the problem of rational acceptance and in moral philosophy. And a very promising analysis of inductive inference, relying on the legitimacy of the notion of subjective probability – a notion that can be developed from *SEU* theory – has been described. The outline has been incomplete, of course. Among the things not discussed are applications of the normative theory to rational betting and information acquisition (Adams & Rosenkrantz 1980) and the possibility of its application in political philosophy (Rawls 1971). And the theory of subjective probability has been applied in analyses of causal beliefs (e.g., Cartwright 1979, Skyrms 1980*a*, and Chapter 7, below) and the explication of actual, historical scientific occurrences (Dorling 1979).

Up to now, I have been relying on a rather vague and crude characterization of *SEU* theory. In the next chapter, we look at the theory in more detail.

3

Bayesian decision theories:
some details

In this chapter, the basic elements of three developments of Bayesian decision theory will be presented: the theories of Ramsey's, Savage's and Jeffrey's. (Since the subsequent chapters will focus on Jeffrey's theory, some readers may wish to concentrate only on the third section of this chapter.) Not all the details will be given, and the discussion will be, for the most part, informal. However, sufficient detail will be given to make possible a discussion of the relative merits of the three theories. The two main problems to which the theories provide different answers are: (i) What are the entities to which the agent's subjective probabilities and desirabilities attach? And (ii) How are these subjective probabilities and desirabilities measured? The points of comparison among the three theories on which this chapter will focus involve the nature of the basic entities assumed by the theories and how they enter into the calculation of subjective expected utility.

In his essay, 'Truth and Probability' (1926), Ramsey is primarily concerned with the problem of defining 'degree of belief', and he suggests a method of measuring an agent's subjective probabilities and desirabilities from his preferences. The basic entities in Ramsey's theory are: outcomes, propositions, gambles and a preference relation on the set of outcomes and gambles. Ramsey calls the outcomes 'possible worlds'; so the outcomes should be thought of as maximally specific relative to the set of eventualities which the agent considers to be relevant to his happiness. They are "the different *totalities* of events between which our subject chooses – the ultimate organic unities" (1926: 176–7, my italics). Gambles are constructed from outcomes and propositions. A gamble is an arrangement under which the agent gets some specified outcome if a given proposition is true and another specified outcome if the proposition is false. I will symbolize gambles according to the following pattern: '$[O_i, p, O_j]$' denotes the gamble: The agent gets outcome O_i if proposition p is true and outcome O_j if p is false. Note that a gamble $[O_i, p, O_j]$ is the same as $[O_j, -p, O_i]$. Also note that, as pointed out earlier, outcomes can be thought of as gambles of a kind: an outcome O_i can be thought of as the gamble $[O_i, p, O_i]$, or $[O_i, p \lor -p, O_i]$. It is assumed that the agent ranks all the outcomes and gambles he considers in one list according to preference and that his preferences satisfy certain constraints. In the example to be given shortly, some of these constraints will be noted.

In Ramsey's theory, desirabilities attach to outcomes and gambles, and probabilities attach to propositions. His measurement technique proceeds in two steps. First, from the agent's preferences, desirabilities for the outcomes and gambles are determined. And second, from the preference data together with the previously determined desirabilities, probabilities for the propositions are determined. To carry out the first step, Ramsey assumes that there exists what he calls 'an ethically neutral proposition believed to degree $\frac{1}{2}$'; this is his first axiom. A proposition p is *ethically neutral* if, and only if, if two outcomes differ only with respect to the truth value of p, then the agent is indifferent between the two outcomes. Intuitively, an ethically neutral proposition is one whose truth value is irrelevant to the agent's happiness, all other things being equal. For example, if you are indifferent between the outcomes 'white wine with chicken on a red checkered tablecloth' and 'white wine with chicken on a nonred checkered tablecloth', then 'The tablecloth is red' is an ethically neutral proposition for you. An ethically neutral proposition p is *believed to degree* $\frac{1}{2}$ if, and only if, the agent is indifferent between the gambles $[O_i, p, O_j]$ and $[O_j, p, O_i]$, yet is not indifferent between the outcomes O_i and O_j, for some O_i and O_j. It is assumed as an axiom that if this is true of some pair of outcomes, then it is true of all such pairs. As an example, most of us would be indifferent between the gambles (i) receiving \$100 if a fair coin lands heads on its next fair toss and receiving nothing otherwise and (ii) receiving nothing if the coin lands heads and \$100 otherwise. Our rationale for indifference between these two gambles is that $P(\text{Heads}) = P(\text{Not-heads}) = \frac{1}{2}$, so that we should be indifferent between staking our chances of getting the \$100 on heads or tails. Also, assuming that someone is indifferent between the two gambles and that the person ranks gambles according to *SEU*, we can calculate that his probability of heads must be $\frac{1}{2}$. Indifference between the two gambles implies equality of their *SEU*s:

$$P(\text{Heads})D(\$100) + P(\text{Not-heads})D(\$0)$$
$$= P(\text{Heads})D(\$0) + P(\text{Not-heads})D(\$100).$$

This equation is true if, and only if,

$$P(\text{Heads})D(\$100) + (1 - P(\text{Heads}))D(\$0)$$
$$= P(\text{Heads})D(\$0) + (1 - P(\text{Heads}))D(\$100)$$

if, and only if,

$$2P(\text{Heads})(D(\$100) - D(\$0)) = D(\$100) - D(\$0)$$

if, and only if,

$$P(\text{Heads}) = \tfrac{1}{2}.$$

Note that I have denoted the desirabilities of the outcomes involved in the gambles by '$D(\$100)$' and '$D(\$0)$', rather than by '$D(\$100$ with the coin's landing heads)', '$D(\$100$ with the coin's landing tails)', and so on. This is because, for most of us, the proposition 'The coin lands heads' is ethically neutral: all other things (e.g. how much money we get) being equal, whether or not the coin lands heads is irrelevant to our happiness. For most of us, the proposition 'The coin lands heads' is an ethically neutral proposition believed to degree $\frac{1}{2}$.

To illustrate Ramsey's technique of determining desirabilities, consider this simple example. After coming home late from work, our agent wants something to drink. His preferences are, in part: Scotch is preferred to Beer and Beer is preferred to Water. We can arbitrarily make the assignments $D(\text{Scotch}) = 1$ and $D(\text{Water}) = 0$. Part of the problem, then, is, as Jeffrey (1965*b*) puts it, to *calibrate* the desirability scale between the outcomes of Scotch and Water, i.e., to assign appropriate desirabilities to outcomes which, like Beer, are preferred to Water and to which Scotch is preferred. Let p be any ethically neutral proposition believed by the agent to degree $\frac{1}{2}$, and consider the gamble [Scotch, p, Water]. Ramsey assumes by way of an axiom that for every gamble, there is some outcome between the gamble and which the agent is indifferent.

Thus, the agent might be indifferent between [Scotch, p, Water] and the outcome Coffee. If so, assign desirability $\frac{1}{2}$ to Coffee. The rationale for this is that if the agent is indifferent between Coffee and [Scotch, p, Water], then their *SEU*s must be equal, i.e., $D(\text{Coffee}) = P(p)D(\text{Scotch}) + P(-p)D(\text{Water}) = \frac{1}{2} \cdot 1 + \frac{1}{2} \cdot 0 = \frac{1}{2}$. To find the desirability of Beer, see whether Beer is preferred to Coffee or Coffee is preferred to Beer. If Beer is preferred to Coffee, we know that $1 > D(\text{Beer}) > \frac{1}{2}$. To narrow down the desirability of Beer further, consider the gamble [Scotch, p, Coffee]. According to Ramsey's axiom, there must be some outcome between this gamble and which the agent is indifferent, say Tomato Juice. Then $D(\text{Tomato Juice}) = P(p)D(\text{Scotch}) + P(-p)D(\text{Coffee}) = \frac{1}{2} \cdot 1 + \frac{1}{2} \cdot \frac{1}{2} = \frac{3}{4}$. If the agent prefers Tomato Juice to Beer, then we can conclude that $\frac{3}{4} > D(\text{Beer}) > \frac{1}{2}$. Next, we consider the gamble [Tomato Juice, p, Coffee] to narrow down $D(\text{Beer})$ even further. Proceeding in this way, $D(\text{Beer})$ can be narrowed down as accurately as we please. The "limit" is $D(\text{Beer})$. In this way, an appropriate desirability between 0 and 1 can be found for any outcome which, like Beer, is preferred to Water and to which Scotch is preferred.

As to assigning desirabilities to outcomes that are preferred to Scotch and to outcomes to which Water is preferred, an axiom of Ramsey's guarantees that there is an outcome, say Martini, such that the agent is indifferent between Scotch and [Martini, p, Water], where p is an ethically neutral proposition believed to degree $\frac{1}{2}$. We assign desirability 2 to Martini and calibrate the desirability scale between the outcomes of Martini and Scotch as before. Also, Ramsey's axiom guarantees the existence of an outcome, say Day Old Coffee, such that the agent is indifferent between Water and [Scotch, p, Day Old Coffee], where p is an ethically neutral proposition believed to degree $\frac{1}{2}$. We assign desirability -1 to Day Old Coffee and calibrate the desirability scale between Water and Day Old Coffee as before. Now, assuming that for every gamble there is an outcome between which and the given gamble the agent is indifferent, Ramsey has given a method for attaching desirabilities to all outcomes and to all gambles.

Of course Ramsey's method does not yield a *unique* desirability assignment, for the choice of zero-point and the unit of desirability was arbitrary. Instead of arbitrarily choosing the outcome Water as the one with desirability 0 and Scotch as the outcome with desirability 1, we could, for example, have arbitrarily chosen Beer as the 0-desirability outcome and Martini as the outcome with desirability 1. However, Ramsey's method does guarantee a desirability assignment that is unique up to linear transformations, i.e., if D and D' are two desirability assignments, each obtained by Ramsey's method, then there are real numbers a and b such that for any outcome or gamble X, $D'(X) = aD(X) + b$. In fact, if $D(Y) = 0$ and $D(Z) = 1$, then $a = D'(Z) - D'(Y)$, and $b = D'(Y)$. (Note the similarity between Ramsey's method and deFinetti's method, discussed previously. The difference is that Ramsey assumes only that there is an ethically neutral proposition of subjective probability $\frac{1}{2}$; deFinetti, on the other hand, determines all the probabilities first.)

Probabilities of the propositions can now be measured. To determine the subjective probability of a proposition p (which need not be ethically neutral), consider a gamble $[O_i, p, O_j]$ in which the agent is not indifferent between O_i and O_j. Here, the outcome O_i must include the truth of p, and the outcome O_j must include the falsity of p. Given this, the *SEU* of the gamble is $P(p)D(O_i) + P(-p)D(O_j)$. Let O_k be an outcome between which and $[O_i, p, O_j]$ the agent is indifferent. Then we must have

$$D(O_k) = P(p)D(O_i) + P(-p)D(O_j).$$

Therefore,

$$D(O_k) = P(p)D(O_i) + (1 - P(p))D(O_j),$$
$$D(O_k) - D(O_j) = P(p)(D(O_i) - D(O_j)),$$

and

$$P(p) = \frac{D(O_k) - D(O_j)}{D(O_i) - D(O_j)}.$$

In the above example, if the agent is indifferent between Coffee and [Tomato Juice, p, Water], for some proposition p, then $P(p)$ should be $(\frac{1}{2} - 0)/(\frac{3}{4} - 0) = \frac{2}{3}$.

In summary, Ramsey's measurement technique can be seen to proceed on four basic assumptions. First, it assumes the correctness of the theory that preference goes by *SEU*, as do the other theories to be discussed in this chapter. *SEU* theory can be thought of as a theory that relates desirabilities of maximally specific things to desirabilities of "not-so-specific" things in a particular way *via* a subjective probability assignment. The not-so-specific things (e.g., acts, gambles) lead to different maximally specific things (outcomes) with different probabilities. Ramsey's method of calibrating the desirability scale proceeds on the insight that, according to *SEU* theory, a gamble involving an ethically neutral proposition of subjective probability $\frac{1}{2}$ and outcomes with arbitrarily set or previously inferred desirabilities must have a desirability midway between the desirabilities of the two outcomes. Then, on the assumption that for every gamble there is an outcome between which and the gamble the agent is indifferent, one can continue to calibrate the desirability scale more and more finely: the guaranteed outcome will figure in other gambles used to more finely calibrate the desirability scale. However, for the purpose of calibrating the desirability scale, it actually need not be assumed that for every gamble there is an outcome between which and the gamble the agent is indifferent. We could proceed to more and more finely calibrate the desirability scale by assuming instead that the agent considers "compound" or "higher-level" gambles that have as "outcomes" *other* gambles which, in turn, may have either outcomes or other gambles as "outcomes." However, Ramsey does have to assume that for any two outcomes, O_i and O_j, that the agent considers, the agent must also be able to consider the gamble $[O_i, p, O_j]$, where p is any ethically neutral proposition believed to degree $\frac{1}{2}$ that enters into any other gamble the agent considers. (In fact, Ramsey's first axiom only guarantees the existence of *one* ethically neutral proposition believed to degree $\frac{1}{2}$; logically equivalent propositions can be identified.) The fact that Ramsey must make this assumption about the possibility of the agent considering certain gambles is rather important; this will be discussed later when comparing the theories described in this chapter.

The third assumption is used in determining desirabilities of outcomes that lie outside the arbitrarily defined unit interval: For any two outcomes O_i and O_j, there is an outcome O_k such that the agent is indifferent between O_j and the gamble $[O_i, p, O_k]$, where p is an ethically neutral proposition believed to degree $\frac{1}{2}$. This assumption would seem to be plausible if among the outcomes the agent considers are outcomes like gains and losses of amounts of money. The fourth assumption is used in determining the probabilities of

70

propositions: For every proposition p, there is an outcome O_k and a gamble $[O_i, p, O_j]$ such that the outcome O_i (O_j) includes the truth (falsity) of p and the agent is indifferent between O_k and $[O_i, p, O_j]$ but not between O_i and O_j. This assumption would also seem to be plausible if among the outcomes the agent considers are outcomes like gains and losses of amounts of money.

It is not immediately obvious how *SEU* theory as developed by Ramsey applies to typical decision situations, for the decisions involved in Ramsey's theory are only about which *outcome* or *gamble* to take when given a choice. Ramsey's theory does not explicitly bring in the idea of an *act*. However, we shall see in the next section that if an ordinary decision problem about which course of action to pursue is formulated in a certain way, then the available acts can reasonably be viewed as gambles of a kind.

SAVAGE

In his book, *The Foundations of Statistics* (1954), Savage generalizes and rigorously develops Ramsey's suggestion of a unified approach to probability and utility. For many years, Savage's theory was the most general formulation of *SEU* theory. Also, the book made popular a "Bayesian" approach to statistics (also explored by deFinetti e.g., 1937), which is now a serious rival to the classical "British–American School."

The basic entities of Savage's theory are:

(i) *states, S_i*, sets, E_i, of which are called '*events*',
(ii) *outcomes, O_j*,
(iii) *acts, A_k*, which are functions from the set of states to the set of outcomes, and
(iv) a preference relation, $\leqslant$ ("is not preferred to"), on the set of acts.

The "states" are to be thought of as possible states of the world, possible states of affairs, possible worlds. They (or, perhaps more accurately, "events" of a certain kind, as we shall shortly see) correspond to Ramsey's propositions that control gambles. An "outcome" is "anything that may happen to the person" (1954: 13). They may be thought of as "states of the agent" and can be distinguished from states as being more directly relevant to the happiness of the agent. Thus, its raining today is a state (or, possibly, an event) and getting caught in the rain today is an outcome. The nature of the distinction between states and outcomes will be discussed further later. The "acts" correspond to Ramsey's gambles, but they are more general than the two-component gambles in Ramsey's theory. The acts result in different outcomes with different probabilities. The act A_k results in outcome O_j with the probability of the event $\{S_i: A_k(S_i) = O_j\}$. Savage's preference relation is on the set of acts while Ramsey's is on the set of gambles *and* outcomes. However, just as we may think of outcomes O_j as gambles, $[O_j, p, O_j]$, of a kind, so we can sometimes think of Savage's outcomes O_j as acts of a kind, namely, constant functions: $A_k(S_i) = O_j$, for all states S_i. Thus, Savage's preference relation can be thought of as on the set of acts and, in a sense, outcomes. (Savage's theory actually requires the agent to rank all "constant acts" in his preference ordering. This is needed to extend definitionally the preference relation to the set of outcomes. This feature of Savage's theory will be discussed later in this chapter.)

Probabilities attach to events (just as Ramsey's probabilities attach to propositions, his events), and desirabilities attach to outcomes and, derivatively *via* Savage's *SEU* formula, to acts. One reason why, officially, probabilities attach to events rather than states is that there may be an infinity of relevant states, each with zero probability. In such a situation, nevertheless, positive probabilities may attach to subsets of the set of states. The following rather artificial example illustrates this: The probability that any given point on a dartboard will be hit is zero even though the probability that the point hit will be within three inches of the bullseye is positive (assuming that the dartboard will be hit, that the points on the dartboard are describable in the standard way by arbitrary pairs of real numbers within some interval and that each point is equally likely to be hit).

When the set of states is finite, however, probabilities may harmlessly be thought of as attaching to states. In order to motivate Savage's official definition of $SEU(A_k)$, let us, as a first approximation, take the formula for *SEU* on Savage's theory to be

$$SEU(A_k) = \sum_i P(S_i)D(A_k(S_i)),$$

or, writing 'O_{ki}' for the outcome that results from performing A_k

in state S_i,

$$SEU(A_k) = \sum_i P(S_i)D(O_{ki}).$$

In fact, when the set of states considered by the agent is finite, this formula is equivalent to the official definition of *SEU*. Also, the official formula for *SEU* has exactly the same *form* as this one, the main difference being that in the official formula, events of a certain kind substitute for the states in the above formula. Note that an important consequence of Savage's analysis is the *Principle of Dominance*: If, for every state S_i, the outcome of act A_k in S_i (i.e., $O_{ki} = A_k(S_i)$) is more desirable that the outcome of act $A_{k'}$ in S_i (i.e., $O_{k'i} = A_{k'}(S_i)$), then A_k is more desirable than $A_{k'}$.

As an example of how states, outcomes and acts figure in decision problems, Savage offers the following:

Your wife has just broken five good eggs into a bowl when you come in and volunteer to finish making the omelet. A sixth egg, which for some reason must either be used for the omelet or wasted altogether, lies unbroken beside the bowl. You must decide what to do with this unbroken egg. Perhaps it is not too great an oversimplification to say that you must decide among three acts only, namely, to break it into the bowl containing the other five, to break it into a saucer for inspection, or to throw it away without inspection. (1954: 13)

The decision problem can be represented, as Savage suggests, by the decision matrix of Table 6. If the desirabilities of the outcomes, O_{ki}, $k = 1, 2, 3$, $i = 1, 2$, and the probabilities of the states, S_i, $i = 1, 2$, are known, then the *SEU*s of the acts, A_k, $k = 1, 2, 3$, can be calculated.

Table 6

State Act	Good (S_1)	Rotten (S_2)
Break into bowl (A_1)	Six-egg omelet (O_{11})	No omelet, and five good eggs destroyed (O_{12})
Break into saucer (A_2)	Six-egg omelet, and a saucer to wash (O_{21})	Five-egg omelet, and a saucer to wash (O_{22})
Throw away (A_3)	Five-egg omelet, and one good egg destroyed (O_{31})	Five-egg omelet (O_{32})

Before describing Savage's technique of measuring probabilities and desirabilities, I would like to point out three important assumptions that are implicit in Savage's approach. (They are also implicit in Ramsey's theory, but I shall discuss them only in relation to Savage's and, later, Jeffrey's theories, the last of which does not require them.) They are, in terminology like that of Adams and Rozenkrantz' (1980):

> *Outcome-functionality*: Each act-state pair determines a unique outcome; that is, for each act A_k and state S_i, performing A_k in state S_i results, with probability 1, in a unique outcome $O_{ki} = A_k(S_i)$;
> *Act-independence*: Which state obtains is not influenced by which act is performed; and
> *Path-free desirabilities*: The desirabilities of the outcomes are not influenced by which act-state pair brings them about.

What happens when these assumptions fail? As to outcome-functionality, consider again Savage's omelet example. Savage himself is of course aware that "a person may not know the consequences of the acts open to him in each state of the world. He might be so ignorant, for example, as not to be sure whether one rotten egg will spoil a six-egg omelet" (1954: 15). In that case, the agent may think, for example, that act A_1 performed in state S_2 may result in outcome O_{11} (say with probability $\frac{1}{10}$) or in outcome O_{12} (say with probability $\frac{9}{10}$). If this is what he thinks, then clearly Table 6 does not accurately represent the decision situation as the agent perceives it and Savage's formula for *SEU* is clearly inapplicable. Savage's resolution to this kind of problem will be discussed below.

As to act-independence, recall that Savage's analysis has as a consequence the principle of dominance, stated previously. But consider this decision problem, posed by Jeffrey (1977). There are only two available acts: smoke two packs a day (S) or quit altogether (Q). And there are just two relevant states: live at least to the age of 65 (L) or die before you reach 65 (K). The relevant outcomes are: living at least to the age of 65 enjoying the pleasures of smoking (SL); living to an age of less than 65 enjoying the pleasures of smoking (SK); living at least to the age of 65 without the pleasures of smoking (QL); and living to an age of less than 65 without the pleasures of smoking (QK). In the same way as Savage's omelet example is represented by Table 6, this decision problem can be represented by the following decision matrix:

	L	K
S	SL	SK
Q	QL	QK

For someone who gets pleasure from smoking, SL is preferred to QL and SK is preferred to QK: all other things being equal, the person would prefer to smoke. Thus, for each of the two states, the outcome of S in that state is preferred to the outcome of Q in that state. So the principle of dominance, a consequence of Savage's analysis, implies that S is preferred to Q, that a rational person who prefers, all other things being equal, to smoke should smoke. This recommendation can easily be seen to be a direct consequence of Savage's analysis by noting that the SEUs of the available acts, on Savage's analysis, are:

$$SEU(S) = P(L)D(SL) + P(K)D(SK);$$
$$SEU(Q) = P(L)D(QL) + P(K)D(QK).$$

Clearly, if $D(SL) > D(QL)$ and $D(SK) > D(QK)$, then $SEU(S) > SEU(Q)$. But surely if one believed that S is a very efficacious *cause* of K, one's desirabilities for the outcomes could be as hypothesized even if, in the end, one rationally prefers Q to S. Obviously, the failure of Savage's analysis to recommend Q over S results from the states' not being independent of the acts, i.e., from failure of the act-independence assumption. A possible resolution to this kind of problem will be discussed below.

Finally, as to the assumption of path-free desirabilities, it is possible, in Savage's omelet example, that the outcome of a five-egg omelet has different desirabilities given the different act-state pairs (A_3, S_1), (A_2, S_2) and (A_3, S_2). The representation of the decision problem in Table 6 is sensitive to this possibility: the outcomes are specified in sufficient detail. A general way of making formulations of decision problems sensitive to this, and thus of ensuring that path-freedom of desirabilities holds, is to include in the specification of the outcomes the act and the state under which they arise. In some cases, this may, of course, force an enlargement of the antecedently thought-up set of outcomes.

Savage's answer to the problem of the possible failure of outcome-functionality in his omelet example is: "nothing could be simpler than to admit that there are four states in the world corresponding to the two states of the egg and the two conceivable answers to the culinary question whether one bad egg spoils a six-egg omelet" (1954: 15). Thus, for example, the act of breaking the egg into the bowl together with the state corresponding to the egg's being rotten and a negative answer to the culinary question results, with probability 1, in the outcome of an edible six-egg omelet.

Actually, Savage's formalism deals generally with the problems of guaranteeing outcome-functionality and act-independence in a somewhat different way. Recall that in Savage's theory, probabilities really attach to events and not to states. In fact, in Savage's theory, the formula given for *SEU* is:

$$SEU(A_k) = \sum_j P(\{S_i : A_k(S_i) = O_j\})D(O_j),$$

or, letting 'E_{kj}' denote the event under which act A_k leads to outcome O_j,

$$SEU(A_k) = \sum_j P(E_{kj})D(O_j)$$

(1954: 70–3). Thus, each state is to be thought of as so specific that, under it, each act results, with probability 1, in a unique outcome. The set of all states which, together with a given act A_k, result in a given outcome O_j is an event E_{kj} that is appropriate to enter into the calculation of $SEU(A_k)$. So, any act together with an event E_{kj} which is, in this sense, appropriate for the calculation of the subjective expected utility of that act determines, with probability 1, a unique outcome. This device would also seem to guarantee act-independence of appropriate events E_{kj}: plausibly, whether or not an act A_k would result in outcome O_j if A_k were the act performed (i.e., whether or not E_{kj} obtains) is unaffected by whether or not A_k is the act actually performed.

Calculating $SEU(A_k)$ relative to the events E_{kj} requires, of course, that the *SEU*s of different acts be calculated relative to different partitions of the states into events. $SEU(A_k)$ is calculated relative to the partition $\{E_{k1}, E_{k2}, \ldots\}$ and $SEU(A_{k'})$ is calculated relative to the partition $\{E_{k'1}, E_{k'2}, \ldots\}$. Jeffrey (1977) suggests a way of partitioning the set of states into events so that the same set of events can be used for the calculation of the SEU of each act. (See also Krantz *et al* (1971: 414–16) in this connection.) Instead of making the events specific enough only to determine the unique outcome of the act whose SEU is being calculated, make the events specific enough so that each determines a unique outcome for *each* act. Thus, instead of using the events E_{kj}, use events

$$E_I = \{S_i : A_k(S_i) = O_{I(k)}, k = 1, \ldots r\}$$

$$= \bigcap \{E_{kj} : I(k) = j\},$$

where I is a function from $\{1, 2, \ldots r\}$ into $\{1, 2, \ldots m\}$, r being the number of available acts and m being the number of possible outcomes. Thus, two states are in the same event if, and only if, they pair the same outcomes with the same acts. The states must be so specific that they determine, in the appropriate way, functions I from the set of acts to the set of states; two states are in the same event if, and only if, they determine, in the appropriate way, the same function. Using basically this device, Jeffrey shows that a decision problem can always be reformulated so that (i) outcome-functionality holds, (ii) act-independence holds (at least this is plausible), (iii) path-free desirabilities holds if the outcomes are sufficiently specific and (iv) the same set of events can be used in the calculation of the SEU of each act.

I will now give a very rough outline of how subjective probability and desirability assignments are derived in Savage's theory. The probability assignment is determined first. To get the (quantitative) probability assignment, a *qualitative* probability relation on the events is first determined. A qualitative probability is a relation $\preccurlyeq$ ("is not more probable than") that satisfies deFinetti's necessary axioms (A1)–(A4), given previously. (DeFinetti's axioms (A1)–(A4) are stated in terms of '$\succ$' and '$\sim$' – "is more probable than" and "is just as probable as" – but '$\succ$' and '$\sim$' can be defined in terms of '$\preccurlyeq$', and vice versa: $E \succ E'$ if, and only if, not $E \preccurlyeq E'$; and $E \sim E'$ if, and only if, $E \preccurlyeq E'$ and $E' \preccurlyeq E$; and $E \preccurlyeq E'$ if, and only if, $E' \succ E$ or $E \sim E'$. Thus, (A1)–(A4) can easily be restated in terms of '$\preccurlyeq$'; also, they could be stated in terms of '$\prec$' and '$\sim$' or in terms of '$\succcurlyeq$', whose interpretations are obvious.)

Savage gives the following definition: For events E and E', $E \leqslant E'$ if, and only if $A \leqslant A'$ for all acts A and A' for which there are outcomes O and O' such that

$$A(S) = O' \text{ for all } S \text{ in } E,$$

$$A'(S) = O' \text{ for all } S \text{ in } E',$$

$$A(S) = O \text{ for all } S \text{ not in } E,$$

$$A'(S) = O \text{ for all } S \text{ not in } E', \text{ and}$$

$$O \geqslant O'.$$

'$O < O'$' is equivalent, of course, to 'not $A_k \leqslant A_{k'}$' where A_k is the "constant act" with outcome O' and $A_{k'}$ is the "constant act" with outcome O. Note that the acts A and A' in the definition can be thought of as the gambles $[O', E, O]$ and $[O', E', O]$, respectively. The rationale for the definition is, of course, that if you prefer to stake your chances of getting the more desirable outcome, O', on E' rather than on E, this must be because you think that E' is at least as probable as E.

Savage's first five postulates, which I shall not state here, guarantee that $\leqslant$ is indeed a qualitative probability. The derivation of a (quantitative) probability assignment is similar to deFinetti's procedure, described previously. Savage advances a ("nonnecessary") postulate that is used in much the same way as deFinetti's nonnecessary condition (A5) to derive a unique probability assignment P such that for any events E and E', $E \leqslant E'$ if, and only if, $P(E) \leqslant P(E')$. One additional postulate makes it possible to prove that there exists a desirability assignment, D, on consequences such that for any two acts A and A', $A \leqslant A'$ if, and only if, $SEU(A) \leqslant SEU(A')$, where SEU is calculated, using the formula for SEU given above, in terms of D and the previously derived probability assignment. The desirability assignment is unique up to linear transformations, i.e., if $A \leqslant A'$ if, and only if, $SEU(A) \leqslant SEU(A')$, both when SEU is calculated in terms of P and D and when SEU is calculated in terms of P and D', then there exist real numbers a and b such that for any outcome O_j, $D'(O_j) = aD(O_j) + b$. The proofs of both the existence and the uniqueness results are based on theorems of von Neumann and Morgenstern's (1947). For details, see Savage (1954).

78

In Jeffrey's decision model, developed in his *The Logic of Decision* (1965*b*), acts, states and outcomes are considered to be entities of the same kind, to which both probabilities and desirabilities attach: propositions. *Acts*, or *act-propositions*, are propositions to the effect that the agent performs certain acts. *States*, or *state-propositions*, are propositions that say that certain states of the world obtain. Let $\{S_1, \ldots S_n\}$ be the finite set of mutually exclusive and collectively exhaustive states considered by the decision maker. *Outcomes*, or *outcome-propositions*, say that a certain outcome, or consequence, results. Let $\{O_1, \ldots O_m\}$ be the finite set of mutually exclusive and collectively exhaustive outcomes the agent considers in his decision situation. Propositions in the Boolean closure of the set of acts, states and outcomes will be called '*decision-relevant propositions*'.

The agent's subjective probability assignment P and desirability assignment D are assumed to satisfy the standard probability axioms and the *desirability axiom*: For any two propositions X and Y, if $P(X \ \& \ Y) = 0$, then

$$P(X \vee Y)D(X \vee Y) = P(X)D(X) + P(Y)D(Y).$$

Of course it follows that if $X_1, \ldots X_r$ are mutually exclusive propositions, then

$$D\left(\bigvee_{i=1}^{r} X_i\right) = \frac{\sum_{i=1}^{r} P(X_i)D(X_i)}{P(\bigvee_{i=1}^{r} X_i)}.$$

Now, where A is any proposition (an especially interesting case is where A is an act), $S_1 \ \& \ A, \ldots S_n \ \& \ A$ are mutually exclusive propositions with disjunction equivalent to A. Thus,

$$D(A) = \frac{\sum_{i=1}^{n} P(S_i \ \& \ A)D(S_i \ \& \ A)}{P(A)}$$

$$= \sum_{i=1}^{n} \frac{P(S_i \ \& \ A)}{P(A)} D(S_i \ \& \ A)$$

$$= \sum_{i=1}^{n} P(S_i | A)D(S_i \ \& \ A),$$

where $P(S_i | A)$ is the probability of S_i conditional on A, or $P(S_i \ \& \ A)/P(A)$. In fact, each of the following four formulas is a consequence of Jeffrey's axioms:

$$D(A) = \sum_{i=1}^{n} P(S_i \mid A) D(S_i \ \& \ A),$$

$$D(A) = \sum_{j=1}^{m} P(O_j \mid A) D(O_j \ \& \ A),$$

$$D(A) = \sum_{i=1}^{n} \sum_{j=1}^{m} P(S_i \ \& \ O_j \mid A) D(S_i \ \& \ O_j \ \& \ A), \qquad \text{and}$$

$$D(A) = \sum_{i=1}^{n} P(S_i \mid A) \sum_{j=1}^{m} P(O_j \mid S_i \ \& \ A) D(O_j \ \& \ S_i \ \& \ A).$$

Terms in these four formulas involving probabilities conditional on a proposition whose probability is 0 are not counted as part of the summation.

If the states and outcomes considered by an agent in a decision situation are as above, then his *conditional expected utility* of an act A, in symbols, $CEU(A)$, is, by definition, given by the expression on the right in the third formula above (or, equivalently, by the expression on the right in the last of the four formulas). Thus, the agent's conditional expected utility of an act is calculated from his desirabilities for maximally specific decision-relevant propositions and his subjective probabilities. The *principle of maximizing conditional expected utility* (*PMCEU*, for short) states that rational preference goes by conditional expected utility and that a rational agent chooses an act that has the greatest conditional expected utility. Conditional expected utility is one interpretation of subjective expected utility. It is called '*conditional* expected utility' because the probabilities that enter into the calculation of subjective expected utility are subjective probabilities *conditional* on the relevant act. *PMCEU* is a version of the subjective expected utility maximization theory. Jeffrey's axioms guarantee that the values denoted by the expressions on the right in the four formulas given above are all equal to $CEU(A)$ and to $D(A)$. Since, for any proposition X, $D(X)$ *is* the agent's desirability of X, an alternative statement of *PMCEU* is: For all propositions X, $D(X) = CEU(X)$.

As to measurement, Ethan Bolker (1967) has proved the following theorems. (See Jeffrey (1978) for another discussion of the theorems and their relation to the logic of decision, and see Appendix 1 for

80

definitions of some of the terms used in the statements of the theorems.)

Existence Theorem

Assume that $\mathcal{D}$, the set of decision-relevant propositions, is a complete, atom-free Boolean algebra. And assume that $>$ ("preference") and $\sim$ ("indifference") are relations on $\mathcal{D}$ such that:

(i) (Transitivity) for all X, Y and Z in $\mathcal{D}$, if $X > Y$ and $Y > Z$, then $X > Z$;

(ii) (Trichotomy) for all X and Y in $\mathcal{D}$, exactly one of the following holds: $X > Y$, $Y > X$, $X \sim Y$;

(iii) (Averaging) for all X and Y in $\mathcal{D}$, if X and Y are disjoint, then: (a) if $X > Y$, then $X > X \vee Y > Y$, and (b) if $X \sim Y$, then $X \sim X \vee Y \sim Y$;

(iv) (Impartiality) for all X, Y and Z in $\mathcal{D}$, if X, Y and Z are pairwise disjoint, $X \sim Y \sim Z$ and $X \vee Z \sim Y \vee Z$, then for all W disjoint from X and Y, $X \vee W \sim Y \vee W$; and

(v) (Continuity) for all $X_1, X_2, \ldots Y$ and Z in $\mathcal{D}$, if $(X_i)_{i=1,2,\ldots}$ is an increasing (or decreasing) sequence in $\mathcal{D}$, $X = \bigvee_{i=1}^{\infty} X_i$ (or $\bigwedge_{i=1}^{\infty} X_i$) and $Y > X > Z$, then $Y > X_i > Z$ for all i larger than some number.

Then there exist a probability assignment P and a (desirability) assignment D on $\mathcal{D}$ such that for all X and Y in $\mathcal{D}$, $X > Y$ if, and only if, $CEU(X) > CEU(Y)$, where CEU is calculated in terms of P and D. In fact, $D = CEU$, so Jeffrey's axioms are satisfied.

Uniqueness Theorem

Suppose

(i) for all X and Y in $\mathcal{D}$, $X > Y$ if, and only if, $CEU(X) > CEU(Y)$, where CEU is calculated in terms of probability assignment P and desirability assignment D, and

(ii) for all X and Y in $\mathcal{D}$, $X > Y$ if, and only if, $CEU(X) > CEU(Y)$, where CEU is calculated in terms of probability assignment P' and desirability assignment D'.

Then there exist real numbers a, b, c and d such that $ad > bc$ and, for all X in $\mathcal{D}$,

$$D'(X) = \frac{aD(X) + b}{cD(X) + d}; \qquad P'(X) = P(X)(cD(X) + d).$$

Note that in the existence theorem, the "necessary" assumptions are (i), (ii), (iii) and (iv). The "nonnecessary" ones are (v) and that $\mathcal{D}$ is a complete, atom-free Boolean algebra. The nonnecessary axioms imply that $\mathcal{D}$ is infinite and contains all infinite conjunctions and disjunctions. But more recently, Domotor (1978) has given necessary and sufficient conditions for representing, in the same way, a preference relation on a *finite* Boolean algebra.

Several advantages of Jeffrey's decision model over Ramsey's and Savage's can now be noted. First, in Jeffrey's theory, the decision maker need not formulate his decision problem in such a way that the assumptions of outcome-functionality, act-independence and path-free desirabilities hold, as he must to apply the Savage theory. Indeed, a Savage-type formulation is a special case of the more general kind of formulation allowed in Jeffrey's theory. A Jeffrey formulation is a Savage formulation when the following conditions hold, where the "states" are, for Savage, "events":

(i) For each act-state pair (A_k, S_i), there is an outcome O_j such that $P(O_j | S_i \ \& \ A_k) = 1$;

(ii) For each act A_k and state S_i, $P(S_i | A) = P(S_i)$, i.e., each state is probabilistically independent of each act; and

(iii) For each outcome O_j, state S_i and act A_k, $D(O_j \ \& \ S_i \ \& \ A_k) = D(O_j)$.

(i) guarantees outcome-functionality, (ii) act-independence and (iii) path-free desirabilities, Jeffrey-style. As Adams and Rozenkrantz (1980) point out, when assumptions (i), (ii) and (iii) are met, the more general Jeffrey formula for *CEU* reduces to the Savage formula, where the probabilities of the states (or events) are not conditional on the relevant act and the desirabilities are of just an outcome. Of course, as pointed out previously, it is always possible to reformulate a decision problem so that Savage's theory applies. Jeffrey (1977) shows in detail how the reformulation can always be done, and, indeed, he shows that after reformulation, the Savage formula for expected utility yields the same values as Jeffrey's does both before and after the reformulation. But this would seem to indicate that reformulation into Savage's standard form is not really worth doing. Why not just apply Jeffrey's formula? In Jeffrey's theory, $CEU(A_k)$ is the same no matter how all possibilities (Savage's states) are partitioned into states (Savage's events). That is, if $\{S_1, \ldots S_n\}$ and $\{S'_1, \ldots S'_{n'}\}$ are two sets of mutually exclusive and collectively exhaustive state-propositions, then $CEU(A_k)$ calculated in terms of the first partition is equal to $CEU(A_k)$ calculated in terms of the second. (And the same goes for partitions of outcomes.) The fact that Jeffrey's decision model is less sensitive to problem formulation than Savage's constitutes one advantage of Jeffrey's theory over Savage's.

An advantage of Jeffrey's system over Ramsey's is that it makes no use of the notion of a gamble. Why is this an advantage? Jeffrey points out (1965b: 146) that a gamble $[O_i, p, O_j]$ is in effect if there is a causal relationship between p, O_i and O_j in virtue of which O_i accrues to the relevant agent if p obtains and O_j accrues otherwise. For example, if I bet you a dollar at even money that p is true, and you accept the bet, then we have set up a causal relationship between p, O_i (you pay me a dollar when we learn whether or not p is true) and O_j (I pay you a dollar when we learn whether or not p is true). It was pointed out earlier that, on Ramsey's theory, if the agent considers outcomes O_i and O_j, then he must also be able to consider the gamble $[O_i, p, O_j]$, where p is any ethically neutral proposition believed to degree $\frac{1}{2}$ that enters into any other gamble the agent considers. For example, Jeffrey points out that if the agent considers the outcomes (O_i) that there will be a thermonuclear war next week and (O_j) that there will be fine weather next week and if he considers any gambles at all on the ethically neutral proposition (p) that this coin will land heads, then he must also be able to consider the gamble, $[O_i, p, O_j]$, that there will be a thermonuclear war next week if this coin lands heads and fine weather otherwise. But, since the gamble is a causal relationship, it would require the agent to revise his causal beliefs in quite bizarre ways, to say the least, for him to consider that this gamble was in effect. Jeffrey's theory, however, does not require that the agent imagine any causal relationship to exist that he does not believe exists. An important advantage of Jeffrey's propositional formulation is that it makes no use of a gamble or other such causal notion.

Suppes (1960) points out a similar difficulty that attends Savage's model. It is not very surprising that a similar difficulty should attend Savage's theory since, as pointed out previously, Savage acts are generalized Ramsey gambles. Savage's system requires that for each outcome, there is an act that invariably results in that outcome. That is, for each outcome O_j that the agent considers, he must also consider an act A_k such that for every state S_i, $A_k(S_i) = O_j$. This is required to extend the preference relation from acts to outcomes, as noted previously. But again, in order for the agent to consider all such acts and include them in his preference ranking, he would sometimes have to revise his causal beliefs in some quite bizarre ways. For example, in Savage's omelet example, in order for Savage's representation results to be applicable, the man would have to rank among the acts shown in Table 6 the act which, whether the egg is good or rotten, results in a good six-egg omelet.

Finally, another advantage of Jeffrey's system over Savage's has to do with the distinction between states and outcomes, which Savage formally incorporates into his system. How is the formal distinction supposed to manifest itself in practical decision problems? As noted earlier, Savage characterizes outcomes as "anything that may happen to the person" (1954: 13). But, since the person is part of the world, anything that may happen to the person is surely a thing that may happen to the world. So it would seem that outcomes ("states of the person") are states ("states of the world") of a kind. So it seems that the distinction between outcomes and states is a distinction between things that may happen to the world *and* the person and things that may happen to the world but *not* the person. Yet it is hard to see why any given place of "drawing the line" would not be arbitrary. An agent with not terribly eccentric beliefs may think that *anything* that happens in the world happens to him, temporally or spacially distant things having only very little, nevertheless some, effect on him (he may believe that time is circular). Elsewhere, Savage remarks that outcomes are "what the person experiences and what he has preferences for," but also, in the next sentence, that "this idea of pure experience, as a good or ill, seems philosophically suspect and is certainly impractical." Savage points out that one of the merits of Jeffrey's theory is "escape from this suspect concept" (1967: 306). In Jeffrey's system, no formal distinction between states and outcomes need be drawn. One *can* draw a distinction by assuming that the decision maker considers two partitions: $\{S_1, \ldots S_n\}$ of states and $\{O_1, \ldots O_m\}$ of outcomes. One can draw *no* distinction by assuming that the decision maker considers just one partition: $\{S_1, \ldots S_n\}$ of states or $\{O_1, \ldots O_m\}$ of outcomes. And one can *blur* the distinction by assuming that the decision maker considers just one partition: $\{S_i \ \& \ O_j : i = 1, \ldots n; \ j = 1, \ldots m\}$. This is another way in which Jeffrey's theory is, virtuously, insensitive to problem formulation. Not only is $CEU(A_k)$ the same no matter what partitions of states and outcomes are used in its calculation, it also exists and is the same whether or not, and no matter how, the agent distinguishes between states and outcomes.

It should be pointed out that the "survey" of Bayesian decision theories in this chapter has been quite incomplete. Notably absent are discussions of the utility theory of von Neumann and Morgenstern's (1947) (which is similar to Ramsey's theory, but begins with antecedently known probabilities and defines gambles using probabilities rather than propositions or events), Pfanzagl's (1968) "wager" approach (which generalizes Ramsey's two-component gambles to two-component compound, higher-level gambles which may have other gambles as "outcomes") and the conditional decision approach of Luce and Krantz (1971) – see also Krantz *et al* (1971) – (which is a conditional expected utility approach that involves conditional decisions, functions from subsets of the set of states into the set of outcomes).

In any case, among the three theories discussed in this chapter, Jeffrey's propositional, conditional expected utility formulation appears to be the most general and the most realistic. It is the most general theory because it allows for, but does not require, satisfaction of outcome-functionality, act-independence and path-freedom of desirabilities; in this and other ways indicated in this chapter, it is less sensitive to the way in which decision problems are formulated than are the other theories. It is the most realistic theory because it does not require attributing to the decision maker certain kinds of bizarre causal beliefs implicit in the consideration of some gambles and "constant acts," nor does it require the decision maker to draw a philosophically suspect distinction between outcomes and states.

Despite the apparent generality of Jeffrey's theory, a number of *prima facie* counterexamples to *PMCEU*, all inspired by what has come to be known as Newcomb's paradox, have recently been constructed. Central to the alleged counterexamples is the observation that *PMCEU* seems not to be sensitive to causal beliefs of a certain kind that a decision maker might have, thus suggesting that

Jeffrey's rule should be revised in a way that brings some causal notions into the calculation of expected utility. In the subsequent chapters, we shall examine the alleged counterexamples and the proposed revisions of *PMCEU* with an eye for determining whether the alleged counterexamples are genuine.

4

The counterexamples

In this chapter, I will present two *prima facie* counterexamples to Jeffrey's *PMCEU* of the kind inspired by Newcomb's paradox, briefly describe a number of others of the same general kind and try to clarify their structure. Newcomb's paradox itself will be discussed in Chapter 8.

The *prima facie* counterexamples are best understood as establishing a *prima facie* conflict between *PMCEU* and another intuitively plausible and well-respected principle of choice which, though not very broadly applicable, is almost certainly true. The second principle is a revised version of Savage's principle of dominance that takes into account the possibility that the states are not act-independent. Henceforth, when referring to the principle of dominance (*PDOM*, for short), I shall be referring to the revised version, stated below.

PDOM will here be given a propositional formulation. That is, the acts, states and outcomes referred to in my statement of the principle will be propositions, *à la* Jeffrey, to the effect that the agent performs such and such an act, that such and such state of the world obtains and that such and such an outcome accrues to the agent, respectively. To state *PDOM*, I must first give the following definition: Where A and B are any available acts and $\{F_1, \ldots F_r\}$ is any set of mutually exclusive and collectively exhaustive decision-relevant propositions, A *dominates B in the agent's preferences relative to* $\{F_1, \ldots F_r\}$ if, and only if, $D(A \& F_i) > D(B \& F_i)$, for $i = 1, \ldots r$. *PDOM* states: If (i) some act, A, dominates every other act in your preferences relative to some partition and (ii) you believe that which act you perform does not causally affect which element of that partition is true, then do A.

Let the states and outcomes considered by the agent be as labeled in the section on Jeffrey in the previous chapter. Then a consequence of *PDOM*, a weaker version, relies on the following definition: For any acts A and B, A *dominates B in the agent's preferences* if,

87

and only if, for any two (maximally specific) decision-relevant propositions of the forms $A \& S_i \& O_j$ and $B \& S_i \& O_j$, $D(A \& S_i \& O_j) > D(B \& S_i \& O_j)$. Then the weaker version states: If (i) some act, A, dominates every other act in your preferences and (ii) you believe that which act you perform does not causally affect which proposition of the form $S_i \& O_j$ is true, then do A.

For a simple two-act $(A$ and $B)$, two state $(S$ and $-S)$ decision situation, PDOM can be simply stated as follows: If (i) $D(A \& S) > D(B \& S)$ and $D(A \& -S) > D(B \& -S)$ and (ii) you believe that which of A and B you do will not affect which of S and $-S$ obtains, then do A.

(For a stronger, but slightly more complicated, version of PDOM, A's dominance of B relative to $\{F_1, \ldots F_r\}$ may be defined as: $D(A \& F_i) \geqslant D(B \& F_i)$ for all i and $D(A \& F_i) > D(B \& F_i)$ for some i. But the simpler version stated above will suffice for our purposes.)

PDOM is intuitively attractive. I believe that it accurately prescribes and describes rational behavior. But it is clearly not very broadly applicable. In very few decision situations does one act dominate all the others. And in very few decision situations do all the relevant causal irrelevancies obtain. But it was long thought that for situations in which PDOM is applicable, PMCEU would agree with PDOM's prescriptions. This was based on the assumption that if a proposition X is believed to be *causally* independent of an act A (i.e., if the agent believes that whether or not A is performed does not causally affect whether or not X will obtain), then X would be (subjectively) *probabilistically* independent of A. It is easy to see that if this assumption is true, then PMCEU will always agree with PDOM in situations where PDOM is applicable. Suppose that A dominates all the other acts in the agent's preferences relative to some partition $\{F_1, \ldots F_r\}$ and that the agent believes that which act is performed does not causally affect which F_i is true. Then PDOM prescribes act A, and, given the above assumption relating causal independence of acts to probabilistic independence of acts, we have:

$$CEU(A) = \sum_{i=1}^{r} P(F_i \mid A) D(F_i \& A)$$

$$= \sum_{i=1}^{r} P(F_i) D(F_i \& A),$$

and, for every other act B,

$$CEU(B) = \sum_{i=1}^{r} P(F_i)D(F_i \& B).$$

Clearly, since A dominates B, $CEU(A) > CEU(B)$. Since this holds for all acts B different from A, $PMCEU$ agrees with $PDOM$'s prescription of A.

The *prima facie* counterexamples to $PMCEU$ described below involve decision situations where the assumption relating causal independence of acts to probabilistic independence of acts seems to fail, so that $PDOM$ gives the right answer and $PMCEU$ seems not to.

Brian Skyrms asks us to consider a rational man who, for some good reason, believes the following about the connection between hardening of the arteries and high cholesterol intake ($1980a$: 128–9). The reason for the high statistical correlation between these two things is not that high cholesterol intake causes hardening of the arteries, as previously thought. Rather, the high correlation is due to there being a *common* cause of these two things: lesions of a certain kind in the artery walls. Previous researchers were deceived about the etiology of the disease because the lesions catch cholesterol from the blood and they somehow cause the victim to increase his cholesterol intake. In fact, though, the increased cholesterol intake is beneficial since it actually slows the growth of the lesions. The level of cholesterol intake has no effect on the vascular health of people who do not have the lesion.

Skyrms then asks what a rational man who believed all this would do if offered eggs benedict for breakfast. It seems that if the man wanted to maximize conditional expected utility, he would not eat the eggs. For if he believes that almost all cases of high cholesterol intake are caused by the lesion and that the lesion is very efficacious in producing high cholesterol intake, then it is plausible that his subjective probabilities are such that the probability of having the lesion is higher conditional on high cholesterol intake than conditional on low to medium cholesterol intake. Thus, since the probability of hardening of the arteries conditional on having the lesion is very high and since the desirability of hardening of the arteries is very low, it seems that $PMCEU$ recommends not eating the eggs benedict.

But it is clear that it would be irrational not to eat the eggs, assuming that the man likes eggs benedict. (Let us assume, in fact, that eating the eggs dominates not eating the eggs in the man's preferences: in each of the four jointly possible states of affairs corresponding to having and not having the lesion and developing and not developing hardening of the arteries, eating the eggs is at least slightly better than not eating them.) For even though the probability of the lesion's being present (and thus of hardening of the arteries) may be higher conditional on high cholesterol intake than on low to medium cholesterol intake, eating the eggs does not *cause* the lesion or hardening of the arteries: the probabilistic relations do not mirror the causal relations in the natural way. *PDOM* prescribes eating the eggs; refraining from the eggs in order to maximize *CEU* is, as Skyrms puts it, "a futile attempt to manipulate the cause by suppressing its symptoms" (1980a: 129).

(One might want to modify the example by assuming that the man must decide between a *life-long policy* of eggs benedict for breakfast and a *life-long policy* of fruit and juice for breakfast.)

Alan Gibbard and William Harper (1978) present the following counterexample. King Solomon wants another man's wife. But he is not sure whether he should summon her, because that would be an unjust act and kings who act unjustly usually face revolts. Where '*J*' symbolizes that Solomon abstains from the woman and '*R*' symbolizes that there will be a revolt, suppose Solomon's desirabilities are as follows: $D(R \& J) = 0$, $D(R \& -J) = 1$, $D(-R \& J) = 9$ and $D(-R \& -J) = 10$. Now Solomon, a student of psychology and political science, believes that unjust acts do not themselves cause revolts. Rather, revolts and unjust acts are effects of a *common* cause. Solomon believes that there are two basic personality types of kings: charismatic and uncharismatic. Charisma tends to produce just acts, uncharisma unjust acts. And uncharismatic kings tend to face revolts while charismatic kings do not. But the revolts against the uncharismatic kings are not caused by their unjust acts but rather by their uncharismatic "sneaky, ignoble bearing." Which personality type a king has depends on genetic make-up and early childhood experiences and cannot be changed in adulthood. Solomon does not know whether or not he is charismatic.

So, Solomon believes that just acts are signs of charisma and thus of being non-revolt-prone, and he believes that unjust acts are signs of uncharisma and thus of being revolt-prone. Since Solomon does not know whether or not he has charisma, his subjective probabilities are such that $P(R|J) < P(R|-J)$. Suppose that $P(R|J) = a$ and $P(R|-J) = a + \varepsilon$ and $\varepsilon > \frac{1}{9}$. Then,

$$CEU(J) = P(R|J)D(R \& J) + P(-R|J)D(-R \& J)$$

$$= 0 + 9(1 - a) = 9 - 9a;$$

$$CEU(-J) = P(R|-J)D(R \& -J) + P(-R|-J)D(-R \& -J)$$

$$= 1(a + \varepsilon) + 10(1 - a - \varepsilon) = 10 - 9a - 9\varepsilon.$$

So, $CEU(J) - CEU(-J) = 9\varepsilon - 1$, which is positive, since $\varepsilon > \frac{1}{9}$. Thus, $CEU(J) > CEU(-J)$; $PMCEU$ appears to recommend act J.

But again, it is clear that J is the wrong recommendation. Solomon knows that unjust acts such as sending for the woman do not cause revolts. So, since all Solomon cares about in his decision situation is having the woman and not having a revolt and since sending for the woman would in no way tend to produce a revolt, he should, as $PDOM$ prescribes, send for her. Again, $PMCEU$ seems to recommend a course of action that is a futile attempt to manipulate the cause (of revolts) by suppressing its (uncharisma's) symptoms (unjust acts). As Gibbard and Harper put it, "Sending for her would be an indication that Solomon lacked charisma, and hence an indication that he will face a revolt. To abstain from the woman for this reason, though, would be knowingly to bring about an indication of a desired outcome without in any way bringing about the desired outcome itself. That seems clearly irrational" (1978: 137).

Skyrms describes a number of other examples of the same general kind. The statistician Ronald Fischer once suggested that the correlation between smoking and lung cancer might be due to a genetic common cause. Assuming this hypothesis were true, then, even though smoking does not cause cancer, still the probability of cancer is higher conditional on smoking than conditional on not smoking. Should one smoke? Calvinism is sometimes thought to involve the thesis that election for salvation and a virtuous life are effects of a common cause: a certain kind of soul. Thus, while leading a virtuous life does not cause one to be elected, still the probability of salvation is higher conditional on a virtuous life than conditional on an unvirtuous life. Should one lead a virtuous life? Also, while going for a medical examination does not usually cause illness, the probability of illness is higher conditional on an examination than conditional on no examination. Should one go to the doctor? And Newcomb's paradox involves a decision situation of the same general kind.

At this point, I would like to introduce some conventions that will simplify the ensuing discussion and also clarify some of the structure of the decision situations of the kind in which I am interested. Skyrms' cholesterol case and Gibbard and Harper's charisma case can be seen to be "isomorphic." For the cholesterol case, let '*L*', '*T*' and '*I*' symbolize propositions to the effect that the lesion is present, that hardening of the arteries develops and that high cholesterol foods are eaten, respectively. For the charisma case, let '*C*' symbolize that Solomon has charisma. We already know what '*R*' and '*J*' symbolize. *L*, *T* and *I* play the same role in the cholesterol case as *C*, $-R$ and *J* play in the charisma case, respectively. *L* and *C* are factors that are not within the agent's control and that cause, independently of what the agent does, *T* and $-R$, respectively. *L* and *C* also cause the acts *I* and *J*, respectively. (I shall freely use expressions like '*L* causes *T*' and '*L* causes *I*', meaning, of course, that the lesion causes atherosclerosis and the lesion causes high cholesterol intake, respectively.) I shall call states that play the same role as *L* and *C* in situations of the kind in question '*common causes*'. I shall call propositions that play the same role as *I* and *J* – acts that are symptomatic of the presence of the common cause – in situations of the kind in question '*symptomatic acts*'. And propositions like *T* and $-R$ – outcomes that are symptomatic of the presence of the common cause – will be called '*symptomatic outcomes*'. When I wish to speak of an arbitrary decision situation of the kind in question – the "general case" – I will use the expressions '*CC*', '*SA*' and '*SO*' to symbolize propositions to the effect that the common cause is present, the symptomatic act is performed and the symptomatic outcome obtains, respectively. And finally, I shall call decision situations of the kind in question '*Newcomb situations*'.

Thus, the causal structure of Newcomb situations can be diagrammatically represented as follows:

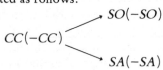

The diagram is to be interpreted as meaning that CC causes SO and SA and (possibly) $-CC$ causes $-SO$ and $-SA$. I do not know if CC's causing SO and SA implies that $-CC$ causes $-SO$ and $-SA$; for instance, it is unclear that the absence of the lesion in the cholesterol case actually *causes* one *not* to have hardening of the arteries. Thus, perhaps, in some Newcomb situations not all of the causal relations indicated in the above diagram will hold; in others, they will all clearly hold. But this does not seem to me to mark an important difference between kinds of Newcomb situations.

Since the distinction between states and outcomes is blurry, the decision situations dicussed above can be characterized in a variety of ways: two-state $(CC$ and $-CC)$ two-outcome $(SO$ and $-SO)$ two-act $(SA$ and $-SA)$; four-state $(CC \& SO, \ CC \& -SO, \ -CC \& SO, \ -CC \& -SO)$ two-act $(SA$ and $-SA)$; four-outcome two-act (as above, considering the states to be outcomes); two-state $(CC$ and $-CC)$ two-act $(SA$ and $-SA)$; or two-outcome $(SO$ and $-SO)$ two-act $(SA$ and $-SA)$. In the last two cases, the utility or disutility of the outcomes or states not explicitly considered is to be thought of as attaching appropriately – given the agent's causal and probabilistic beliefs – to the states or outcomes explicitly considered. All of the above characterizations of Newcomb situations will be used in the ensuing discussion.

I think it would be illuminating to present a recipe for concocting two-state, two-act Newcomb situations. This will help to clarify their structure and show that they are probably not uncommon. I shall say (loosely) that a state S *swamps an act A in an agent's preferences* if $D(-S \& A) - D(S \& A)$ and $D(-S \& -A) - D(S \& -A)$ are both positive or both negative and are large compared to $D(-S \& A) - D(-S \& -A)$ and $D(S \& A) - D(S \& -A)$, which are also both positive or both negative. Then, to construct a Newcomb situation, just find a state S and an act A such that

  (i) A dominates $-A$ in the agent's preferences;
 (ii) S swamps A in the agent's preferences;
(iii) S is very bad compared to $-S$;
(iv) A, like $-A$, causes neither S nor $-S$;

and

  (v) $P(S|A) > P(S|-A)$.

(i), (ii) and (iii) together are equivalent to (ii) plus the assumption that the differences used in defining 'swamps' are all positive. The rationale for (v) is that S causes A. By (i), (iv) and *PDOM*, A is the rational act. But $CEU(-A) > CEU(A)$ if, and only if,

$$P(S|-A)D(S \& -A) + P(-S|-A)D(-S \& -A)$$
$$> P(S|A)D(S \& A) + P(-S|A)D(-S \& A)$$

if, and only if,

$$P(S|-A)D(S \& -A) + (1 - P(S|-A))D(-S \& -A)$$
$$> P(S|A)D(S \& A) + (1 - P(S|A))D(-S \& A)$$

if, and only if,

$$P(S|-A)(D(S \& -A) - D(-S \& -A)) + D(-S \& -A)$$
$$> P(S|A)(D(S \& A) - D(-S \& A)) + D(-S \& A)$$

if, and only if,

$$P(S|A)(D(-S \& A) - D(S \& A)) - D(-S \& A)$$
$$> P(S|-A)(D(-S \& -A) - D(S \& -A)) - D(-S \& -A).$$

It is easy to see that this last relationship holds if S sufficiently swamps A, S is bad enough compared to $-S$ and the difference between $P(S|A)$ and $P(S|-A)$ is great enough. In that case, S is the common cause and A is the symptomatic act in a two-state, two-act Newcomb situation.

So far, I have described only simple, or pure, Newcomb situations. There are also more complex, mixed cases. The man in Skyrms' cholesterol case may think that high cholesterol intake, though often caused by the atherosclerosis lesion, also has some tendency to produce such lesions. Or he may think that high cholesterol intake has a tendency to cause hardening of the arteries, though the primary cause of this is the lesion. Or he may not know what the causal structure of his decision situation is, having partial beliefs in several hypotheses as to what that causal structure is. And these three possibilities are not mutually exclusive.

5

Causal decision theories

To accommodate decision problems of the kind discussed in the previous chapter, a number of philosophers have advocated revising Jeffrey's theory in a way that brings causal notions into the calculation of expected utility. Basically, these philosophers advocate a return to something very much like Savage's theory. In the new "causal decision theories," the probabilities of some states enter into the calculation of expected utility unconditional on the act. As in Savage's theory, these states must be chosen in a special way, a way that guarantees, for example, their causal independence from the acts. The desired effect is that the new theories will agree with the principle of dominance whenever the latter is applicable *and*, being principles prescribing the maximization of an expectation of a kind, be broadly applicable, as the principle of dominance is not.

In this chapter, I will discuss the causal decision theories of Alan Gibbard and William Harper's, Brian Skyrms' and David Lewis'. For another discussion of these theories, as well as the theory of Jordan Howard Sobel's, see David Lewis' 'Causal decision theory' (1981). Also, Nancy Cartwright (1979) gives a related theory, and, "for the record," Richard Jeffrey (1981*b*) sketches a "causalized" version of *PMCEU*.

GIBBARD AND HARPER

The theory of Gibbard and Harper (1978) is based on using probabilities of counterfactual, or subjunctive, conditionals in the evaluation of expected utility instead of conditional probabilities. Where '$A \rightarrow C$' symbolizes the counterfactual conditional 'If A were, then C would be' and $\{O_1, \ldots O_m\}$ is a set of mutually exclusive and collectively exhaustive outcomes containing the possible outcomes of the act A, the *U-expectation* of A, $U(A)$, is given by:

$$U(A) = \sum_j P(A \rightarrow O_j)D(O_j).$$

95

I shall call the Gibbard–Harper rule, which says that preference goes by U-expectation and that one should choose an act that has the greatest U-expectation, 'the *principle of maximizing U-expectation*' (hereafter, '*PMUE*').

In the charisma case, the U-expectations are as follows:

$$U(J) = P(J \mathbin{\Box\!\!\to} R)D(J \,\&\, R) + P(J \mathbin{\Box\!\!\to} -R)D(J \,\&\, -R);$$
$$U(-J) = P(-J \mathbin{\Box\!\!\to} R)D(-J \,\&\, R) + P(-J \mathbin{\Box\!\!\to} -R)D(-J \,\&\, -R).$$

(The outcomes can be thought of as really of the form $A \,\&\, O_j$, and we can assume that $P(A \mathbin{\Box\!\!\to} (A \,\&\, O_j)) = P(A \mathbin{\Box\!\!\to} O_j)$.) Since unjust acts do not in any way tend to bring about revolts, $-J$'s holding would not tend to bring about R. Thus $P(-J \mathbin{\Box\!\!\to} R) = P(R)$. (This depends on a "nonbacktracking" interpretation of counterfactuals. This feature of the Gibbard–Harper approach will be discussed below.) Similarly, $P(J \mathbin{\Box\!\!\to} R) = P(R)$ and $P(-J \mathbin{\Box\!\!\to} -R) = P(J \mathbin{\Box\!\!\to} -R) = P(-R)$. So,

$$U(J) = P(R)D(J \,\&\, R) + P(-R)D(J \,\&\, -R);$$
$$U(-J) = P(R)D(-J \,\&\, R) + P(-R)D(-J \,\&\, -R).$$

Since $D(-J \,\&\, R) > D(J \,\&\, R)$ and $D(-J \,\&\, -R) > D(J \,\&\, -R)$, $U(-J) > U(J)$, agreeing with the recommendations of *PDOM* and our intuitions. And it is easy to see that *PMUE* can be applied in the same way to the cholesterol case and to the other Newcomb situations discussed in the previous chapter and that it will yield the correct recommendation in each case.

Note that the couterfactual conditionals $A \mathbin{\Box\!\!\to} O_j$ play the same role in Gibbard and Harper's analysis as Savage's appropriate events E_{kj} play in his. Just as one of Savage's events E_{kj} together with the act A_k determines a unique outcome O_j, so one of Gibbard and Harper's "events" $A \mathbin{\Box\!\!\to} O_j$ together with the act A determines a unique outcome O_j. And just as the probabilities of the E_{kj}s enter into the calculation of Savage expected utility unconditional on an act, so the probabilities of the $A \mathbin{\Box\!\!\to} O_j$s enter into the calculation of U-expectation unconditional on an act. Recall that in Savage's theory, a partition of E_{kj}s (with constant k, varying j) is appropriate only for the calculation of the expected utility of the act A_k, and not for that of other acts. Similarly, a partition of $A \mathbin{\Box\!\!\to} O_j$s (with constant A, varying j) is appropriate only for the calculation of the U-expectation of the act A, and not for that of other acts. (That such a set of $A \mathrel{\square\!\!\rightarrow} O_j$s *is* a partition is an important assumption of Gibbard and Harper's which will be discussed below.) But just as Jeffrey suggested a method of getting a partition of E_is that is appropriate for the calculation of the Savage expected utilities of all the acts, David Lewis has suggested a method of getting a partition of "full patterns" of counterfactuals that is appropriate for the calculation of the U-expectations of all the acts. A full pattern is a set (or it can be thought of as a conjunction) of counterfactuals $A \mathrel{\square\!\!\rightarrow} O_j$ containing exactly one such counterfactual for each available act, i.e., if A is an available act, then exactly one counterfactual conditional $A \mathrel{\square\!\!\rightarrow} O_j$ with that act as antecedent is in a full pattern. This idea will be discussed more fully in the section on Lewis' causal decision theory.

PMUE's success in the simple Newcomb situations of Chapter 4 is due to the fact that it is sensitive to some causal aspects of such decision situations in a way in which it appears that *PMCEU* is not. Thus, in general, it appears that $P(SA \mathrel{\square\!\!\rightarrow} CC) = P(-SA \mathrel{\square\!\!\rightarrow} CC)$, $P(SA \mathrel{\square\!\!\rightarrow} SO) = P(-SA \mathrel{\square\!\!\rightarrow} SO)$, and so on, while $P(CC|SA) > P(CC|-SA)$, $P(SO|SA) > P(SO|-SA)$, and so on, so that *PMUE* will follow the principle of dominance but *PMCEU* may not. Also, it appears that we cannot modify the Gibbard–Harper rule to get back something like the Jeffrey rule (and still always get the right answer) by taking the probabilities of counterfactuals $A \mathrel{\square\!\!\rightarrow} O_j$ conditional on the act in the calculation of expected utility. Gibbard and Harper argue, in fact, that $P(A \mathrel{\square\!\!\rightarrow} O_j|A) = P(O_j|A)$. Thus, for example, $P(J \mathrel{\square\!\!\rightarrow} R|J) = P(R|J)$, $P(J \mathrel{\square\!\!\rightarrow} -R|J) = P(-R|J)$, $P(-J \mathrel{\square\!\!\rightarrow} R|-J) = P(R|-J)$ and $P(-J \mathrel{\square\!\!\rightarrow} -R|-J) = P(-R|-J)$. This is not implausible, for it would seem that J is an indication of R to the same degree as it is an indication that R would result from performing J, and so on. Thus, maximizing the expectation

$$\sum_j P(A \mathrel{\square\!\!\rightarrow} O_j|A)D(O_j)$$

would lead to the same acts as *PMCEU* does.

Thus, *PMUE* assimilates the agent's causal information in Newcomb situations through the use of probabilities of counterfactuals rather than conditional probabilities in the evaluation of expected utility. It is obvious that, as pointed out earlier, the counterfactuals used in evaluating U-expectation must be given a "nonbacktracking" interpretation. An appropriate interpretation must disallow the following kind of reasoning: It is highly probable that if Solomon were to send for the woman, he would be the kind of person who would, i.e., uncharismatic and thus revolt-prone; it is less probable that he would be the kind of person who would send for her, i.e., uncharismatic and thus revolt-prone, if he were to abstain from her; therefore, $P(-J \mathrel{\square\!\!\!\rightarrow} R) > P(J \mathrel{\square\!\!\!\rightarrow} R)$. The interpretation must be such that if an act A has no causal efficacy in producing either the state S or the state $-S$, then $P(A \mathrel{\square\!\!\!\rightarrow} S)$ equals $P(-A \mathrel{\square\!\!\!\rightarrow} S)$. Conditional probabilities "backtrack," but nonbacktracking counterfactuals do not. It is the nonbacktracking interpretation of counterfactual conditionals that makes *PMUE* sensitive to causal information that the agent has in Newcomb situations, such causal information to which it appears *PMCEU* is insensitive.

While it is easy to express what is required of an interpretation of counterfactuals for it to be appropriate for Gibbard and Harper's purpose, it is quite a different problem to construct a theory of counterfactuals that has the desired nonbacktracking effect. Gibbard and Harper state that they do not appeal to any theory of counterfactuals, but rather to their readers' intuitions. However, it is not clear that this is satisfactory, for in the first place, our intuitions are weak here (at least mine are) and in the second place, some agents might have to suppress strong backtracking intuitions to apply *PMUE* and get the right answer. To these agents, a nonbacktracking interpretation may be quite unintuitive in some cases. I think this point will be born out if we look at a sketch of a Stalnaker-like theory of counterfactuals that Gibbard and Harper give to guide our intuitions:

Let a be an act which I might decide at time t to perform. An a-*world* will be a possible world which is like the actual world before t, in which I decide to do a at t and do it, and which obeys physical laws from time t on. Let W_a be the a-world which, at t, is most like the actual world at t. Thus W_a is a possible world which unfolds after t in accordance with physical law, and whose initial conditions at time t are minimally different from conditions in the actual world at t in such a way that 'I do a' is true in W_a. The differences in initial conditions should be entirely within the agent's decision-making apparatus. Then 'I do $a \mathrel{\square\!\!\!\rightarrow} S$' is true [if, and only if,] S is true in W_a. (1978: 127)

There are two difficulties with this theory – and, I suspect, with any theory that tries to build in the nonbacktracking feature – that bear directly on Gibbard and Harper's analysis. The first has to do with the requirement that the differences in initial conditions "should be entirely within the agent's decision-making apparatus." It seems that this could be interpreted *either* as a requirement that all the initial conditions with respect to which the two worlds differ should be within the agent's influence to affect *or* as a requirement that all the initial conditions with respect to which the two worlds differ should be, as it were, "in the agent's head," i.e., that all the differences should be differences in the agent's decision making process. What I have to say about the requirement, however, applies, I believe, to both interpretations.

Looking at the Charisma case, suppose Solomon believes that the conjunction of some set of factors that are *outside* his decision making apparatus – say $-C$ (lack of charisma) together with some other factors $F_1, \ldots F_n$ (he may not know what these other factors are) – are physically incompatible with J, and with having done J. In part, he may believe this because he believes that $-C$ together with the other factors invariably cause $-J$. But he may also believe that J invariably causes things which $-C, F_1, \ldots F_n$ together invariably prevent (or, what is the same thing, that $-C, F_1, \ldots F_n$ together invariably cause things which J invariably prevents). Thus, Solomon (who, let us say, has weak intuitions about counterfactuals and is seeking guidance from the above sketch of a theory) believes that no possible world that obeys physical laws from time t (the time at which he either does J or does $-J$) on and in which $-C, F_1, \ldots F_n$ are all true (before at and after t) is sufficiently different in initial conditions from one in which he either has charisma or one of the F_is is false that 'Solomon does J' is true in it. (Below, I will discuss the possibility that physical laws are suspended in W_a at or around time t.)

How should such a case be handled? Of course it will not do to say that W_a is undefined if every possible world that obeys physical laws from time t on and in which 'I do a' is true differs from the actual world in initial conditions that are not within the agent's decision making apparatus. For then, how should Solomon interpret $J \boxrightarrow C$ and $J \boxrightarrow -C$? If Solomon lacks charisma and $F_1, \ldots F_n$ are all true, W_J is undefined and, thus, so are the truth values of $J \boxrightarrow C$ and $J \boxrightarrow -C$. If Solomon does not know the truth values of $-C, F_1, \ldots F_n$, he does not even know if the truth values of $J \boxrightarrow C$ and $J \boxrightarrow -C$ are defined, so it hardly seems appropriate for him to attach probabilities to them.

Another possibility is that in defining the truth values of $J \Rightarrow C$ and $J \Rightarrow -C$, we consider a world $W_{J,C}$: the world which obeys physical laws from time t on and which is minimally different from the actual world at t in such a way that (i) 'Solomon does J' is true in it and (ii) C has the same truth value in it as it has in the actual world. Thus, in evaluating the truth values of $J \Rightarrow C$ and $J \Rightarrow -C$ we may have to consider a world that differs from the actual world in initial conditions that are outside the agent's decision making apparatus but not one that differs with respect to the truth value of C. There are at least three problems with this suggestion. First, it seems rather arbitrary to define the truth value of the counterfactuals $J \Rightarrow C$ and $J \Rightarrow -C$ with reference to a world in which C – as opposed to one or more of the other factors $F_1, \ldots F_n$ – has the same truth value as it has in the actual world. For the agent may think that it is the truth value of C that would most likely be different were he to do J and not those of other factors. And even assuming that it is reasonable to consider a world in which the truth value of C is the same as it is in the actual world, on what basis is it to be decided *which* of $F_1, \ldots F_n$ should be false in the world used to define the truth values of $J \Rightarrow C$ and $J \Rightarrow -C$ (if $-C, F_1, \ldots F_n$ are true in the actual world)? (This problem will be discussed more fully below.) Second, under this suggestion, $J \Rightarrow C$ and $J \Rightarrow -C$ are equivalent to C and $-C$, respectively. So, why not just use $P(C)$ and $P(-C)$ in the evaluation of expected utility instead of $P(J \Rightarrow C)$ and $P(J \Rightarrow -C)$? Then, U-expectation threatens to reduce to Skyrms' K-expectation, which will be discussed in the next section of this chapter. And third, what is the criterion according to which we would define the truth value of a counterfactual $A \Rightarrow S$ with reference to a world in which the truth value of S is the same as it is in the actual world? Certainly if Solomon believed that J caused C, we would not want to define the truth value of $J \Rightarrow C$ or $J \Rightarrow -C$ with reference to the world $W_{J,C}$, defined above. If the criterion is whether S is within the influence of A, then U-expectation begins to look even more like Skyrms' K-expectation.

Another possibility is to give up the requirement that the differences in initial conditions should be entirely within the agent's decision making apparatus and to define W_a just as the world which obeys physical laws from time t on and which is minimally different from the actual world at t in such a way that 'I do a' is true in it.

Under this suggestion there is no reference to factors that are not within the agent's decision making apparatus. Now Solomon believes that the conjunction of $-C, F_1, \ldots F_n$ is physically incompatible with J: that in every possible world which obeys physical laws from T on and in which $-C, F_1, \ldots F_n$ are true, $-J$ is true. Therefore, in W_J at least one of $-C, F_1, \ldots F_n$ must be false. But again, we ask, "Which ones?" Presumably, this would depend on the truth values of $-C, F_1, \ldots F_n$ in the actual world. If at least one of them is false in the actual world, then perhaps their truth values in W_J would be the same as their truth values in the actual world. But if they are all true in the actual world, then which are false in W_J? There are $2^{n+1}-1$ possibilities. On the sketched theory of counterfactuals, the ones that are false in W_J are those whose falsehood leaves W_J most similar to the actual world. But how is similarity to be characterized? This problem will be discussed below.

We are assuming, of course, that Solomon does not know the truth values of $-C, F_1, \ldots F_n$. But he believes that at least one of $-C, F_1, \ldots F_n$ must be false in W_J. This alone is enough to make it reasonable to think that Solomon believes that C is more probable in W_J than it is in W_{-J}, so that $P(J \mathbin{\square\!\!\rightarrow} C)$ is actually greater than $P(-J \mathbin{\square\!\!\rightarrow} C)$. And if Solomon believes that the conjunction of C with some other factors, $F_1', \ldots F_m'$, is physically incompatible with $-J$, then it seems even more reasonable to think that Solomon thinks that C is more probable in W_J than it is in W_{-J}, so that again $P(J \mathbin{\square\!\!\rightarrow} C) > P(J \mathbin{\square\!\!\rightarrow} -C)$. And this contradicts what is essential to the Gibbard–Harper analysis.

Someone sympathetic to U-expectation might try to meet the above objections by saying, "You are imagining a situation in which Solomon has some positive degree of belief in the proposition that he will be completely determined to do one of the available acts. But in this case, we do not have a decision problem. If Solomon really believed that he is free to choose, he must believe that neither all of $-C, F_1, \ldots F_n$ are true nor are all of $C, F_1', \ldots F_m'$ true. Only if he believed this could he believe that he is free to do whichever of J and $-J$ he determines to be the rational act. And only then is there a real decision problem. And in this case there is no problem about which of $C, F_1, \ldots F_n, F_1', \ldots F_m'$ are true in W_J and W_{-J}. As you pointed out above they all have the same truth values in W_J and W_{-J} as they have in the actual world."

My reply is three-fold. First, it might simply be the case that Solomon attaches some positive probability to the proposition (F^*) that either all of $-C, F_1, \ldots F_n$ or all of $C, F'_1, \ldots F'_m$ are true. And there is still a real decision problem, for Solomon's degree of belief in this proposition may not be 1. And it is consistent, reasonable and desirable for one to try to determine what the rational act is knowing full well that one may or may not be able to do that act. Second, it seems unrealistic – and un-Bayesian – for the agent to just *assume* that he is completely free to do any of the acts that he considers in his decision making process. In fact, such an assumption might lead to the wrong act. Consider the somewhat eccentric person who gets extra utility from an act the more likely he thinks that he is determined to do some other act. And third, if the decision maker *is* to assume F^* away, what is the decision-theoretic mechanism by which this should be accomplished? Should one, for decision purposes, make all probabilities conditional on $-F^*$? Or should Solomon consider counterfactuals whose antecedents are conjunctions of an act-proposition and $-F^*$ instead of just an act-proposition? Or should some other method be used? It is unclear how promising any of these methods are.

Another way of meeting the above objections might be: "You have misinterpreted the sketched theory of counterfactuals. If, in the actual world, $-C, F_1, \ldots F_n$ are all true and if they are all outside the agent's decision making apparatus, then they are all true in W_J even if $-C, F_1, \ldots F_n$ are, together, physically incompatible with J. For W_J only has to obey physical laws at times before and after Solomon performs J. If there is a physical law to the effect that $-C$, $F_1, \ldots F_n$ together invariably cause $-J$, then this law is suspended in W_J when Solomon performs J. And if there are laws to the effect that $-C, F_1, \ldots F_n$ together invariably cause S and that J invariably causes $-S$, then the second law is suspended in W_J when Solomon performs J. Since $-C, F_1, \ldots F_n$ are outside the agent's decision making apparatus, and since they together invariably cause S, then S is also outside the agent's decision making apparatus and, hence, is true in W_J. The only ways in which W_J and the actual world differ are with respect to J and with respect to things that J, in W_J, causes that are not prevented by factors outside Solomon's decision making apparatus."

Two points ought to be made here. First, aside from difficulties Solomon (and others whose intuitions about counterfactuals are weak and need guidance) may have in envisaging worlds in which physical laws break down, it would seem in some cases to be rather unintuitive to analyze counterfactuals in terms of the truth or falsity of their consequences in such worlds. Indeed, many people would, I think, consider the question "What would be the case if I were to do A?" to be equivalent to the question "What would be the case, given physical law, if I were to do A?" That is, they would think that a counterfactual of the form $A \mathrel{\Box\!\!\!\to} C$ has the same truth value as the corresponding one of the form $(A \mathrel{\&} L_1 \mathrel{\&} L_2 \mathrel{\&} \ldots \mathrel{\&} L_n) \mathrel{\Box\!\!\!\to} C$, where the L_is are true physical laws. At least this shows that an analysis of counterfactuals involving lawlike statements would have to be different from the sketched theory.

Also, consider acts that take a long time to finish, like taking an ocean voyage, and consider a counterfactual conditional of the form 'I take an ocean voyage' $\mathrel{\Box\!\!\!\to} S$, for some consequent S. It seems rather unintuitive to say that this conditional is, by definition, true if S is true in some particular world in which physical laws are suspended during my trip.

The second point that ought to be made is that the response under discussion invokes the notion of a state's being outside the agent's decision making apparatus. The notion is invoked to characterize how W_J and the actual world differ after time t. According to the response, if a state is outside the agent's decision making apparatus, then, for any act A, its truth value in W_A is the same as its truth value in the actual world, so that if some state S is outside the agent's decision making apparatus, $A \mathrel{\Box\!\!\!\to} S$ has the same truth value as S. So, as queried previously, why not just use $P(S)$ in the evaluation of expected utility instead of $P(A \mathrel{\Box\!\!\!\to} S)$ for such states and use $P(S|A)$ for the other states. Then, perhaps, we will not need, in addition to the notion of states' being outside the agent's decision making apparatus, a theory of counterfactuals. This, basically, is Skyrms' approach, in which the notion of a state's being outside the influence of the available acts is central. At the end of the next section, on Skyrms, the two approaches will be compared.

A second difficulty with the sketched theory concerns the notion of "minimal difference" between a world W_a and the actual world at a given time. Making sense of this notion depends, for one thing, on making sense of comparing worlds with respect to their degrees of similarity to the actual world. The problems involved in characterizing this kind of similarity are well-known. For example, should the comparison be made on the basis of the number of properties the worlds share? But then which properties of which kinds count for this purpose? And which properties of which kinds count most? And how should we compare properties and kinds of properties with respect to their importance as a basis for comparing degrees of similarity?

But also, if there is to be a world W_a that is *minimally* different from the actual world at a time, then the similarity relation must not be dense. That is, the similarity relation must be such that it is not the case that for every a-world, there is another a-world that is more similar to the actual world than the first. Solomon must not believe, for example, that for every J-world in which C holds there is a more similar J-world in which $-C$ holds and for every J-world in which $-C$ holds there is a more similar J-world in which C holds. Thus, either the similarity relation or the specifications of possible worlds must be sufficiently "coarse." But how coarse can they be for *PMUE* still to yield the correct prescription?

And even assuming that such a similarity relation can be adequately explicated, Gibbard and Harper's analysis further requires that there be a *unique* minimally different a-world. Solomon must not think, for example, that there are *both* minimally different J-worlds in which C holds *and* minimally different J-worlds in which $-C$ holds. As Gibbard and Harper point out, their Axiom 2, $(A \boxright -S) \leftrightarrow -(A \boxright S)$ (Stalnaker's principle of conditional excluded middle), which is crucial to their analysis, depends on the uniqueness assumption. Their Axiom 2 is crucial to their analysis because if it does not hold, then their formula for U-expectation is not a formula for an expectation at all; it would neglect the possibility that none of the $A \boxright O_j$s (A fixed, j varying) holds, a possibility to which the agent may attach some, perhaps high, probability. The uniqueness assumption may be challenged on two counts. First, if it holds, then no two worlds having, at t, different initial conditions can both be minimally different, with respect to their pasts, from the actual world; and this would seem to be questionable. And second, even if the similarity relation has this feature, it must further be the case that there is only one way in which a world minimally different at t from the actual world can unfold *after* t; and the indeterminist challenges this. Gibbard and

Harper state that in circumstances in which their Axiom 2 breaks down, a more general approach than theirs is needed. Later, we shall look at David Lewis' suggestion for generalizing Gibbard and Harper's approach.

It should perhaps be pointed out again that Gibbard and Harper do not appeal to the theory of counterfactuals they sketch (except as a rationale for their Axiom 2) or to any other theory, but rather to their readers' intuitions. They do not regard the principles that follow from the sketched theory as self-evident: "Our reason for casting the rough theory in a form which gives these principles is that circumstances where these can fail involve complications which it would be best to ignore in preliminary work" (1978: 128). My point here is that the intuitions appealed to must be constrained, and perhaps strained, for their analysis to come out right. It would be desirable to have a theory of decision that can be applied by decision makers with weak intuitions about counterfactuals, or strong backtracking intuitions. And it is questionable whether a clear, plausible theory of counterfactuals that has the desired non-backtracking effect can be constructed. Without such a theory, there is always the possibility of other interpretations of the subjunctive by decision makers. As Skyrms points out, "The latitude for interpretation that subjunctives allow makes this a kind of minimal theory, to the effect that there is a way of resolving the ambiguity of the subjunctive that gives the right answer" (1980a: 132).

Giving the right answer is not the same as giving the right answer for the right reason. The crucial thing about pure, simple Newcomb situations is a certain causal feature: the absolute causal independence of the chance of the symptomatic outcome SO (or of the chance of the common cause CC) from the symptomatic act SA. But, as Jeffrey (1981a) points out, the Gibbard–Harper analysis does not deal directly with this causal feature but rather with something which, given a suitable theory of counterfactuals, would be a consequence of the fact that Newcomb situations have that feature: namely, the equality of $P(SA \mathbin{\square\!\!\rightarrow} SO)$ and $P(-SA \mathbin{\square\!\!\rightarrow} SO)$ and of $P(SA \mathbin{\square\!\!\rightarrow} CC)$ and $P(-SA \mathbin{\square\!\!\rightarrow} CC)$. In order to get to the causal heart of the matter with a U-expectation approach, one must construct a suitable theory of counterfactuals which is sensitive in the right way to a state's being within or outside of the agent's influence and which has these equalities as a consequence. These equalities are crucial for the Gibbard–Harper analysis, and it is clear that they make the analysis work in the simple Newcomb situations discussed in Chapter 4. But, as Jeffrey points out, if the analysis gets the right answer for the right reason, then the analysis should be broadly applicable.

Consider, for example, the three mixed Newcomb situations described at the end of Chapter 4. In these examples, it is clear that under a theory of counterfactuals that is suitable for Gibbard and Harper's decision rule, the relevant equalities of probabilities of counterfactuals should not hold. What is not clear is whether or not the Gibbard–Harper rule would give the correct prescriptions in these more complicated decision situations. We have no guarantee.

A representation theorem for *PMUE* of the kind described earlier for the *CEU* approach would go a long way in support of a claim that *PMUE* is broadly applicable, assuming of course that the qualitative assumptions of the theorem would be intuitively plausible, as those of the *CEU* representation theorems are. One advantage that a successful *CEU* approach to Newcomb situations would have over the *U*-expectation approach is evidence of broad applicability given by the *CEU* representation theorems. This is related to another advantage: namely, that *PMCEU* does not require decision makers to make counterfactual judgments. When a representation theorem for *U*-maximization is found, it would seem that its qualitative assumptions would have to involve a new primitive in addition to the preference relation that can capture the force of the subjunctive judgments expressed on the quantitative side with the connective □→. Perhaps the new primitive would be one that theories of counterfactuals invoke, perhaps a similarity relation on possible worlds. In any case, in view of the controversial nature of counterfactuals, perhaps we can expect the new primitives and the new assumptions of a *PMUE* representation theorem also to be controversial.

SKYRMS

Skyrms suggests that in a decision situation we may classify factors (states) according to whether they are "outside the influence of our action" or "may be influenced by our actions." In the cholesterol case, for example, having or not having the atherosclerosis lesion is a factor outside the influence of the agent's available acts. Skyrms suggests the following:

Let K_is be maximally specific specifications of the factors outside our influence at the time of decision which are causally relevant to the outcome of our actions, and let C_js be specifications of factors which may be influenced by our actions. Then I suggest that we should maximize the K-expectation:

$$U_K(A) = \sum_i Pr(K_i) \sum_j Pr(C_j \text{ given } K_i \ \& \ A) \, \text{Utility} \, (C_j \ \& \ K_i \ \& \ A)$$

$$= \sum_{i,j} Pr(K_i) Pr(C_j \text{ given } K_i \ \& \ A) \, \text{Utility} \, (C_j \ \& \ K_i \ \& \ A)$$

(1980a: 133).

For a K_i to be a specification of some factor F is for K_i either to imply F or to imply $-F$. K_i will be a specification of F if either F is a conjunct of K_i or $-F$ is a conjunct of K_i. Thus, K_i is a maximally specific specification of the factors outside our influence which are causally relevant to the outcome of our action if, for every such factor F, either F or $-F$ is a conjunct of K_i. The K_is form a partition, as do the C_js.

In our notation, the K-expectation of an act A is given by:

$$U_K(A) = \sum_i P(K_i) \sum_j P(C_j | K_i \ \& \ A) D(C_j \ \& \ K_i \ \& \ A)$$

$$= \sum_{i,j} P(K_i) P(C_j | K_i \ \& \ A) D(C_j \ \& \ K_i \ \& \ A).$$

Note that

$$\sum_j P(C_j | K_i \ \& \ A) D(C_j \ \& \ K_i \ \& \ A)$$

is just $CEU(K_i \ \& \ A)$ and is, thus, the same no matter what partition of C_js is used in calculating it. Thus, the K-expectation of A can be expressed as:

$$U_K(A) = \sum_i P(K_i) CEU(K_i \ \& \ A).$$

Where the K_is are as described above, it is uncontroversial that $CEU(K_i \ \& \ A) = D(K_i \ \& \ A)$. Thus,

$$U_K(A) = \sum_i P(K_i) D(K_i \ \& \ A).$$

This formula for K-expectation has the same form as Savage's formula for expected utility. And, as in Savage's theory, the partition of factors whose probabilities enter into the calculation of

107

expected utility unconditional on the act must be chosen in a special way.

It is easy to see that maximizing K-expectation will always agree with *PDOM* in situations in which the latter is applicable. By the definition of the K_is, which act you perform does not affect which K_i is true. So, if an act A dominates every other act relative to the partition of K_is, *PDOM* will recommend act A, and so, obviously, will Skyrms' suggestion.

In the cholesterol case, for example, L and T are factors that are outside the influence of the agent's actions, and they are causally relevant to the outcome of his action in the sense that they are causally relevant to his eventual level of happiness. If we consider T and $-T$ to be the outcomes, we may allow that they are causally relevant, in a degenerate sense, to themselves. This will simplify the calculation of $U_K(I)$ and $U_K(-I)$ below. So each K_i should have either L or $-L$ as a conjunct and either T or $-T$ as a conjunct. The K-expectations of the acts I and $-I$ are as follows:

$$U_K(I) = P(L \ \& \ T)D(L \ \& \ T \ \& \ I) + P(L \ \& -T)D(L \ \& -T \ \& \ I)$$
$$+ P(-L \ \& \ T)D(-L \ \& \ T \ \& \ I)$$
$$+ P(-L \ \& -T)D(-L \ \& -T \ \& \ I);$$
$$U_K(-I) = P(L \ \& \ T)D(L \ \& \ T \ \& -I)$$
$$+ P(L \ \& -T)D(L \ \& -T \ \& -I)$$
$$+ P(-L \ \& \ T)D(-L \ \& \ T \ \& -I)$$
$$+ P(-L \ \& -T)D(-L \ \& -T \ \& -I).$$

Clearly, having the eggs benedict maximizes K-expectation, since I dominates $-I$. And in the charisma case, where C and R are outside the influence of the available acts and $-J$ dominates J in Solomon's preferences, it is easy to check that maximizing K-expectation agrees with the principle of dominance, *PMUE* and our intuitions that Solomon should send for the woman.

Note that if we blur the distinction between outcomes and states, the K-expectation and the U-expectation of an act can be seen to be equal, at least for the simple examples of Newcomb situations presented in Chapter 4. That is, if we set

$$U(A) = \sum_{ij} P(A \ \Box\!\!\rightarrow (S_i \ \& \ O_j))D(A \ \& \ S_i \ \& \ O_j),$$

then the K- and U-expectations of acts considered in the two main examples of Chapter 4 are equal. For instance, in the cholesterol case, considering T and $-T$ to be outcomes,

$$
\begin{aligned}
U(I) = {} & P(I \mathbin{\square\!\!\rightarrow} (L \mathbin{\&} T))D(L \mathbin{\&} T \mathbin{\&} I) \\
& + P(I \mathbin{\square\!\!\rightarrow} (L \mathbin{\&} -T))D(L \mathbin{\&} -T \mathbin{\&} I) \\
& + P(I \mathbin{\square\!\!\rightarrow} (-L \mathbin{\&} T))D(-L \mathbin{\&} T \mathbin{\&} I) \\
& + P(I \mathbin{\square\!\!\rightarrow} (-L \mathbin{\&} -T))D(-L \mathbin{\&} -T \mathbin{\&} I) \\
= {} & P(L \mathbin{\&} T)D(L \mathbin{\&} T \mathbin{\&} I) + P(L \mathbin{\&} -T)D(L \mathbin{\&} -T \mathbin{\&} I) \\
& + P(-L \mathbin{\&} T)D(-L \mathbin{\&} T \mathbin{\&} I) \\
& + P(-L \mathbin{\&} -T)D(-L \mathbin{\&} -T \mathbin{\&} I),
\end{aligned}
$$

and similarly for $U(-I)$.

Of course K-expectation has to get more complicated than characterized above, for in some decision situations an agent may not know which factors are outside his influence. To handle this, Skyrms says that we should construct hypotheses about what is outside our influence whose truth values are also outside our influence. The suggestion is to get a set of mutually exclusive and collectively exhaustive hypotheses H_n – whose truth values are outside our influence – such that according to H_n, K_{ni}s are maximally specific and collectively exhaustive factors that are outside the agent's influence and C_{nj}s are mutually exclusive and collectively exhaustive factors which may be influenced by the agent's actions. Then the new maximally specific specifications of factors that are outside our influence are of the form $H_n \mathbin{\&} K_{ni}$. These are the new "K_is." Letting the new "C_js" be propositions of the form $H_n \mathbin{\&} C_{nj}$ and plugging into the formula given for K-expectation, the K-expectation of an act A is:

$$
\begin{aligned}
& \sum_{nmij} P(H_n \mathbin{\&} K_{ni})P(H_m \mathbin{\&} C_{mj} \mid H_n \mathbin{\&} K_{ni} \mathbin{\&} A) \\
& \qquad \times D(H_m \mathbin{\&} C_{mj} \mathbin{\&} H_n \mathbin{\&} K_{ni} \mathbin{\&} A) \\
& = \sum_{nij} P(H_n \mathbin{\&} K_{ni})P(C_{nj} \mid H_n \mathbin{\&} K_{ni} \mathbin{\&} A)D(C_{nj} \mathbin{\&} H_n \mathbin{\&} K_{ni} \mathbin{\&} A) \\
& = \sum_{ni} P(H_n \mathbin{\&} K_{ni})CEU(H_n \mathbin{\&} K_{ni} \mathbin{\&} A).
\end{aligned}
$$

(No matter how one reads 'may', it is not clear that the H_n & C_{nj}s are "specifications of factors which may be influenced by our actions," for the H_ns are, by hypothesis, outside the influence of our actions. Also, it is not easy to see how an H_n can be a factor which is *causally* relevant to the outcome of our action, of which the K_is are supposed to be maximally specific specifications. But later on in this section, I will give what I think are more satisfactory characterizations of what the K_is and C_js should be, according to which the H_n & K_{ni}s are indeed K_is and the H_n & C_{nj}s are indeed C_js.)

Thus, Skyrms' causal decision theory has a device for dealing with the kind of mixed Newcomb situation about whose causal structure the agent is uncertain: ultimately, the K_is are of the form H_n & K_{ni}. I shall call Skyrms' rule, which says that preference goes by K-expectation and that one should choose an act that has the greatest K-expectation, 'the *principle of maximizing K-expectation*' (hereafter, '*PMKE*').

It is clear that *PMKE* gives the correct prescriptions in the pure Newcomb situations discussed in Chapter 4, and, as just noted, *PMKE* is equipped for dealing with at least one kind of mixed Newcomb situation. We shall eventually have to consider other kinds of mixed Newcomb situation in connection with *PMKE*. But let us first note an unclarity in Skyrms' characterization of what kinds of causal relations the K_is and C_js are supposed to have with the available acts.

Let us assume, for now, that the agent has full belief in one of the H_ns: he knows what the causal structure of his decision situation is. Thus, the K_is may be thought of as of the simple form K_{ni} and the C_js as of the simple form C_{nj}. Since the agent concentrates all his belief in just one H_n, though, we may drop the subscript 'n' on the 'K's and 'C's.

Precisely what features of an agent's causal beliefs are supposed to determine whether a factor should be specified in the K_is or may be left to be specified in the C_js instead? The K_is have to specify enough but not too much. They must specify the factors that are outside the influence of the acts, but to which the acts may be probabilistically relevant, so that the probabilities of specifications of these factors will never occur conditional on an act in the evaluation of K-expectation; this is so that *PMKE* will agree with *PDOM*. But they must not specify too much: they must not specify factors that are within the influence of the acts: the K_is have to be act-independent, as Savage's events must be. But exactly *which* actions must a factor be within the influence of for it to be left unspecified in the K_is? I shall consider three suggestions of necessary and sufficient conditions for whether a factor must be left unspecified in the K_is: (i) a factor is to be left unspecified in the K_is if, and (obviously) only if, it is within the influence of *at least one* of the available acts, (ii) a factor is to be left unspecified in the K_is (obviously) if, (but also) and only if, it is within the influence of *all* of the available acts, and (iii) a factor is to be left unspecified in the K_is if, and only if, it is within the influence of the act *whose K-expectation is being calculated.*

Adopting (i) cannot, by itself, solve the problem. Consider this modification of the cholesterol case. It is a mixed Newcomb situation; for future reference, I shall call it 'DS_1'. The agent considers just two states: L (presence of the lesion) and $-L$ (absence of the lesion). In this decision situation, however, there are three available acts. The agent may decide on a policy of high cholesterol intake (this act, caused by L, has no effect on whether or not the lesion is present); he may decide on a policy of low to medium cholesterol intake (this act also has no effect on whether or not the lesion is present); or he may stop eating altogether. In this last case, no lesion can develop and any lesion he already has will dissolve; but, of course, he will soon die. Here, the presence or absence of the lesion is a factor that is within the influence of at least one of the available acts. Thus, according to suggestion (i), L is not to be specified in the K_is. But taking L and $-L$ to be C_js, it is easy to see that *PMKE* will prescribe the wrong act: refraining from eggs benedict but not from food in general.

Another example showing the inadequacy of (i) is the following, which I shall call 'DS_2'. It is a mixed Newcomb situation that is exactly like the original cholesterol case except that the agent believes that high cholesterol intake has a very, very small, negligible tendency to produce the lesion and that low to medium cholesterol intake has a very, very small, negligible tendency to prevent and dissolve such lesions. Since the acts' influence on L is so small as to be negligible, the correct act should be the same whether we neglect the fact of the influence or not. The correct act, that is, is I. But since L is, nevertheless, within the influence of the acts, we should, according to (i), leave L unspecified in the K_is. But taking L and $-L$ to be C_js, it is again easy to see that

111

PMKE will recommend the incorrect act: low to medium cholesterol intake.

Also, adopting (ii) is no solution. Consider another modification of the cholesterol case, which, for future reference, I shall call '*DS₃*'. In it, the agent considers just the two states L and $-L$. There are three available acts. First, the agent may decide to eat only high cholesterol foods that have been treated by an inexpensive procedure that makes high cholesterol foods dissolvers of lesions; only high cholesterol foods can be so treated. Second, he may decide to eat untreated high cholesterol foods. And third, he may decide to eat only low to medium cholesterol foods. So, the presence or absence of the lesion is within the influence of the first act but not within the influence of the other two. Clearly, since, by hypothesis, the agent likes high cholesterol foods more than low to medium cholesterol foods and since he does not like the lesion, he should opt for the first act. But, under suggestion (ii), since L is not within the influence of *all* of the available acts, L should be specified in the K_is. In this decision situation, then, the K_is are just L and $-L$, and *PMKE* will, relative to this partition of K_is, prescribe the act of eating only low to medium cholesterol foods, an incorrect act. Clearly, the probabilities of L and $-L$ should occur conditional on the first act in the evaluation of its expected utility.

This example suggests that (iii) may be a way out. To adopt (iii) is to adopt a more general rule of maximizing K-expectation where the hypotheses H_n are replaced with more complex hypotheses H_n^* about which states are outside of or within the influence *of which acts*. For each hypothesis H_n^* and each act A, let K_{nAi}s be maximally specific specifications of the factors which are, according to H_n^*, outside the influence of act A and let C_{nAj}s be specifications of factors which may, according to H_n^*, be influenced by act A. Then the suggestion is to modify the K-expectation of an act A to:

$$\sum_{nij} P(H_n^* \ \& \ K_{nAi}) P(C_{nAj} | H_n^* \ \& \ K_{nAi} \ \& \ A)$$

$$\times D(C_{nAj} \ \& \ H_n^* \ \& \ K_{nAi} \ \& \ A).$$

This will not work. It introduces a kind of distortion into the evaluation of an act. To see this, consider, for example, this decision situation, which, for future reference, I shall denote by '*DS₄*'. It is a two-state, two-act decision situation. A coin will be tossed. If it lands heads (state S), the agent wins \$100. If it lands tails (state $-S$), the agent gets nothing. Now the agent may either cheat (act A), for example by replacing the fair coin with a two-headed coin, or not cheat (act $-A$). Reasonably, it would seem, the agent has full belief in one hypothesis H_n^*: the one according to which S and $-S$ are within the influence of act A and are outside the influence of act $-A$. Since the agent has full belief in this one hypothesis, we may drop the subscript n on the 'K's and 'C's. Thus, S and $-S$ are C_{Ai}s, and they are also K_{Ai}s. Now the agent believes that if he cheats, the probability will be 1 that heads will come up: $P(S|A) = 1$ and $P(-S|A) = 0$. And he believes that if he does not cheat, the chances of heads are even: $P(S|-A) = P(-S|-A) = 0.5$. Suppose also that, all else being equal, the agent prefers not to cheat. Suppose, in fact, that his desirabilities for this decision situation are: $D(S \& -A) = 4$, $D(S \& A) = 3$, $D(-S \& -A) = 1$ and $D(-S \& A) = 0$. Thus, we have, according to the suggested revision of K-expectation,

$$U_K(A) = P(S|A)D(S \& A) + P(-S|A)D(-S \& A)$$
$$= (1)(3) + (0)(0)$$
$$= 3,$$

and

$$U_K(-A) = P(S)D(S \& -A) + P(-S)D(-S \& -A).$$

Now if the agent is initially completely uncertain about which act he will perform, then it is plausible that $P(A) = P(-A) = 0.5$. Since it is a general truth that $P(S) = P(A)P(S|A) + P(-A)P(S|-A)$, we have $P(S) = (0.5)(1) + (0.5)(0.5) = 0.75$ and $P(-S) = 0.25$. Thus,

$$U_K(-A) = (0.75)(4) + (0.25)(1)$$
$$= 3.25.$$

The suggested revision of *PMKE* prescribes not cheating. However,

$$CEU(A) = U_K(A) = 3,$$

113

and

$$CEU(-A) = P(S|-A)D(S \& -A) + P(-S|-A)D(-S \& -A)$$
$$= (0.5)(4) + (0.5)(1)$$
$$= 2.5.$$

PMCEU recommends cheating.

It seems clear that the *CEU* evaluations are the correct ones in this situation: maximization of the revised version of *K*-expectation leads to the wrong act. (As a rough check of this, note that *PMUE* also recommends cheating.) The problem, of course, is that the weighting of the desirabilities is wrong in the *K*-expectation of the act $-A$. For $P(S)$ has both an act A component ($P(S \& A)$) and an act $-A$ component ($P(S \& -A)$), and the same goes for $P(-S)$. In calculating the expected utility of $-A$, the act A components of $P(S)$ and $P(-S)$ should be ignored. That, in fact, is the effect of using the probabilities of S and $-S$ *conditional on* $-A$ in the evaluation of $CEU(-A)$. Any application of the suggested revision of *PMKE* that involves a hypothesis H_n^* that is not equivalent to one of the old hypotheses H_n and that has positive subjective probability will involve a distortion of this kind.

Anyway, there is intuitive reason to think that one should not believe any hypothesis H_n^* that is not equivalent to one of the old hypotheses H_n. It is not unreasonable to think (though I do not insist) that if a factor is within the influence of one of the available acts, it is within the influence of them all. For example, if an act A causes a state S, then a way to prevent S – i.e. to cause $-S$, thereby influencing whether or not S obtains – would be to perform $-A$. And if it is true that 'within the influence of one' implies 'within the influence of all', then if a factor is *outside* the influence of at least one of the available acts, it is outside the influence of *all* the available acts. Thus, we should also have: 'outside the influence of one' implies 'outside the influence of all'. Henceforth, when I refer to *K*-expectation or to *PMKE*, I shall be referring to the original versions.

Note that if we accept the conditionals, 'within (outside) the influence of one act' implies 'within (outside) the influence of all the acts', of the previous paragraph, DS_1 and DS_2 still retain their force and, in DS_3, the *K*-expectation ordering of the two non-optimal acts will be wrong; in DS_4, *PMKE* will prescribe the correct act. However, DS_1, DS_2 and DS_3 are not counterexamples to *PMKE*. As Skyrms has suggested in discussion, we can introduce an additional partition $\{L', -L'\}$, where L' is the proposition to the effect that the agent already, at the time of decision, has the lesion. This will change the three decision situations, formally, into four-state decision situations. Plausibly, L' and $-L'$ are factors that are outside the influence of all the available acts. And the agent will believe this if he believes that "backwards causality" is impossible, i.e., if he believes that a cause cannot be future to its effect. Thus, taking L' and $-L'$ to be the K_is, their probabilities will never occur conditional on any of the acts in the evaluations of K-expectation. The propositions L ('The lesion is or will be present') and $-L$ are factors that are within the influence of (at least one of) the available acts in DS_1, DS_2 and DS_3, so, in the evaluation of K-expectation, their probabilities will occur conditional on the act whose K-expectation is being evaluated *but also on one of L' and $-L'$*. But the probability of L (or $-L$) conditional on one of L' and $-L'$ and on the act of eating (ordinary) high cholesterol foods should be the same as its probability conditional on the same one of L' and $-L'$ and the act of eating only low to medium cholesterol foods. That is, $P(L|L' \& I) = P(L|L' \& -I)$ and $P(L|-L' \& I) = P(L|-L' \& -I)$. (Note that I have committed a kind of abuse of notation here, for in the cases of DS_1 and DS_3, in addition to I and "$-I$," there is a third available act: stopping eating altogether in DS_1 and eating treated high cholesterol foods in DS_3.) So, since also the probabilities of L' and $-L'$ occur only unconditional on an act in the evaluation of K-expectation, all the probabilities occurring in the K-expectations of the available acts will mirror the agent's causal beliefs in just the right way and, as is easy to see, *PMKE* will give the correct prescription when the K-expectations are calculated relative to L' and $-L'$ being the K_is and L and $-L$ being C_is.

What this shows is that we cannot always expect to be able to construct K_is that are appropriate for a given decision situation as conjunctions of propositions and negations of propositions that the agent initially, naively considers to be decision-relevant. Sometimes it will be necessary to *enrich* the set of decision-relevant propositions in order to express distinctions that are not expressable in terms of the initially considered propositions. The problem of characterizing what goes into the K_is and what may be left for the C_is is *not* just the problem of saying how they should be constructed from the initially considered decision-relevant propositions, for those propositions may be inadequate as a basis from which to get appropriate K_is and C_js.

In what follows, I shall address both the problem of *characterizing* appropriate partitions and that of *finding* such partitions. Note that the problem of finding appropriate partitions of K_is and C_js is really just the problem of finding the K_is. Once these have been found, it will not matter which partition of C_js we use; this was pointed out earlier. But as to characterization, a partition of K_is is appropriate in virtue both of which factors get specified in them and which factors do not get specified in them. Recall that the K_is must specify enough *but not too much*. So I think that the problem of characterization is best thought of, at least initially, as the problem of characterizing appropriate *pairs* of partitions of K_is and C_js. Another reason for framing the characterization problem in this way is that, in the first stages of the investigation, it will be useful to consider not only what causal relations appropriate K_is have to the acts but also what causal relations anything that goes unspecified in the K_is (e.g., the C_js) should have to the acts and what ternary causal relations the K_is, C_js and acts should have to each other.

The problem of finding appropriate K_is is two-fold. First, there is the problem of how to go about suitably enriching the set of propositions that the agent initially, perhaps naively, considers to be decision-relevant, so that appropriate K_is may be expressable in terms of the enriched set. Second, there is the problem of characterizing which elements may appropriately serve as K_is and which as C_js. The second problem is that of finding what I shall call 'the appropriateness conditions' for pairs of partitions of K_is and C_js: it is the characterization problem. These conditions will specify what kinds of causal relations appropriate K_is and C_js will have to the available acts and to each other. Applying these appropriateness conditions to *find* an appropriate pair of partitions presupposes a solution to the first problem, that of how to suitably enrich the set of decision-relevant propositions. However, a solution to the second problem does not presuppose a solution to the first. I will put off until later a discussion of the first problem. Now, by considering various ways of enriching the set of decision-relevant propositions in particular examples, I shall seek to isolate the appropriateness conditions. A solution to this second problem will,

116

of course, be useful in seeking a solution to the first, for the enriched set of propositions must be just rich enough so that partitions that satisfy the appropriateness conditions can be expressed in terms of it. Also, the conditions will play an essential role in the main argument of Chapter 7.

(The assumption that the agent is certain about the causal structure of his decision situation is still in effect.)

One of the appropriateness conditions is obvious and hardly needs comment at this point. Since the probabilities of the K_is are taken unconditional on the act in K-expectation, the K_is must be causally independent of the acts: they must be outside the influence of the available acts. Just as Savage's events must be act-independent since their probabilities enter into his formula for expected utility unconditional on the act, the same must hold for Skyrms' K_i's. We know that our condition must specify *causal* independence of acts, and not merely *probabilistic* independence, because Newcomb situations seem to show that these two kinds of independence of acts are not coextensive. But, of course, the acts need not be causally independent of the K_is: the common causes in Newcomb situations should be counted as K_is (or at least as specified in the K_is). The fact that the appropriate K_is we eventually came up with for DS_1, DS_2 and DS_3 were outside the influence of *all* the available acts is an indication that we should always try to come up with K_is that are outside the influence of all the available acts. (Also, as pointed out earlier, it is not unreasonable to think that – though I do not insist that – if a factor is outside the influence of at least one of the available acts, it is outside the influence of all of the available acts.) The first appropriateness condition is:

AC_1: While the acts may be within the influence of the K_is (according to the agent's beliefs), the K_is are not within the influence of any of the available acts (according to the agent's beliefs).

Of course more conditions are needed – the satisfaction of AC_1 alone is clearly not sufficient to guarantee the appropriateness of a pair of partitions. Consider DS_1 again and let us introduce the following new partition of factors that are outside the influence of all the available acts: $\{L'', -L''\}$, where L'' is the proposition that the sun is losing mass. If we calculate K-expectation relative to this being the partition of K_is and $\{L, -L\}$ being the partition of C_j's,

PMKE will prescribe a wrong act. Even though L'' and $-L''$ are outside the influence of the available acts and L and $-L$ are within the influence of (at least one of) the available acts, still *PMKE* gives a wrong recommendation when K-expectation is calculated relative to these partitions. This is because even if we fix one of the K_is, high cholesterol intake is still an indication of the presence of the lesion.

Also, the satisfaction of AC_1 and a condition to the effect that the K_is be *about* the current state of the agent's arteries is not sufficient to guarantee the appropriateness of a pair of partitions. Consider the proposition L''': 'The agent presently has the lesion but only in arteries in his left thumb'. If we introduce, as the partition of K_is, the partition $\{L''', -L'''\}$, and again consider L and $-L$ to be C_js, then *PMKE* will recommend an incorrect act in DS_1 and DS_2, low to medium cholesterol intake, and in DS_3, the K-expectation ordering of the two non-optimal acts will be incorrect. This is because fixing the very probable – and therefore decisive – K_i, $-L'''$, high cholesterol intake is still evidence for L: there would just have to be a lesion elsewhere than in the agent's left thumb for both L and L''' to be true.

In this example, $L(L|-L''' \& I) > P(L|-L''' \& -I)$ not because I causes L but rather because, even fixing $-L'''$, L can still obtain and cause I: lesions not confined to the left thumb still cause high cholesterol intake. (Note that I have committed the same abuse of notation as before: in the cases of DS_1 and DS_3, in addition to I and "$-I$", there is also a third act. Also, if you think that, because the third act causes $-L$, I must be considered to have some tendency to produce L, then still the *main* reason for the above inequality is not that I has this small tendency: the main reason is still that L causes I, even given $-L'''$. And the same goes for DS_2, in which the two acts have a very small, negligible influence on L.) This example suggests the following as an appropriateness condition:

AC_2: For every i, j and act A, the difference between $P(C_j|K_i \& A)$ and $P(C_j|K_i \& -A)$ reflects the extent to which the agent believes that A is positively or negatively causally relevant to C_j (given K_i); it is not a reflection of the extent to which the agent may believe that C_j is positively or negatively relevant to A (given K_i).

Of course a positive difference between the two probabilities is supposed to reflect belief in positive causal relevance of A to C_j, given K_i, i.e., belief that either A causes C_j given K_i or $-A$ causes $-C_j$ given K_i. And a negative difference is supposed to indicate belief in negative causal relevance of A to C_j given K_i, i.e., belief that, given K_i, either A causes $-C_j$ or $-A$ causes C_j. Note that the extent to which the agent believes that something X is causally relevant to something Y has two parts: first, how strong the agent's belief is that X is causally relevant to Y and, second, how efficacious one of X and $-X$ is in bringing about one of Y and $-Y$, according to the agent's beliefs.

One way to arrange for the satisfaction of AC_2 is to arrange for the K_is to be specific about the C_js that the agent believes are causally relevant to the acts. That is, if the agent believes that some C_j is causally relevant to the acts, then revise the K_is so that each will have as a conjunct that C_j or its negation. *More accurately*, the K_is should be made specific relative to the *ways of the C_js' being true* that the agent believes are causally relevant to the acts. This, essentially, is what we did in introducing the partition L', $-L'$ into DS_1, DS_2 and DS_3. Note that L – a C_j – is equivalent to the disjunction of the following three propositions:

L_1: The lesion is already, at the time of decision, present, and it will be present in the future;

L_2: The lesion is already, at the time of decision, present, but it will be absent in the future;

L_3: The lesion is, at the time of decision, absent, but it will be present in the future;

and $-L$ is equivalent to:

L_4: The lesion is, at the time of decision, absent, and it will be absent in the future.

What are the ways of L's being true that are causally relevant to the agent's action? Clearly (if we rule out "backwards causality"), the lesion can cause high cholesterol intake only if it is already, at the time of decision, present. Thus, L_1 and L_2 are the ways of L's being true that are causally relevant to the agent's action. So we could make the K_is specify L_1 and L_2 to obtain satisfaction of AC_2. However, which of L_1 and L_2 is true, if either is, is within the influence of our acts in DS_1, DS_2 and DS_3. So we should make the K_is specify the disjunction $L_1 \lor L_2$. Note that $L_1 \lor L_2$ is equivalent to L'. Previously, it was by making the K_is specify L' that got us satisfaction of AC_1 and AC_2.

More generally, this way of arranging for the satisfaction of AC_2 is by arranging for the satisfaction of:

AC_2^*: While the C_js may be within the influence of the acts whether or not a K_i is fixed (according to the agent's beliefs), the acts are not within the influence of the C_js once a K_i is fixed (according to the agent's beliefs).

Satisfaction of AC_2^* guarantees satisfaction of AC_2: if the agent believes that, given K_i, act A is outside the influence of C_j, then a difference between $P(C_j|K_i \& A)$ and $P(C_j|K_i \& -A)$ *cannot* be a reflection of a belief that C_j is causally relevant to A, given K_i, for the agent has no such belief. Also, note that satisfaction of AC_2^* will be consistent with satisfaction of AC_1 if there is no "two-way causality," i.e., if the ways of a C_j's being true that must be specified in the K_is because they are causally relevant to the acts cannot also be ways of the C_j's being true to which the acts are causally relevant. Later, we shall consider the question of whether there are ways in which AC_2 may be satisfied other than by way of satisfaction of AC_2^*.

The satisfaction of AC_1 and AC_2 is still not enough to guarantee appropriateness of a pair of partitions of K_is and C_js. Consider this decision situation, which I shall call 'DS_5'. It is a mixed Newcomb situation that is the same as the cholesterol case except that the agent believes that the act I has a slight tendency to produce hardening of the arteries, the state T. The agent considers it to be a two-state (T and $-T$), two-act (I and $-I$) decision situation; that is, his decision relevant propositions are, initially, just T and I and their Boolean combinations. Taking the partition of K_is to be just $\{p \vee -p\}$ and the partition of C_js to be $\{T, -T\}$, it is easy to see that the K_is and C_js satisfy AC_1 and AC_2. But, of course, relative to these partitions, *PMKE* will give the wrong recommendation. Here, $P(T|K_1 \& I)$ is greater than $P(T|K_1 \& -I)$, but not just because the agent believes that I causes T – and not at all because he believes that T causes I, since he does not believe this. The *main* reason is that he believes that there is a common cause of I and T. The agent's believing that C_j is causally relevant to A is not the only reason why, for some K_i, $P(C_j|K_i \& A)$ may be quite different from $P(C_j|K_i \& -A)$ in cases where the agent does not believe that

A is causally relevant to C_j: he may believe that there is a common cause of both one of A and $-A$ and one of C_j and $-C_j$. That is why AC_2 together with AC_1 is not alone sufficient to guarantee the appropriateness of a pair of partitions. This example suggests the following as an appropriateness condition:

AC_3: For every i, j and act A, the difference between $P(C_j|K_i \& A)$ and $P(C_j|K_i \& -A)$ does not reflect the extent to which the agent may believe that some factor is causally relevant to both A and C_j (given K_i).

One way to arrange for the satisfaction of AC_3 is to arrange for the K_is to be specific relative to factors that are causally relevant both to some act and to some C_j. That is, if some factor F is causally relevant both to some act and to some C_j, then each K_i should have either F or $-F$ as a conjunct. Again, more accurately, the K_is should specify the ways of such factors F being true that are commonly causally relevant both to an act and to a C_j. For example, if we revise the K_is in DS_4 so that they specify L' (not L, note), thus making DS_5 a four-state, two-act decision situation, it is easy to see that the partitions will satisfy AC_1, AC_2, and AC_3.

More generally, satisfaction of AC_3 will be guaranteed by the satisfaction of:

AC_3^*: The acts are not within the influence of any cause of any C_j once some K_i is fixed (according to the agent's beliefs);

if the agent believes that A is not within the influence of any cause of C_j given K_i, then a difference between $P(C_j|K_i \& A)$ and $P(C_j|K_i \& -A)$ *cannot* reflect a belief that some factor is commonly causally relevant to both A and C_j given K_i, for the agent has no such belief. Again, satisfaction of AC_3^* will be consistent with the satisfaction of AC_1 if there is no two-way causality, i.e., if no act can influence some way of some factor's being true which, because it is commonly causally relevant to the act and a C_j, is specified in the K_is. Later we shall consider the question of whether there are ways in which AC_3 can be satisfied other than by way of satisfaction of AC_3^*.

I think that AC_1, AC_2 and AC_3 are the really crucial features of an appropriate choice of K_is and C_js. The important thing, of course, is that the two partitions be chosen in such a way that the probabilities that enter into the calculation of K-expectation reflect the agent's causal beliefs in the right way. There are two kinds of probability terms in K-expectation: terms of the form $P(K_i)$ and terms of the form $P(C_j | K_i \ \& \ A)$. AC_1 guarantees that it is appropriate to take the probabilities of the K_is unconditional on the act, for, according to AC_1, the acts do not affect which K_i is true. Using $P(K_i)$ in the calculation of the K-expectation of every act makes K-expectation sensitive to the fact that, while the acts may be subjectively probabilistically relevant to the K_is, the acts do not causally affect the chances of the K_is. And AC_2 and AC_3 guarantee that the differences between probabilities $P(C_j | K_i \ \& \ A)$ and probabilities $P(C_j | K_i \ \& -A)$ reflect only the extent to which the agent believes that A is causally relevant to C_j (given K_i) for all C_j, K_i and A, assuming the *subjective common cause principle*: Two logically independent things, X and Y, can be subjectively probabilistically relevant to each other only to the extent that the agent believes one or more of the following: X is causally relevant to Y, Y is causally relevant to X, and there is some other factor which is commonly causally relevant to both X and Y. This principle would seem to be plausible in decision contexts. But I do not know how to argue for it except to say that it seems that subjective probabilities are determined just by the agent's deductive and inductive (causal) beliefs. AC_2 guarantees that the difference between a $P(C_j | K_i \ \& \ A)$ and a $P(C_j | K_i \ \& -A)$ is not a result of the agent's believing that C_j causes A (given K_i), and AC_3 guarantees that the difference is not a result of the agent's believing that there is a factor that is causally relevant commonly to both A and C_j (given K_i). Therefore, the common cause principle tells us that the difference reflects only the extent to which the agent believes that A is causally relevant to C_j. Thus, the differences between the values of corresponding probabilities in the K-expectations of different acts will reflect only the extent to which the agent believes that the different acts are differently causally relevant to the various K_is and (given a K_i) C_js.

I believe that if the partitions of K_is and C_js satisfy the appropriateness conditions, then K-expectation will be sensitive to the relevant causal distinctions in just the right way: I believe that *PMKE will always give the correct prescription in any decision situation as long as the partitions of K_is and C_js used in the calculation of K-expectation satisfy AC_1, AC_2 and AC_3.* Henceforth, I shall say that a pair of partitions, one of K_is and the other of C_js, is *appropriate* if the partitions jointly satisfy the appropriateness conditions AC_1, AC_2

and AC_3. We have already seen that relative to appropriate partitions, $PMKE$ gives the correct recommendations in DS_1, DS_2, DS_3 and DS_5. In DS_4, the partition $\{S, -S\}$ is appropriate as a partition of C_is; no partition of K_is is needed for DS_4, i.e., one may just use $\{p \vee -p\}$. This indicates, incidentally, that the important thing in connection with the C_is is not that the acts can influence which of them turns out to be true, but rather that neither they nor their causes can influence which act is performed when some K_i is fixed.

What about decision situations about whose causal structure the agent is not certain? Recall that Skyrms' K_is must ultimately be of the form H_n & K_{ni}, where H_n is a hypothesis about which states are outside the influence of the agent's actions. Now it seems reasonable to change the form of the H_ns and consider them to be hypotheses to the effect that a certain pair of partitions, $\{K_{ni}\}_i$ and $\{C_{nj}\}_j$, satisfies the appropriateness conditions. If the H_ns state that a pair of partitions satisfies AC_2 (as opposed to AC_2^*) or AC_3 (as opposed to AC_3^*), then it would seem reasonable to use objectivized versions of AC_2 and AC_3 when they occur in the context of an H_n: in this context, interpret the 'P's objectively (perhaps as relative frequency or "objective chance") and omit the phrase 'the agent believes that'. Let 'C', for 'chance', denote the objective distribution. Further, if the H_ns say that a pair of partitions satisfies AC_2 or AC_3, let the H_ns give the values of the (objectivized) probabilities, the $C(C_{nj}|K_{ni}$ & $A)$s and the $C(C_{nj}|K_{ni}$ & $-A)$s, that occur in the objectivized AC_2 and AC_3. If the H_ns just say that a pair of partitions satisfies AC_1, AC_2^* and AC_3^*, then there would seem to be no call to revise the conditions.

Since the H_ns are, plausibly, outside the influence of the agent's actions, the pair of partitions $\{H_n$ & $K_{ni}\}_{n,i}$ and $\{H_n$ & $C_{nj}\}_{n,j}$ will satisfy the appropriateness conditions. It is straightforward to verify this if the H_ns just say that a pair of partitions satisfies AC_1, AC_2^* and AC_3^*: in this case, in fact, the partitions $\{H_n$ & $K_{ni}\}_{n,i}$ and $\{H_n$ & $C_{nj}\}_{n,j}$ will satisfy AC_1, AC_2^* and AC_3^* and thus also AC_2 and AC_3. If the H_ns state that some pair of partitions satisfies the objectivized versions of AC_2 and AC_3 (and thus also give values for the (objectivized) probabilities $C(C_{nj}|K_{ni}$ & $A)$ and $C(C_{nj}|K_{ni}$ & $-A)$), then consider this *principle connecting objective and subjective probabilities*: If the proposition X implies that the objective probability of Y given Z is p, then the subjective probability of

Y conditional on X & Z is equal to p. Assuming this principle, the partitions $\{H_n \& K_{ni}\}_{n,i}$ and $\{H_n \& C_{nj}\}_{n,j}$ will satisfy AC_1, AC_2 and AC_3. So, I believe that if K-expectation is evaluated relative to these partitions, *PMKE* will give correct prescriptions.

So far, in our examples, we have only seen satisfaction of AC_2 and AC_3 by a pair of partitions *by way of satisfaction of AC_2^* and AC_3^**. Is it possible for a pair of partitions to satisfy AC_2 and AC_3 *without satisfying AC_2^* and AC_3^**? David Lewis (1981) points out that there are different ways of construing Skyrms' "factors." Lewis' causal decision theory is very much like Skyrms' if 'factor' is given a "broad" construal. Lewis' theory and the broad construal will be discussed in the next section. Under the "narrow" construal of 'factor', a factor is a "[proposition asserting the obtaining of a] localized occurrence – event, state, omission, etc. – that we normally think of as a cause," or (I should like to add) as being caused. I believe that if the K_is and C_js are thought of as specifications of factors under the narrow construal of 'factor', then the only way that a pair of partitions may satisfy AC_2 and AC_3 is by way of satisfying AC_2^* and AC_3^*. Even under a somewhat broader construal of 'factor' where a hypothesis H_n – of one of the types discussed just above – may be a factor, still I think the only way a pair of partitions may satisfy AC_2 and AC_3 is by way of satisfying AC_2^* and AC_3^*.

Let us consider the narrowest construal first. Suppose a pair of partitions of K_is and C_js – where these are specifications of factors, narrowly construed, and thus themselves factors, narrowly construed – fails to satisfy AC_2^*. Thus, for some K_i, C_j and A, the agent believes that C_j is causally relevant to A, given K_i. Then, since the agent's subjective probabilities – his subjective degrees of belief – can surely be assumed to reflect his causal beliefs, it would seem that the difference between $P(C_j|K_i \& A)$ and $P(C_j|K_i \& -A)$ would have to reflect, for one thing, his belief in the causal relevance of C_j to A, given K_i. If he believes that C_j is positively causally relevant to A, the difference between these two probabilities is greater than if he believed that C_j was causally irrelevant to A. And if he believes that C_j is negatively causally relevant to A, then the difference between these two probabilities is less (or more negative) than they would be if he believed that C_j was causally irrelevant to A. In either case, the difference between the two probabilities reflects the extent to which he believes that

C_j is, given K_i, causally relevant to A, and AC_2 is violated. (If the agent believes that C_j is causally relevant to A given K_i but he does not know whether this relevance is positive or negative, then these two effects may cancel each other. But still, the small resulting difference between the two probabilities is a result of his belief that C_j is causally relevant to A, given K_i). Parallel reasoning shows that if AC_3^* is violated by a pair of partitions whose elements specify factors, narrowly construed, then AC_3 will be violated.

Now let us turn to the somewhat broader construal, under which hypotheses H_n count as factors. In this case, the K_is and C_js are of the forms $H_n \& K_{ni}$ and $H_n \& C_{nj}$, respectively. Recall that a hypothesis H_n asserts that K_{ni}s and C_{nj}s satisfy the appropriateness conditions; the K_{ni}s and C_{nj}s are specifications of factors, narrowly construed, and, hence, are themselves factors, narrowly construed. The question is this: Can the partitions $\{H_n \& K_{ni}\}_{n,i}$ and $\{H_n \& C_{nj}\}_{n,j}$ satisfy one of AC_2 and AC_3 without also satisfying the corresponding one of AC_2^* and AC_3^*?

Suppose these partitions violate AC_2^*. Then for some n, i, j and act A, the agent believes that $H_n \& C_{nj}$ is causally relevant to A, given $H_n \& K_{ni}$. Recall that it is factors, *narrowly* construed, that can be causes or effects. Thus, the agent must believe that C_{nj} is causally relevant to A, given $H_n \& K_{ni}$. So, if the agent has any positive degree of belief in H_n, then H_n must be a hypothesis of the kind that asserts that the partitions of K_{ni}s and C_{nj}s satisfy the objectivized version of AC_2 and not one of the kind that asserts that the partitions satisfy AC_2^*. Also, H_n must give values for the objective chances of the C_{nj}s given the $K_{ni} \& A$s and given the $K_{ni} \& -A$s. Suppose the agent believes that C_{nj} is *positively* causally relevant to A, given $H_n \& K_{ni}$. Then it would seem that he could have belief in H_n only if, according to H_n, $C(C_{nj}|K_{ni} \& A) = C(C_{nj}|H_n \& K_{ni} \& A) > C(C_{nj}|K_{ni} \& -A) = C(C_{nj}|H_n \& K_{ni} \& -A)$, where, as before, '$C$' denotes the objective distribution that H_n asserts is correct. For if the agent believes that C_{nj} causes A, given $H_n \& K_{ni}$, then he should believe that the objective chance of C_{nj} given $H_n \& K_{ni} \& A$ is greater than the objective chance of C_{nj} given $H_n \& K_{ni} \& -A$: the objective chance of the cause is greater given the effect than given the absence of the effect. Surely this is true if objective chance is thought of as relative frequency. And similar reasoning applies if the agent thinks that $-C_{nj}$ causes $-A$, given $H_n \& K_{ni}$. The inequality should reflect C_{nj}s causal relevance to A, given H_n & K_{ni}. But H_n says that the K_{ni}s and C_{nj}s satisfy the objectivized version of AC_2, according to which the difference between $C(C_{nj}|K_{ni}$ & $A)$ and $C(C_{nj}|K_{ni}$ & $-A)$ (and thus between $C(C_{nj}|H_n$ & K_{ni} & $A)$ and $C(C_{nj}|H_n$ & K_{ni} & $-A)$) does not reflect C_{nj}s causal relevance to A, given K_{ni} (given H_n & K_{ni}). Thus, the agent should have no belief at all in H_n. Similar reasoning applies if the agent believes that C_{nj} is *negatively* causally relevant to A, given H_n & K_{ni}.

What this shows is that the agent should have no belief at all in any H_n according to which a pair of partitions satisfies the objectivized version of AC_2 unless the agent believes that such an H_n implies that the partitions also satisfy AC_2^*. And, as pointed out earlier, for a partition of such hypotheses, the partitions $\{H_n$ & $K_{ni}\}_{n,i}$ and $\{H_n$ & $C_{nj}\}_{n,j}$ will satisfy AC_2^*. Parallel reasoning shows that these partitions must also satisfy AC_3^* if they satisfy AC_3.

Thus, if the K_is and C_js in K-expectation are specifications of factors, narrowly or, in the sense given above, somewhat more broadly construed, the only way for them to satisfy AC_1, AC_2 and AC_3 is for them to satisfy AC_1, AC_2^* and AC_3^*. Can such K_is and C_js always be found?

It will be illuminating at this point to give a new appropriateness condition whose satisfaction is, in the presence of the satisfaction of AC_1, equivalent to the satisfaction of AC_2^* and AC_3^* and which characterizes the appropriateness of K_is independently of C_js. It is:

AC_4^*: The acts are not within the influence of any factor once a K_i is fixed (according to the agent's beliefs).

Obviously, AC_4^* implies AC_2^*, for no matter how the agent partitions into C_js, if a C_j is the kind of thing that can be causally relevant to the acts, then it should be thought of as a factor. Thus, if the acts are outside the influence of all factors once a K_i is fixed, then they are outside the influence of the C_js once a K_i is fixed. And AC_4^* implies AC_3^*, for if any factor is commonly causally relevant to an act and a C_j, it is causally relevant to the act.

In the presence of AC_1, the conditions AC_2^* and AC_3^* together imply AC_4^*. Suppose some K_is and C_js satisfy AC_1, AC_2^* and AC_3^*. And let F be any factor. What is to be shown is that the acts are not within the influence of F once some K_i is fixed. As pointed out several times earlier, if a pair of partitions of K_is and C_js is appropriate, then for any other partition, $\{C_k'\}_k$ the K_is together

126

with the C'_ks will be appropriate. Thus, let us consider the pair of partitions $\{K_i\}_i$ and $\{F, -F\}$. This pair must be appropriate, and must, therefore, satisfy AC_1, AC_2^* and AC_3^* (if I was right earlier in isolating the appropriateness conditions for the case in which 'factor' is either narrowly or "somewhat more broadly" construed). By AC_2^*, then, the acts are not within the influence of F once a K_i is fixed.

(Just for the record, the corresponding "unstarred" version of AC_4^* is:

AC_4: For every i, proposition C and act A, the difference between $P(C|K_i \,\&\, A)$ and $P(C|K_i \,\&\, -A)$ is not a reflection of the agent's believing of any factor that it is causally relevant to A.

From what has gone before, it is easy to see that the only way in which some K_is can satisfy AC_4 – when they are specifications of factors, narrowly or, in the sense given previously, somewhat more broadly construed – is by way of satisfaction of AC_4^*.)

Thus, we now have complete appropriateness conditions for the K_is. Appropriate K_is have now been characterized independently of C_js. And satisfaction of AC_4^* will be consistent with satisfaction of AC_1 if there is no two-way causality, i.e., if the acts can influence no factor which, because it is causally relevant to the acts, must be specified in the K_is.

So now the question is this: Can we always find a partition of K_is that satisfy AC_1 and AC_4^*? Skyrms gives something of a recipe for concocting the K_is: they are "maximally specific specifications of the factors outside our influence at the time of decision which are causally relevant to the outcome of our actions" (1980a: 133). Looking at AC_4^*, however, it appears that it is not always necessary to specify in the K_is *everything* that is outside our influence that is causally relevant to the outcome of our actions: we need only specify such things *that are also causally relevant to our action*. If a factor is not causally relevant to our action, then it need not be specified in the K_is.

Of course it will not hurt to specify too much in the K_is as long as we do not specify the wrong things, namely, factors that are within our influence. Suppose that K_is are maximally specific specifications of the factors that are all three of the following: outside the influence of our actions, causally relevant to the outcome

127

of our action and causally relevant to our action. And suppose that K'_ks are maximally specific specifications of all the factors that are outside our influence and are causally relevant to the outcome of our action. Thus, the K_is specify all the factors in the set:

$\mathscr{F} = \{F\colon F$ is outside our influence &

$\quad\quad F$ is causally relevant to the outcome

$\quad\quad\quad$ of our action &

$\quad\quad F$ is causally relevant to our action};

and the K'_ks specify all the factors in the set:

$\mathscr{F}' = \{F\colon F$ is outside our influence &

$\quad\quad F$ is causally relevant to the outcome of our action}.

Thus, since $\mathscr{F}'$ has more members than $\mathscr{F}$ does, the K'_ks specify more than the K_is do; the K'_ks are more specific. Also, since the K'_ks specify everything that the K_is do, each K'_k implies some K_i. Furthermore, I claim that for every i, k and act A, $P(K'_k|K_i \& A) = P(K'_k|K_i \& -A) = P(K'_k|K_i)$. This is because the K_is are specific enough: they specify everything that is causally relevant to A. Thus, given a K_i, a K'_k cannot be causally relevant to A. Also, if there is a factor that is commonly causally relevant to both K'_k and A, then it is causally relevant to A and, therefore, specified in each K_i. So, by the common cause principle, stated previously, the equalities follow. Therefore, for any act A,

$$U_k(A) = \sum_i P(K_i)CEU(K_i \& A)$$

$$= \sum_i P(K_i) \sum_k P(K'_k|K_i \& A)CEU(K'_k \& K_i \& A)$$

$$= \sum_i P(K_i) \sum_k P(K'_k|K_i)CEU(K'_k \& K_i \& A)$$

$$= \sum_{ik} P(K'_k \& K_i)CEU(K'_k \& K_i \& A)$$

$$= \sum_k P(K'_k)CEU(K'_k \& A).$$

Thus, though the partition of K_is is sufficiently specific, it does not harm to calculate K-expectation in terms of the partition of the more specific K'_ks, as the passage from Skyrms, quoted above, suggests we do.

The passage from Skyrms suggests that we make the K_is specify only factors that are causally relevant to the outcome of our action. But if 'factor causally relevant to the outcome of our action' means 'factor causally relevant to our eventual level of satisfaction', it seems that the factors causally relevant to the outcome of our action are just the decision-relevant propositions: the propositions that the agent deems it necessary to consider in his decision situation. If this is so, and I think it is, then, if we think of F as ranging over the decision-relevant propositions, $\mathscr{F}$ is the same set as

$$\mathscr{F}'' = \{F: F \text{ is outside our influence } \&$$

$$F \text{ is causally relevant to our action}\}.$$

Now AC_4^* just says that we must specify in the K_is the factors that influence our action. Those are the only things that AC_1 or AC_4^* say we *must* specify in the K_is. AC_1 just says that the things that get specified in the K_is must be outside the influence of our actions. Assuming that the factors that influence our action are outside the influence of our action (so that joint satisfaction of AC_1 and AC_4^* is possible), a partition of K_is will be appropriate (together with any partition of C_js) if the K_is specify the elements of the set:

$$\mathscr{F}''' = \{F: F \text{ is causally relevant to our action}\}.$$

Thus, the two crucial features of the K_is are: (i) they specify all the elements in $\mathscr{F}'''$ and (ii) the elements of $\mathscr{F}'''$ are outside the influence of our action. Can such K_is always be found?

There are two things that may stand in the way of finding such K_is. First, the elements of $\mathscr{F}'''$ must make all the relevant causal distinctions. This was seen earlier in the discussion of DS_1, DS_2 and DS_3. If, in these decision situations, $\mathscr{F}'''$ contained only L and $-L$, then, by (i) the K_is must specify (in fact, be) L and $-L$. But in these decision situations, L and $-L$ are within the influence of our actions so that (ii) is violated. We saw earlier how this can be remedied. There is a way in which L can be true (a "*sub*-factor" of L) which is outside our influence and influences our action. Recall that L is equivalent to $L_1 \vee L_2 \vee L_3$, where the disjuncts are as described earlier. $L_1 \vee L_2$ (which, recall, is equivalent to L') is outside our influence and influences our action. If $\mathscr{F}'''$ contained L_1, L_2, L_3 and L_4 and their Boolean combinations (or just L, L_3 and Boolean combinations thereof, or just L' and $-L'$), then the right causal distinctions would be expressible in terms of $\mathscr{F}'''$. This is the feature that a set of decision-relevant propositions must have for it to be *rich* enough that appropriate K_is can be expressed in its terms. Thus, the first thing that may stand in the way of finding appropriate K_is is that the set $\mathscr{F}'''$ may not be rich enough to make the right causal distinctions.

Note that we can now specify more precisely in virtue of what a set of decision-relevant propositions is sufficiently rich: roughly, the set is sufficiently rich if, for every decision-relevant factor F (e.g., L, L_1), if ways of F's being true can affect the actions and the actions can affect F (according to the agent's beliefs), then there must be some decision relevant factor F' (like L') such that $F \& F'$ ($L \& L'$) is outside the influence of the acts (according to the agent's beliefs) *or* a factor F'' (like L_2) such that $F \vee F''$ ($L_1 \vee L_2$) is outside the influence of the acts (according to the agent's beliefs). I know of no procedure whereby a given set of decision-relevant propositions can always be so enriched. But perhaps, for most ordinary decision situations, this can be accomplished by adding, for each factor F, a proposition F' something like 'F is true only in virtue of the way the world already, at the time of decision, is' and a proposition F'' something like 'Only those implications of F that may hold in virtue of the way the world already, at the time of decision, is are true'. Then, if backwards causality is the only kind of two-way causality the agent may believe in and if we rule out the possibility that he believes in backwards causality, we may have done the trick.

The second thing that may stand in the way of constructing appropriate K_is is that we may not want to rule out, *a priori*, the possibility that a rational agent may believe in nonbackwards two-way causality. And we may not want to rule out, *a priori*, that a rational agent may believe in backwards causality. Indeed, David Lewis (1981) asks us to consider an agent with eccentric beliefs who thinks that the influence of his actions extends into all of the future, but fades. This agent also believes that time is circular, so that the far future includes all of the past and the influence of his actions extends into all of space and time. Suppose, for example, that the agent in the original cholesterol case believes that his present action has some very slight influence on whether or not he presently has the lesion. What, for this situation, would be appropriate K_is?

Thus, we have discovered a number of complexities involved in the construction of partitions of decision-relevant propositions that are appropriate for the application of *PMKE*. The main problem is that of suitably enriching the set of propositions that the agent initially, perhaps naively, considers to be decision-relevant. Such K_is must be constructable from the enriched set that the agent believes there is no two-way causality between them and the acts. Note that one form of two-way causality is rendered eliminable by construing 'factor' "somewhat more broadly" so that hypotheses H_n count as factors. An agent may believe that a factor F causes an act A and that A causes F as a result of having partial belief in two hypotheses H_n, one of which is consistent (in the presence of the agent's other beliefs) with F's causing A but not with A's causing F and the other of which is consistent (in the presence of the agent's other beliefs) with A's causing F but not with F's causing A. Under the somewhat more broad construal of 'factor', the two H_ns are factors that should be specified in the K_is. And note that for neither of the two hypotheses will both of the following hold: the agent believes that F causes A given H_n and the agent believes that A causes F given H_n. Construing 'factor' in such a way that hypotheses H_n count as factors is a way of enriching the set of decision-relevant propositions. In the next section, on Lewis' causal decision theory, we shall consider an even broader construal of 'factor' that results in a further enrichment of the set of decision-relevant propositions. Given this broader construal, it is plausible that we will always be able to construct partitions that satisfy AC_1, AC_2, AC_3 and AC_4 that do not necessarily also satisfy AC_2^*, AC_3^* and AC_4^*. Also, given this construal, it will be plausible that *PMKE* will be able to deal even with bizarre decision situations like the one involving Lewis' agent with the eccentric beliefs.

Meanwhile, I would like to point out that the problem of finding and characterizing appropriate partitions would not even arise on a possible successful *CEU* resolution of the problem, for the conditional expected utility of an act does not vary according to how the space of probabilities is partitioned, as its K-expectation does. Jeffrey's axioms guarantee that for any proposition X, $CEU(X) =$

$D(X)$, no matter what partition may be used in calculating $CEU(X)$.

Before moving on to Lewis' theory, I would like to point out some other important implications of enriching the set of decision-relevant propositions so as to include hypotheses H_n and to compare this approach with Gibbard and Harper's.

An apparent advantage of Skyrms' approach over Gibbard and Harper's is that while the Gibbard–Harper rule assimilates the causal information characteristic of Newcomb situations – namely, that SA is causally irrelevant to SO and to CC – *indirectly*, by appealing to an appropriate (nonbacktracking) interpretation of counterfactual conditionals, Skyrms' rule assimilates this information by appealing *directly* to the notion of a state's being outside the influence of acts. Skyrms suggests, though, that the notion of a state's being outside the influence of an act "may involve subjunctive judgments, but the problem is more sharply circumscribed if the judgments required are restricted in this way" (1980*b*: 132). Thus, for example, Skyrms does not invoke a full theory of counterfactuals which, together with the causal independence of a K_i from an act A, has as a consequence the equality $P(A \mathbin{\square\!\!\rightarrow} K_i) = P(-A \mathbin{\square\!\!\rightarrow} K_i)$. Rather, because of the causal independence of K_i from A, Skyrms' rule simply advocates the use of $P(K_i)$ both in the evaluation of the expected utility of A and in the evaluation of the expected utility of $-A$.

Does the notion of a state's being outside the influence of the available acts involve counterfactual judgments? It is plausible that under an interpretation of $\mathbin{\square\!\!\rightarrow}$ that would be appropriate for the Gibbard–Harper analysis, a hypothesis H_n might be equivalent to something like:

$$\bigwedge_{i,j,k} (P(A_k \mathbin{\square\!\!\rightarrow} K_{ni}) = P(K_{ni}) \ \& \ P(A_k \mathbin{\square\!\!\rightarrow} C_{nj} | K_{ni}) = P(C_{nj} | K_{ni} \ \& \ A_k)),$$

or perhaps to something like:

$$\bigwedge_{i,j,k} (((A_k \mathbin{\square\!\!\rightarrow} K_{ni}) \leftrightarrow (-A_k \mathbin{\square\!\!\rightarrow} K_{ni})) \ \& \ (K_{ni} \rightarrow ((C_{nj} \mathbin{\square\!\!\rightarrow} A_k)$$

$$\leftrightarrow (-C_{nj} \mathbin{\square\!\!\rightarrow} A_k)))).$$

In the second expression, the first conjunct inside the big conjunction sign is supposed to imply causal independence of the K_{ni}s from the acts, so that the K_is satisfy appropriateness condition AC_1. The second conjunct is supposed to imply that AC_2^* is satisfied (or, if the C_{nj}s are sufficiently specific, that AC_4^* is satisfied). But if the H_ns are explicated in some such way as these, they will involve counterfactual conditionals with act antecedents that must be given a nonbacktracking interpretation; and we have already seen some of the difficulties that attend the explication of such counterfactuals.

How else could the hypotheses H_n be explicated? Another possibility is that H_n is just equivalent to the statement that the best way to compare acts A is by comparing

$$\sum_{i,j} P(K_{ni})P(C_{nj} \mid A \& K_{ni})D(A \& K_{ni} \& C_{nj})$$

for the various acts A. Then H_n is a statement that a certain rule is the best in the situation at hand. $H_{n'}$ is the statement that some other rule, namely, the maximization of

$$\sum_{i,j} P(K_{n'i})P(C_{n'j} \mid A \& K_{n'i})D(A \& K_{n'i} \& C_{n'j})$$

is the best rule. But then what exactly does 'best' in H_n mean? Clearly it must mean 'best in view of the causal facts'. But what are the causal facts, and are counterfactual judgments required for their explication?

Of course we could just leave the explication of the H_ns at 'The K_{ni}s are outside our influence and the C_{nj}s may be influenced by our actions', or rather, if I was right earlier, 'The K_{ni}s and C_{nj}s satisfy the appropriateness conditions', thus leaving the notion of a state's being outside the influence of an act unexplicated. In this case, if a set of such mutually exclusive and collectively exhaustive hypotheses could always be found, then *PMKE* would be, I believe, a broadly applicable and correct principle of choice.

But, as pointed out previously, it is far from clear that finding appropriate partitions will always be a routine matter. This is one advantage that a successful *CEU* approach would have over the *K*-expectation approach.

But also, leaving the notion of a state's being outside the influence of the acts unexplicated means that the *K*-expectation approach introduces into *SEU* theory a new primitive corresponding to a controversial and not very well-understood notion. Note that in *PMCEU*, the formalism involves only the nonlogical constants P, D, $+$, and $\cdot$ and the set of decision-relevant propositions closed under the usual sentential connectives. In *PMKE*, we have all this

133

plus the connective 'is outside the influence of' connecting acts and states. And in *PMUE* we have all the primitives of *PMCEU* plus the connective $\Box\!\!\rightarrow$ relating acts and states (or outcomes).

As prescriptive theories, *PMUE* and *PMKE* have to assume that the agent has, and understands, the notions of $\Box\!\!\rightarrow$ and 'is outside the influence of'. As descriptive theories, the philosopher or psychologist has to understand these notions and attribute the understanding of them to decision makers. In view of the controversial and not very well-understood nature of the additional concepts involved in the *U*- and *K*-expectation approaches, I consider these observations to indicate another important advantage that a successful *CEU* approach to Newcomb situations would have.

Finally, it should be pointed out that we have, as yet, no theoretical guarantee that *PMKE* is broadly applicable. The class of decision situations in which appropriate partitions exist has not been characterized in a clear way. For *PMCEU* on the other hand, we have representation theorems, the satisfaction of whose intuitive qualitative preference axioms guarantees applicability of *PMCEU*. No theorem of this kind has yet been found for *PMKE*. And, as pointed out previously in connection with *PMUE*, it would seem that when such a theorem is found, its qualitative assumptions would have to involve a primitive in addition to the preference relation. They would have to involve a new primitive that can capture the force of causal or (more or less sharply circumscribed) counterfactual judgments expressed on the quantitative side with the connective 'is outside the influence of'. Perhaps the new primitive would be a partition of a certain kind or a similarity relation on possible worlds. But, in any case, in view of the controversial nature of causal and counterfactual notions, perhaps we can reasonably expect the new primitive and the qualitative conditions involving it also to be quite controversial.

LEWIS

The causal decision theories of Gibbard and Harper's and of Skyrms' share at least one common idea. They are both articulations of the view that causal distinctions of a certain kind need to be incorporated into the calculation of expected utility. On the face of it, however, the two proposals look quite different. More recently, David Lewis has proposed a version of causal decision theory, compared it with others and argued convincingly that they are all basically the same.

I shall call the kind of expectation of which Lewis advocates maximization '*L-expectation*'. (Lewis calls it U-expectation, but I want to distinguish it from Gibbard and Harper's proposal.) And I shall call the rule that says that preference goes by L-expectation and that one should choose an act that has the greatest L-expectation 'the *principle of maximizing L-expectation*' (hereafter, '*PMLE*'). Lewis' formula for L-expectation is identical to Skyrms' formula for K-expectation: For any act A,

$$U_L(A) = \sum_i P(K_i)CEU(K_i \,\&\, A)$$

$$= \sum_{ij} P(K_i)P(C_j|K_i \,\&\, A)D(C_j \,\&\, K_i \,\&\, A).$$

As in Skyrms' theory, the K_is form a partition of a special kind and the C_js are any partition whatsoever. In Lewis' theory the K_is are "dependency hypotheses": hypotheses about how the things the agent cares about (e.g., the lesion, hardening of the arteries, charisma, revolts) do and do not depend on which course of action he pursues.

Lewis defines 'dependency hypothesis' as follows:

Suppose someone knows all there is to know about how the things he cares about do and do not depend causally on his present actions. If something is beyond his control, so that it will obtain – or have a certain chance of obtaining – no matter what he does, then he knows that for certain. And if something is within his control, he knows that for certain; furthermore, he knows the extent of his influence over it and he knows what we must do to influence it one way or another ... Let us call the sort of proposition that this agent knows – a maximally specific proposition about how the things he cares about do and do not depend causally on his present actions – a *dependency hypothesis*. (1981)

Later on, we will take a look at Lewis' more specific proposal for the form of a dependency hypothesis. Meanwhile, from the quoted passage, it seems that we may think of a dependency hypothesis as having three parts. First, there is a hypothesis H_n – just like Skyrms' H_ns (not the ones that assert of a pair of partitions that they satisfy the appropriateness conditions) – which says which factors are within and which factors are outside of the influence of the agent's actions (at the time of decision). Again, let 'K_{ni}'

denote maximally specific specifications of factors which, according to H_n, are outside the influence of the agent's actions, and let 'C_{nj}' denote elements of a partition of factors which, according to H_n, are within the influence of the agent's actions. The second part of a dependency hypothesis is a hypothesis G_{nm} which says what the chances of the K_{ni}s are. These chances are, according to the first part of the dependency hypothesis, independent of which course of action is pursued. One way of thinking of the G_{nm}s is as specifying "objective chance" distributions for the K_{ni}s. The third part of a dependency hypothesis is a hypothesis G'_{no} which specifies the extent and direction of each act's influence on each C_{nj}. The G'_{no}s can be thought of as saying, for each act and each C_{nj}, from what to what the act, by way of its causal influence, raises or lowers the objective chance of C_{nj}. (Later, we shall see why the G'_{no}s must specify "base" objective chances for the C_{nj}s in addition to the magnitude and direction in which the acts change these chances.) Thus, Lewis' dependency hypotheses, his K_is, can be thought of as of the form H_n & G_{nm} & G'_{no}.

What is the relation between *PMLE* and *PMKE*? Formally, the proposals look identical. But recall that (ultimately) Skyrms' K_is consist of two parts: first, a hypothesis H_n saying which factors are within and which factors are outside of the influence of the agent's actions and, second, a maximally specific specification, K_{ni}, of the factors which, according to H_n, are outside the influence of the agent's actions. Skyrms' K_is are of the form H_n & K_{ni}. Thus, both Skyrms' and Lewis' K_is specify an H_n. Skyrms' go on to specify a K_{ni}; Lewis' do not. And Lewis' go on to specify a G_{nm} and a G'_{no}; Skyrms' do not.

Do Skyrms' K_is specify enough? Do Lewis'? Or should we adopt what might be a more general theory whose K_is are of the form H_n & G_{nm} & G'_{no} & K_{ni}?

A theory whose K_is are of the form H_n & G_{nm} & G'_{no} & K_{ni} would be equivalent to Lewis' theory, as the following chain of equalities shows (it depends on one assumption which will be noted below). For all acts A,

$$U_L(A) = \sum_{nmo} P(H_n \,\&\, G_{nm} \,\&\, G'_{no}) CEU(H_n \,\&\, G_{nm} \,\&\, G'_{no} \,\&\, A)$$
$$= \sum_{nmo} P(H_n \,\&\, G_{nm} \,\&\, G'_{no}) \sum_i P(K_{ni} | H_n \,\&\, G_{nm} \,\&\, G'_{no} \,\&\, A)$$
$$\times CEU(H_n \,\&\, G_{nm} \,\&\, G'_{no} \,\&\, K_{ni} \,\&\, A)$$

$$= \sum_{nmo} P(H_n \,\&\, G_{nm} \,\&\, G'_{no}) \sum_i P(K_{ni} | H_n \,\&\, G_{nm} \,\&\, G'_{no})$$
$$\times CEU(H_n \,\&\, G_{nm} \,\&\, G'_{no} \,\&\, K_{ni} \,\&\, A)$$

$$= \sum_{nmoi} P(H_n \,\&\, G_{nm} \,\&\, G'_{no} \,\&\, K_{ni})$$
$$\times CEU(H_n \,\&\, G_{nm} \,\&\, G'_{no} \,\&\, K_{ni} \,\&\, A).$$

The only assumption on which this chain of equalities relies (aside from the probability axioms) is:

(i) For every n, m, o, i and act A, $P(K_{ni} | H_n \,\&\, G_{nm} \,\&\, G'_{no} \,\&\, A)$
    $= P(K_{ni} | H_n \,\&\, G_{nm} \,\&\, G'_{no})$.

This assumption should be expected to hold because H_n says that the chance of K_{ni} is causally independent of whether or not A is the act performed and G_{nm} says what this independent-of-A chance is; so, given H_n and G_{nm}, the probability of K_{ni} should be judged to be the same whether conditional on A or not conditional on A. Plausibly, in fact, $P(K_{ni} | H_n \,\&\, G_{nm} \,\&\, G'_{no} \,\&\, A) = P(K_{ni} | H_n \,\&\, G_{nm} \,\&\, G'_{no}) =$ what G_{nm} says the independent-of-A chance of K_{ni} is, for each n, m, o, i and A. The above chain of equalities, then, shows that as far as the H_ns, G_{nm}s, G'_{no}s and K_{ni}s are concerned, Lewis' K_is specify all that needs to be specified.

Do Skyrms' K_is specify all that needs to be specified? Or should they, in addition to specifying an H_n and a K_{ni}, also specify a G_{nm}, or a G'_{no}, or one of each? In most cases, Skyrms' K_is will be adequate. Indeed, in most decision situations, the following chain of equalities will hold (it depends on one assumption, which will be fully noted below). For any act A,

$$U_K(A) = \sum_{ni} P(H_n \,\&\, K_{ni}) CEU(H_n \,\&\, K_{ni} \,\&\, A)$$
$$= \sum_{ni} P(H_n \,\&\, K_{ni}) \sum_{mo} P(G_{nm} \,\&\, G'_{no} | H_n \,\&\, K_{ni} \,\&\, A)$$
$$\times CEU(G_{nm} \,\&\, G'_{no} \,\&\, H_n \,\&\, K_{ni} \,\&\, A)$$
$$= \sum_{ni} P(H_n \,\&\, K_{ni}) \sum_{mo} P(G_{nm} \,\&\, G'_{no} | H_n \,\&\, K_{ni})$$
$$\times CEU(G_{nm} \,\&\, G'_{no} \,\&\, H_n \,\&\, K_{ni} \,\&\, A)$$
$$= \sum_{nmoi} P(H_n \,\&\, G_{nm} \,\&\, G'_{no} \,\&\, K_{ni})$$
$$\times CEU(H_n \,\&\, G_{nm} \,\&\, G'_{no} \,\&\, K_{ni} \,\&\, A).$$

This chain of equalities depends only on this assumption:

(ii) For every n, m, o, i and act A, $P(G_{nm} \& G'_{no} | H_n \& K_{ni} \& A)$
$= P(G_{nm} \& G'_{no} | H_n \& K_{ni})$.

If assumption (ii) holds, then, Skyrms' theory is as general as a theory whose K_is go on to specify, in addition to an H_n and a K_{ni}, a G_{nm} and a G'_{no}.

But should (ii) be expected to hold in general? In most decision situations it should hold. In the first place, given an H_n and a K_{ni}, the agent should have full (conditional) belief in the one G_{nm} that says that the chance of K_{ni} is 1, which act is performed being irrelevant. And in the second place, while A is surely probabilistically relevant to which factor within the influence of A obtains, usually the extent and direction of that influence (which is what the G'_{no}s specify) should be probabilistically independent of A.

There are situations, however, in which we should not expect (ii) to hold of some agents' beliefs. Such situations are admittedly bizarre, but they do indicate that a theory whose K_is specify a G'_{no} is more general than one whose K_is do not. Consider again Lewis' agent with eccentric beliefs who, for some good reason, thinks that time is circular and that the influence of his actions propagates (weakly) over all of space and time. Suppose this agent is in the two-state (L', and $-L'$), two-act (I and $-I$) cholesterol case decision situation. (Recall that L' is the state in which the agent already has the lesion.) Although the agent believes that L' is a very efficacious, and the predominant, cause of I, he also believes that I has a slight tendency to bring about L'. Now this agent has full belief in just one H_n: the one that says that everything is within his influence except for the one K_{ni}: the necessary proposition. (Hence, I drop the subscript 'n' in discussion of this example.) He also has full belief in just one G_m: the one that says that the independent-of-his-action chance of the necessary proposition is 1. Thus, for this agent in this decision situation, (ii) reduces to: For all o, $P(G'_o | I) = P(G'_o)$.

Some aspects of this agent's causal beliefs can be modeled by the G'_os he considers and their subjective probabilities conditional on the two available acts. Suppose, for simplicity, that he concentrates all of his belief on just two G'_os:

G'_1: Performing I raises the objective chance of L' from 0.8 to 0.81;

138

G_2': Performing I raises the objective chance of L' from 0.2 to 0.21.

Since this agent believes that I has only a slight tendency to bring about L', it is reasonable that he has (partial) belief only in G_o's according to which I raises the chance of L' just a little. Since this agent believes that L' is a very efficacious and the predominant cause of I, I is, for this agent, very strong evidence for L'. Thus, we expect his beliefs to be such that $P(G_1'|I) > P(G_1') > P(G_1'|-I)$ and $P(G_2'|I) < P(G_2') < P(G_2'|-I)$. This, of course, violates (ii).

While this example is bizarre, it does indicate that a theory whose K_is are of the form H_n & G_{nm} & G_{no}' & K_{ni} (or just H_n & G_{nm} & G_{no}') is more general than one whose K_is are of the form H_n & K_{ni}. The example shows the need to incorporate hypotheses G_{no}' into the K_is so that their probabilities will never occur conditional on an act in the calculation of expected utility: while the G_{no}'s are obviously outside the influence of the available acts, it nevertheless appears that which act is performed may be subjectively probabilistically relevant to which G_{no}' obtains.

(Note also that the G_{no}'s in L-expectation must specify the base objective chances for the C_{nj}s. In the example just considered, if G_1' and G_2' just said that I increases the objective chance of L' by 0.01, so that the two would be equivalent, then still $P(L'|G_1'$ & $I) > P(L'|G_1') > P(L'|G_1'$ & $-I)$ with the difference arising *mainly* from the agent's belief that I is strong evidence for L' and not just from the agent's belief that I is positively causally relevant to L'. The difference, in other words, between the first two probabilities would exceed 0.01.)

It can easily be shown, though, that a theory whose K_is are of the form H_n & G_{no}' & K_{ni} would be just as general as one whose K_is are of the form H_n & G_{nm} & G_{no}' & K_{ni}. This can be established by a chain of equalities – like those above – which depends on the assumption:

(iii) For every n, m, o, i and act A, $P(G_{nm}|H_n$ & G_{no}' & K_{ni} & $A)$ $= P(G_{nm}|H_n$ & G_{no}' & $K_{ni})$.

This assumption is plausible because, as noted previously, given an H_n and a K_{ni}, the agent should have full (conditional) belief in the one G_{nm} that says that the chance of K_{ni} is 1, which act is performed being irrelevant.

Assumptions (i) and (iii) are plausible, and they imply that causal decision theories whose K_is are of the forms H_n & G_{nm} & G'_{no}, H_n & G_{nm} & G'_{no} & K_{ni} or H_n & G'_{no} & K_{ni} will all be equivalent. These two assumptions together with (ii), which, as we have seen, is not universally true, imply that all such theories would be equivalent to theories whose K_is are of the forms H_n & K_{ni} or H_n & G_{nm} & K_{ni}. Other conditional-independence-of-acts assumptions will yield other more or less general causal decision theories with more or less specific K_is. As another example, the assumption:

(iv) For every n, m, o, i and act A, $P(K_{ni}|H_n$ & G_{nm} & $A)$
$= P(K_{ni}|H_n$ & $G_{nm})$

implies that a theory whose K_is are of the form H_n & G_{nm} & K_{ni} is equivalent to one whose K_is are of the form H_n & G_{nm}. And (iv) is plausible for the same reason that (i) is.

Lewis points out that there are different ways of construing Skyrms' "factors." On a narrow construal, a factor is a localized event or state: the kind of thing we normally think of as a cause or an effect. Thus, on the narrow construal, things like the lesion and atherosclerosis are factors that are, in Skyrms' cholesterol case, outside the influence of the agent's actions. That the agent may not know the causal structure of the decision situation in which he finds himself shows the need for a somewhat broader construal of 'factor', a construal under which a factor may include a hypothesis about what is within and what is outside of the influence of the available actions. Thus, under the broader construal, things like H_n and H_n & K_{ni} are factors outside the influence of the agent's actions (the latter is counted as a maximally specific such factor). And examples like Lewis' agent with eccentric beliefs shows the need for an even broader construal, a construal under which Lewis' dependency hypotheses count as factors.

Just as Skyrms' H_ns are always outside the influence of the agent's available acts, so are Lewis' dependency hypotheses. Lewis' proof of this:

Suppose [not]. Consider the dependency hypothesis which we get by taking account of the ways the agent can manipulate dependency hypotheses to enhance his control over things. This hypothesis seems to be right no matter what he does. Then he has no influence over whether this hypothesis or another is right, contrary to our supposition that the dependency hypotheses are within his influence. (1981)

140

Thus, under the broad construal, Skyrms' maximally specific specifications of factors that are outside the influence of the available acts are (at any rate *include*) dependency hypotheses, and Skyrms' theory is much the same as Lewis'.

(Whether or not, on the broad construal of 'factor', Skyrms' and Lewis' theories are *identical*, as Lewis claims they are, depends, of course, on what, precisely, a dependency hypothesis is. In particular, it depends on whether or not dependency hypotheses *also include* maximally specific specifications of all factors the agent cares about that are outside the influence of his actions. Lewis says, "Any specification of something outside the agent's influence is included in a dependency hypothesis – recall that they cover what doesn't depend on the agent's actions as well as what does – unless it concerns something the agent doesn't care about" (1981). I have been construing Lewis' dependency hypotheses as specifying only what the *chances* of the things the agent cares about would be given the various actions. And, later on, we will see that on Lewis' more specific (though tentative) proposal for the form of dependency hypotheses, they are conjunctions of counterfactual conditionals with act antecedents and probabilistic consequents which specify just *chances* of the things the agent cares about. Lewis prefers this over conjunctions of counterfactuals with act antecedents and consequents that are specifications of things the agent cares about because it seems that the world is "chancy." But whether the world is chancy or deterministic, maximally specific specifications of the things the agent cares about specify those things and not just their chances, unless all the agent cares about are chances.)

Assume that for every i, j and act A, $P(C_j | K_i \& A)$ equals what K_i says that A, by way of its causal influence, raises or lowers the objective chance of C_j to. (This principle is very much like Lewis' "principle connecting chance and credence," which will be given later.) Since this raising or lowering of the objective chance of a C_j is a result only of A's causal influence, it is clear, assuming the principle, that the difference between $P(C_j | K_i \& A)$ and $P(C_j | K_i \& -A)$, for any i, j and A, reflects only the extent to which the agent believes that A is causally relevant to C_j, given K_i, and thus not the extent to which he believes that C_j is causally relevant to A, given K_i, or the extent to which he believes that some factor is commonly causally relevant to both A and C_j, given K_i, *even if he has these other beliefs*. Thus, under Lewis' broad construal of 'factor', under which dependency hypotheses count as factors, a pair of partitions of K_is and C_js can satisfy appropriateness conditions AC_2 and AC_3 without also satisfying AC_2^* and AC_3^*. In fact, a partition of Lewis' dependency hypotheses will always satisfy AC_1 (since they are outside the influence of the agent's actions) and AC_4 without also having to satisfy AC_4^*. And that is why *PMLE* and – given the broad construal of 'factor' under which dependency hypotheses count as factors – *PMKE* can handle cases in which the agent believes that everything is within his influence but only a little (like the one involving Lewis' agent with eccentric beliefs), but *PMKE* cannot if 'factor' is narrowly, or, in the sense given in the previous section, somewhat more broadly construed.

What is the relation between *PMLE* and *PMUE*? Lewis suggests that dependency hypotheses may take the form of conjunctions of counterfactuals with act antecedents and outcome consequents, where the counterfactuals are given a nonbacktracking interpretation suitable for Gibbard and Harper's analysis and the outcomes specify everything the agent cares about in his particular decision situation. In connection with the charisma case, consider, for example, the conjunction $(J \mathrel{\Box\!\!\rightarrow} R) \mathrel{\&} (-J \mathrel{\Box\!\!\rightarrow} R)$. This is a dependency hypothesis because it says that everything Solomon cares about (i.e., whether or not he will face a revolt) is outside his influence and that a revolt will ensue no matter what he does. As another example, $(J \mathrel{\Box\!\!\rightarrow} -R) \mathrel{\&} (-J \mathrel{\Box\!\!\rightarrow} R)$ says that whether or not a revolt will ensue is within his influence: abstaining from the woman will result in no revolt and sending for her will result in a revolt.

Following Lewis, let us call a counterfactual under an interpretation suitable for Gibbard and Harper's analysis 'a *causal counterfactual*'. And, for the general theory, let $\{O_1, \ldots O_m\}$ be a partition of outcomes where each O_j is a maximally specific specification of each thing the agent cares about in his particular decision problem. For example, if the agent cares about how he brings about the outcome of his action, then each O_j specifies an act. Then a *full pattern* is defined to be a set of causal counterfactuals which contains, for each act A, exactly one causal counterfactual of the form $A \mathrel{\Box\!\!\rightarrow} O_j$. (This is the same as Lewis' definition of 'full pattern' except that, for Lewis, the consequents of counterfactuals in a full pattern (i) are elements of a *rich* partition, i.e., a partition of propositions S_j such that for any dependency hypothesis K_i and any act A, $CEU(K_i \mathrel{\&} S_j \mathrel{\&} A) = CEU(S_j \mathrel{\&} A)$, and (ii) do not specify an act but rather "combinations of occurrences wholly distinct from the actions." Outcomes may then be of the form S_j & A, for such an S_j.) Lewis suggests that the conjunction of (the elements of) any full pattern is a dependency hypothesis.

Is the set of all conjunctions of full patterns a partition? Clearly, two conjunctions of different full patterns are mutually exclusive. If two full patterns are different, then, for some act A, they must differ in the consequent of the counterfactual with that act as antecedent. And if one full pattern contains $A \mathbin{\Box\!\!\rightarrow} O_j$ and another contains $A \mathbin{\Box\!\!\rightarrow} O_{j'}$, where $j \neq j'$, then, since these two counterfactuals are contrary, the two conjunctions of the two full patterns are contraries.

Is the set of all conjunctions of full patterns collectively exhaustive? Clearly it will be if Stalnaker's principle of conditional excluded middle (Gibbard and Harper's Axiom 2) holds: $(A \mathbin{\Box\!\!\rightarrow} -C) \leftrightarrow -(A \mathbin{\Box\!\!\rightarrow} C)$. Let us, for the moment, assume this principle and that dependency hypotheses are conjunctions of full patterns. Given this assumption, *PMLE* is the same as *PMUE*.

Let $\{K_1, \ldots K_n\}$ be the set of dependency hypotheses. Then n is equal to m^r, where r is the number of available acts. For each act A and outcome O_j, let I_{Aj} be the set of indices on dependency hypotheses that have $A \mathbin{\Box\!\!\rightarrow} O_j$ as a conjunct: $I_{Aj} = \{i : A \mathbin{\Box\!\!\rightarrow} O_j$ is a conjunct of $K_i\}$. Then, for each act A, the set of I_{Aj}s is a partition of $\{1, 2, \ldots, m^r\}$, and, for each A and O_j,

$$\sum_{i \in I_{Aj}} P(K_i) = P(A \mathbin{\Box\!\!\rightarrow} O_j).$$

Now if $i \in I_{Aj}$, then $CEU(K_i \ \& \ A) = D(O_j)$. This is because in this case, $K_i \ \& \ A$ implies O_j and O_j is a full description of everything that the agent cares about. Thus, for every act A,

$$U_L(A) = \sum_i P(K_i) CEU(K_i \ \& \ A)$$

$$= \sum_j \sum_{i \in I_{Aj}} P(K_i) CEU(K_i \ \& \ A)$$

$$= \sum_j \sum_{i \in I_{Aj}} P(K_i) D(O_j)$$

$$= \sum_j P(A \mathbin{\Box\!\!\rightarrow} O_j) D(O_j)$$

$$= U(A).$$

Using Lewis' definition of 'full pattern' and given that S_js form a rich partition whose members specify combinations of occurrences wholly distinct from the actions, Lewis shows that for every act A, (in our notation)

$$U_L(A) = \sum_j P(A \mathbin{\square\!\!\!\rightarrow} S_j) D(S_j \,\&\, A).$$

Note that the relation between Gibbard and Harper's $A \mathbin{\square\!\!\!\rightarrow} O_j$s and Lewis' K_is here is the same as the relation between Savage's E_{kj}s and Jeffrey's E_Is, as discussed in the section on Savage in Chapter 3.

As pointed out earlier, a possible objection to Gibbard and Harper's U-maximization approach is that the agent may attach some probability to the possibility that none of the $A \mathbin{\square\!\!\!\rightarrow} O_j$s ($A$ fixed, j varying) holds. Some possible reasons why he may do this were set out previously. In this case, Gibbard and Harper's formula for U-expectation is not a formula for expectation at all: it neglects the probability that none of the relevant counterfactuals holds. Here, there is no unique closest A-world (perhaps no closest A-worlds), Gibbard and Harper's Axiom 2 – Stalnaker's principle of conditional excluded middle – fails and the set of conjunctions of full patterns is not collectively exhaustive. In this case, a more general theory is needed, as Gibbard and Harper point out. Lewis supplies such a generalization.

Lewis assumes ("not without misgivings") that a special version of the principle of conditional excluded middle will always hold. Assuming that there is such a thing as objective chance, let $[C = c]$ be the proposition, called 'a chance proposition', that says that the chances of the outcomes, $O_1, \ldots O_m$ are correctly given by the chance distribution c. The $[C = c]$s form a partition, and the *special principle of conditional excluded middle* that Lewis assumes is: For every act A, the $A \mathbin{\square\!\!\!\rightarrow} [C = c]$s form a partition. (Lewis uses 'C' for credence, or subjective probability, and 'P' and 'p' in the chance propositions; here, I use 'P' for subjective probability and 'C' and 'c' for chance.)

Lewis' tentative suggestion for what dependency hypotheses are is that they are conjunctions of probabilistic full patterns, where a *probabilistic full pattern* is defined to be a set of causal counterfactuals which contains, for each act A, exactly one causal counterfactual of the form $A \mathbin{\square\!\!\!\rightarrow} [C = c]$. If the special principle of conditional excluded middle is true, then the dependency hypotheses, on this characterization of them, clearly form a partition.

144

There are infinitely many $[C = c]$s, infinitely many $A \mathbin{\square\!\!\rightarrow} [C = c]$s for each A and, thus, infinitely many dependency hypotheses. However, if two chance distributions, c and c', over the O_js are approximately the same in the sense that, for every O_j, they assign approximately the same chance to O_j, then the two chance propositions $[C = c]$ and $[C = c']$ may be, for all practical decision purposes, identified: the agent's preference ranking would be the same if all occurrences of $[C = c]$ and $[C = c']$ in the decision-relevant propositions were replaced by the proposition $[C = c] \vee [C = c']$. Thus, it will do no harm to assume that the set of $[C = c]$s and the sets of $A \mathbin{\square\!\!\rightarrow} [C = c]$s are *finite* partitions of cardinality, say, m'.

Let $\{K_1, \ldots K_n\}$ be the set of dependency hypotheses. Then $n = m''$, where, as before, r is the number of available acts. For each act A and chance proposition $[C = c]$, let 'I_{Ac}' denote the set of indices on dependency hypotheses that have $A \mathbin{\square\!\!\rightarrow} [C = c]$ as a conjunct: $I_{Ac} = \{i : A \mathbin{\square\!\!\rightarrow} [C = c]$ is a conjunct of $K_i\}$. Then, for each act A, the set of I_{Ac}s is a partition of the set $\{1, 2, \ldots m''\}$, and, for each A and $[C = c]$,
$$\sum_{i \in I_{Ac}} P(K_i) = P(A \mathbin{\square\!\!\rightarrow} [C = c]).$$
In most cases, the following will hold:

For all i, A, c and j, if $i \in I_{Ac}$, then
$$P(O_j | K_i \ \& \ A) = c(O_j).$$

This is because if $i \in I_{Ac}$, then $K_i \ \& \ A$ implies $[C = c]$, according to which the chance of O_j is $c(O_j)$. Lewis calls this 'the principle connecting chance and credence'. One case in which it would not hold is, as Lewis points out, where the agent believes he has foreknowledge of the outcomes of chance processes. Again, because the O_js fully specify everything that is relevant to the agent's happiness, $CEU(O_j \ \& \ K_i \ \& \ A) = D(O_j)$. Thus, for every act A,

$$
\begin{aligned}
U_L(A) &= \sum_i P(K_i) CEU(K_i \ \& \ A) \\
&= \sum_c \sum_{i \in I_{Ac}} P(K_i) CEU(K_i \ \& \ A) \\
&= \sum_c \sum_{i \in I_{Ac}} P(K_i) \sum_j P(O_j | K_i \ \& \ A) CEU(O_j \ \& \ K_i \ \& \ A) \\
&= \sum_c \sum_{i \in I_{Ac}} P(K_i) \sum_j c(O_j) D(O_j) \\
&= \sum_{jc} P(A \mathbin{\square\!\!\rightarrow} [C = c]) c(O_j) D(O_j).
\end{aligned}
$$

145

Then, letting '$[C(O_j) = d]$' stand for the disjunction of all the $[C = c]$s for which $c(O_j) = d$, we have:

$$U_L(A) = \sum_{jd} P(A \Box\!\!\rightarrow [C(O_j) = d])dD(O_j).$$

Again, with Lewis' definition of 'probabilistic full patterns', where the chance propositions specify chances for elements of a rich partition whose members specify combinations of occurrences wholly distinct from the actions and given that S_js form such a partition, Lewis shows that for every act A, (in our notation)

$$U_L(A) = \sum_{jd} P(A \Box\!\!\rightarrow [P(S_j) = d])dD(S_j \ \& \ A).$$

It is obvious that, given a suitable nonbacktracking (causal) interpretation of the counterfactuals in the probabilistic full patterns and assuming Lewis' principle connecting chance and credence, the partition of conjunctions of probabilistic full patterns together with any other partition will satisfy AC_2 and AC_3 even if they do not satisfy AC_2^* and AC_3^* and the partition of conjunctions of probabilistic full patterns will satisfy AC_4 even if it does not satisfy AC_4^*.

DISCUSSION

I have already indicated some of the advantages that a successful *CEU* approach to Newcomb situations would have over the approaches of Gibbard and Harper's and of Skyrms'. Now that Lewis' causal decision theory has been set out and the various approaches have been compared, some common features have emerged. Here, I shall summarize what I think are the principle advantages that a successful *CEU* resolution of the *prima facie* conflict between *PDOM* and *PMCEU* would have over causal decision theory in general, and I shall indicate some preliminary reasons for doubting that the counterexamples to *PMCEU* are genuine. In the next section, the latter will be taken up in detail.

In causal decision theory, as in Savage's theory, the probabilities of some states enter into the calculation of expected utility unconditional on the act. And, as in Savage's theory, these states (causal decision theory's K_is) must be chosen in a special way, a way that guarantees, for example, their causal act-independence. If the agent calculates causal expected utility in terms of the wrong partition

146

of K_is, then he may, of course, get the wrong prescription. Causal decision theory must, therefore, provide instructions for constructing an appropriate partition of K_is. On a *CEU* approach, however, the agent need not put together a special partition that is sensitive to the relevant causal distinctions.

Of course causal decision theories do provide recipes for constructing appropriate partitions. But the question then is how easy it will be for rational agents to follow the recipes. In Skyrms' theory – if 'factor' is narrowly or "somewhat more broadly" construed – the decision-relevant propositions must be chosen in a special way so that the appropriate causal distinctions are expressible in terms of them: a partition of K_is must be found whose members have no "two-way causality" with the acts. And, as we have seen, it is not clear that this will always be a routine matter. In Gibbard and Harper's theory and in Lewis' probabilistic full pattern formulation of his theory, it seems that the "base" decision-relevant propositions need not be chosen in a special way. But the K_is that are constructed from them must be put together in a special way. This brings me to the second point.

Causal approaches introduce into decision theory some concepts, absent in a *CEU* approach, that are not very well-understood. Causal decision theories invoke all the concepts of a *CEU* approach (subjective probability, desirability, addition, multiplication, factors narrowly construed) *plus* such concepts as: nonbacktracking, causal counterfactuals, the relation between states and acts of "being outside the influence of," objective chance. The counterfactual connective is an ingredient of Gibbard and Harper's K_is; "being outside the influence of" goes into Skyrms'; the counterfactual connective and chance propositions go into the K_is of the probabilistic full pattern formulation of Lewis' theory; and "being outside the influence of" and objective chance go into the K_is of the formulation of Lewis' theory in which they are of the form H_n & G_{nm} & G'_{no}. As prescriptive theories, causal decision theories must assume that the agent has and understands these notions. And as descriptive theories, the philosopher or psychologist must understand them and attribute the understanding of them to the decision makers under study. In view of the controversial and not very well-understood nature of these concepts, these observations would seem to indicate an important advantage to a possible *CEU* approach to Newcomb situations.

147

CEU theory, on the other hand, is fairly well-developed and, as a consequence, fairly well-understood. For it, there exist a number of representation theorems (discussed previously) that tell us, in terms of a qualitative preference relation, precisely where *PMCEU* is applicable. Owing to the intuitive plausibility of the qualitative assumptions of the theorems, it would seem that *PMCEU* is very broadly applicable indeed for agents with rationally related preferences. I believe that representation theorems for causal decision theories will be found. But it seems that the qualitative assumptions of these would have to involve more than just a preference relation: they would need a new primitive that can capture the force of judgments expressed on the quantitative side in terms of the causal counterfactual, 'is outside the influence of' or the chance propositions, depending on the version of causal decision theory in question. So, perhaps we can expect the new primitive also to be not very well-understood and the assumptions framed in terms of it also to be quite controversial.

All of these considerations provide incentive to carefully consider whether or not the *prima facie* counterexamples to *PMCEU* are genuine.

There are certainly reasons for doubting that the counterexamples are genuine. First, it is a fundamental tenet of Bayesianism – generally accepted by the proponents of causal decision theory – that conditionalization models learning, as discussed in Chapter 1. But the truth of this tenet together with the assumption that is essential to the counterexamples – namely, that $P(CC|SA) > P(CC|-SA)$, so that $P(SO|SA) > P(SO|-SA)$ – has some rather strange consequences. Consider the charisma case. If conditionalization models learning and if – as is essential to the counterexamples – the probability of Solomon's having charisma, and thus of having a revolt-free reign, is greater conditional on his abstaining from the woman than on sending for her, then, if Solomon abstains, we would expect Solomon's degrees of belief in the propositions that he has charisma and that he will have a revolt-free reign to increase. And we would expect that by performing other just acts, Solomon could make himself more and more confident that he is charismatic and that he will not face a revolt. But, since Solomon knows that whether or not he abstains from the woman – or performs other just acts – has no effect on whether or not he has charisma or will face a revolt, it seems that his beliefs would not change in this way

148

if he is rational. This throws doubt on the inequalities essential to the *prima facie* counterexamples.

Second, there are some seemingly reasonable ways in which an agent can generate his probabilities in which the condition essential to the counterexamples – i.e., $P(SO|SA) > P(SO|-SA)$ – is disallowed. Take the charisma case again for example. One way in which Solomon might go about evaluating $P(R|J)$ and $P(R|-J)$ is by equating them with hypothetical relative frequencies. Solomon imagines two long sequences of decision situations that he finds himself in – that he might actually find himself in in the future – that are identical to the one he now finds himself in in all respects that he considers relevant to rational decision making. In the situations of sequence 1, of length u, Solomon does not send for the woman. In the situations of sequence 2, of length v, Solomon sends for her. Let u' (v') be the number of situations in sequence 1 (2) in which Solomon imagines that a revolt ensues. Solomon sets $P(R|J)$ equal to u'/u and $P(R|-J)$ equal to v'/v. Because of the causal information that Solomon has (uncharisma, not unjust acts, causes revolts and Solomon has either charisma eternally or uncharisma eternally), it seems clear that $P(R|J)$ should equal $P(R|-J)$. As another possibility, Solomon bases his probabilities on proportions taken from a hypothetical group of kings that are exactly like him in all ways up to the time of decision.

Finally, it seems that on any plausible account as to how a common cause can cause a rational person to perform a symptomatic act, the common cause can cause the act only indirectly: by causing the person to have *reasons* for performing the act. But then, it should not be the performing of the act that is evidence for the presence of the common cause, but rather the nature of the reasons the agent has for performing it. *It seems to me that any approach to the counter-examples that does not deal directly with the nature of the causal relation between the common cause and the symptomatic act in a Newcomb situation cannot really go to the heart of the matter.* In the next section, I will follow up this idea and its implications for a possible *CEU* resolution of the matter.

6

Common causes, reasons and symptomatic acts

In this chapter, I argue that the alleged counterexamples to *PMCEU* are not genuine, that *PMCEU* really gives the correct prescriptions – indeed, the same as those given by *PDOM* and by causal decision theory. Here, the analysis will be confined to pure, simple Newcomb situations, and the analysis will be on a general level in the sense that I shall refer to "the common cause" rather than to, for example, the lesion or charisma, to "the symptomatic act" rather than to, for example, high cholesterol intake or Solomon's sending for the woman, and so on. One may, of course, think 'lesion' when one reads 'common cause', 'high cholesterol intake' when one reads 'symptomatic act', '*L*' when one reads '*CC*', and so on. In Chapter 7, the analysis of this chapter will be generalized in a number of ways: to mixed Newcomb and general decision situations and to cases in which the idealistic assumptions of this chapter do not hold strictly.

It is essential to the counterexamples that the agent's subjective probabilities be such that:

$$P(CC|SA) > P(CC|-SA). \tag{1}$$

Then, either *CC* can be thought of as carrying the bad news or, from (1), it can be argued that $P(SO|SA)$ must be greater than $P(SO|-SA)$. (1) is equivalent to:

$$P(SA|CC) > P(SA|-CC). \tag{2}$$

Is it plausible that our rational agent's beliefs be such that they are accurately characterizable by (1) and (2)? Now the agent does not know whether or not he has the common cause. Let us assume that the agent knows that he does not know whether or not he has the common cause and that he believes that he is rational. And let us

150

abbreviate the expression 'rational people who do not know whether or not they have the common cause' by 'agent-like people'. Then it should be illuminating to consider the question: Is it plausible that (1) and (2) characterize the agent's beliefs about the behavior of agent-like people? (Later I shall discuss in detail precisely what kinds of belief (1) and (2) can be taken as characterizing.)

One thing that might make us think that this *is* plausible is that the agent, of course, thinks that the common cause causes the symptomatic act. It is very natural to think (and indeed very often, though not always, the case) that an effect is more probable given that its cause obtains than given that its cause does not obtain. Thus, the fact that our rational agent believes that the common cause causes agent-like people to perform the symptomatic act would seem to make it plausible that he would (rationally) believe that agent-like people behave in such a way that the probability of their performing the symptomatic act is higher given that they have the common cause than given that they do not.

On the other hand, it is natural to think that a rational person's act – and, indeed, the rational act – is determined by the body of information the person has at hand (by his subjective beliefs and desires) and not by what in fact is the case. An act is rational relative to a possessed body of information; the quality of the information is irrelevant and the actual facts are irrelevant. (Of course we may reasonably insist that for the act to be rational, the agent's beliefs and desires be rationally related *to each other* – e.g., that the beliefs be logically consistent – even though we do not insist that they must have any particular degree of correspondence *to the facts*. Recall that this is the Bayesian sense of rationality discussed in Chapter 1.) Let us assume that our agent believes this. The fact that he believes *this* would seem – at least initially – to make it implausible that (1) and (2) characterize his (rational) beliefs about the behavior of agent-like people. The difference between having and not having the common cause is a difference between one thing's being the case and another thing's being the case: it itself is not a difference between one body of information and another. So how could the agent rationally believe that agent-like people with the common cause are more likely to perform the symptomatic act than agent-like people without the common cause when they are all alike with respect to knowledge about whether the common cause, in each such case, obtains?

I think it is very easy to reconcile the natural view, sketched above, about rational behavior and the rationality of acts with the belief that agent-like people behave in such a way that the symptomatic act is more probable given that the common cause obtains than given that the common cause does not obtain. And I believe that the obvious and natural way to make this reconciliation is to point out that while the difference between the common cause's obtaining and its not obtaining is not *itself* a difference between two bodies of information, still such a difference can *account* for a difference in bodies of information. I propose that the only way in which a common cause can cause an agent-like person to perform the symptomatic act is by suitably affecting his body of possessed information. *I shall assume that the way in which a common cause causes a rational person to perform a symptomatic act is by causing him to have such beliefs and desires that a rational evaluation of the available acts in light of these beliefs and desires leads to the conclusion that the symptomatic act is the best act. And I shall assume that our agent believes this hypothesis about how the common cause causes the symptomatic act.*

According to this hypothesis, the causal structure of Newcomb situations is more complex than indicated earlier. The causal structure can be represented in more detail by the following diagram:

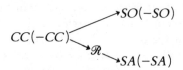

Here, interpret $\mathscr{R}$ as the set of propositions describing the possible sets of beliefs and desires a person might have in the relevant decision situation (more on such propositions later). Then the lower chain is to be interpreted as meaning that $CC(-CC)$ causes $SA(-SA)$ indirectly, i.e., by affecting which element of $\mathscr{R}$ is true: $CC(-CC)$ causes some element of $\mathscr{R}$, which, in turn, causes $SA(-SA)$.

The plausibility of this hypothesis – and thus the plausibility of our rational agent's subscribing to it – would seem, if anything, to reinforce the plausibility of his beliefs being accurately characterizable by (1) and (2). However, (1) and (2) are ambiguous (a fact that I have been deliberately ignoring up until now). There are two possible readings of (1) and (2). Under one reading, (1) and (2) characterize beliefs, the agent's possession of which is very plau-

152

sible. And indeed, the plausibility of the agent's possessing these beliefs might reasonably be though to be reinforced by the plausibility of his subscribing to our hypothesis about how the common cause causes the symptomatic act. But, as we shall see, it is inappropriate to draw conclusions about which act maximizes *CEU* from (1) and (2) taken as characterizations of these beliefs. On the other hand, it would be appropriate to draw conclusions about which act maximizes *CEU* from (1) and (2) if the agent had the beliefs characterized by (1) and (2) under the alternative reading. But we shall see that the assumption that he has *these* beliefs is very implausible given my assumption about how he believes the common cause causes the symptomatic act.

The two readings of (1) and (2) that I have in mind are as follows. Let us concentrate first on (1). According to one reading, (1) characterizes a belief that is roughly equivalent to, or closely approximated by, the belief that

$$\frac{\#\{w : CC(w) \,\&\, SA(w)\}}{\#\{w : SA(w)\}} > \frac{\#\{w : CC(w) \,\&\, -SA(w)\}}{\#\{w : -SA(w)\}},$$

where '$\#$' indicates cardinality, 'w' ranges over all agent-like people – or perhaps just those in some set of agent-like people that the agent thinks is representative of the incidence of the common cause and the symptomatic act – and $CC(w)$ and $SA(w)$ are propositions that say that w has the common cause and w does the symptomatic act, respectively. I shall say that under this reading of (1), (1) characterizes a *type-A* belief. Thus, the type-*A* belief that (1) characterizes is the belief that the common cause occurs with greater frequency among people who do the symptomatic act than among those who do not. Similarly, the type-*A* belief that (2) characterizes is the belief that the symptomatic act is more common among those who have the common cause than among those who do not have it. Henceforth, a characterization of a type-*A* belief will be intended if the relevant symbols in a probabilistic statement are followed by '(a)':

$$P(CC(a)|SA(a)) > P(CC(a)|-SA(a)); \qquad (1')$$

$$P(SA(a)|CC(a)) > P(SA(a)|-CC(a)). \qquad (2')$$

It will be convenient to associate propositions with symbols like '$CC(a)$' and '$SA(a)$' so that there will be no difficulty of interpretation when such a symbol occurs in a probability statement along with symbols that stand for propositions. '$CC(a)$' and '$SA(a)$' can be thought of as symbolizing the propositions 'If I were to randomly select an agent-like person a right now, a would have the common cause' and 'If I were to randomly select an agent-like person a right now, a would be a doer of the symptomatic act', respectively. Of course, 'a' is to be thought of as denoting the same agent-like person in each of the above propositions, since 'right now' is to be thought of as referring to the same time in each of the above propositions. A more elegant method, suggested to me by Charles Chihara, might be to interpret '$CC(a)$' and '$SA(a)$' simply as 'a has the common cause' and 'a does the symptomatic act', respectively, and think of all probabilities as conditional on the proposition 'a is a randomly selected agent-like person'.

According to the other reading of (1), (1) characterizes a belief that is also characterizable as:

$$P(CC(DM)|SA(DM)) > P(CC(DM)|-SA(DM)), \qquad (1'')$$

where $CC(DM)$ and $SA(DM)$ are the propositions to the effect that DM, our particular rational decision maker, has the common cause and does the symptomatic act, respectively. I shall say that under this reading of (1), (1) characterizes a type-B belief. A characterization of a type-B belief of our agent will be intended if the relevant symbols in a probability statement are followed by '(DM)', as in $(1'')$ and

$$P(SA(DM)|CC(DM)) > P(SA(DM)|-CC(DM)). \qquad (2'')$$

The distinction between type-A and type-B beliefs will become clearer as the discussion unfolds.

I hope to show that the assumption that the agent believes my hypothesis about how the common cause causes the symptomatic act makes it plausible that he has the type-A beliefs that $(1')$ and $(2')$ characterize but makes it implausible that he has the type-B beliefs that $(1'')$ and $(2'')$ characterize and in fact makes it very plausible that he has the following (equivalent) type-B beliefs:

$$P(CC(DM)|SA(DM)) = P(CC(DM|-SA(DM)); \qquad (3)$$

$$P(SA(DM)|CC(DM)) = P(SA(DM)|-CC(DM)). \qquad (4)$$

I will also argue that type-B beliefs, and not type-A beliefs, should figure in the agent's calculation of the conditional expected utility of his available acts.

Equations (3) and (4) imply that for simple two-state, two act Newcomb situations K-expectation=U-expectation=CEU, for

$U_K(SA(DM))$

$= P(CC(DM))D(SA(DM) \& CC(DM))$

$+ P(-CC(DM))D(SA(DM) \& -CC(DM));$

$U(SA(DM))$

$= P(SA(DM) \Box\!\!\rightarrow CC(DM))D(SA(DM) \& CC(DM))$

$+ P(SA(DM) \Box\!\!\rightarrow -CC(DM))D(SA(DM) \& -CC(DM))$

$= P(CC(DM))D(SA(DM) \& CC(DM))$

$+ P(-CC(DM))D(SA(DM) \& -CC(DM));$

$CEU(SA(DM))$

$= P(CC(DM)|SA(DM))D(SA(DM) \& CC(DM))$

$+ P(-CC(DM)|SA(DM))D(SA(DM) \& -CC(DM))$

$= P(CC(DM))D(SA(DM) \& CC(DM))$

$+ P(-CC(DM))D(SA(DM) \& -CC(DM)).$

That

$$P(CC(DM)|SA(DM)) = P(CC(DM))$$

and

$$P(-CC(DM)|SA(DM)) = P(-CC(DM))$$

are easy consequences of (3) and (4) and the axioms of probability. So are the equalities

$$P(CC(DM)|-SA(DM)) = P(CC(DM))$$

and

$$P(-CC(DM)|-SA(DM)) = P(-CC(DM)),$$

so that the K-expectation, U-expectation and CEU of $-SA(DM)$ are also equal as a consequence of (3) and (4). Thus, assuming that the rules of maximizing K-expectation and U-expectation (and

PDOM) give the right answer in such decision situations, (3) and (4) establish that *PMCEU* also gives the right answer. (Of course the equality between K-expectation, U-expectation and *CEU* will hold even if *CEU* is evaluated relative to a different selection of decision-relevant propositions, for, as pointed out previously, *CEU* does not vary according to how the space of probabilities is partitioned.)

It is easy to show that the assumption that the agent believes my hypothesis about how a common cause can cause a symptomatic act makes it plausible that he has the type-A beliefs characterized by (1′) and (2′). Let '$R_{CC}(a)$' symbolize the proposition that a has beliefs and desires of the kind that the common cause causes. '$R_{-CC}(a)$' will symbolize the proposition that a does not have beliefs and desires of the kind caused by the common cause. $R_{-CC}(a)$ is equivalent to $-R_{CC}(a)$. Then it is plausible that $P(R_{CC}(a)|CC(a)) > P(R_{CC}(a)|-CC(a))$: it is more probable that a has beliefs and desires of the kind caused by the common cause given that a has the common cause than given that a does not have the common cause. Let $\alpha = P(R_{CC}(a)|-CC(a))$ and let ε be the positive number such that $\alpha + \varepsilon = P(R_{CC}(a)|CC(a))$. Now it is plausible that

$$P(SA(a)|R_{CC}(a)\ \&\ CC(a)) = P(SA(a)|R_{CC}(a)\ \&\ -CC(a))$$

and that

$$P(SA(a)|R_{-CC}(a)\ \&\ CC(a)) = P(SA(a)|R_{-CC}(a)\ \&\ -CC(a)),$$

since the agent believes that a rational person's act is determined by his beliefs and desires and not by what in fact is the case: given that a is rational and has beliefs and desires of such and such a kind, whether some unknown matter of fact obtains or not is irrelevant to which act is rational, to which act is performed by the rational agent a. Also, since the common cause causes beliefs and desires of such a kind that a rational evaluation of the alternatives in light of them leads to the conclusion that the symptomatic act is the correct act, it is plausible that

$$P(SA(a)|R_{CC}\ (a)) > P(SA(a)|R_{-CC}(a)).$$

Thus, let

$$\beta = P(SA(a)|R_{-CC}(a)\ \&\ CC(a)) = P(SA(a)|R_{-CC}(a)\ \&\ -CC(a))$$

156

and let δ be the positive number such that

$$\beta + \delta = P(SA(a)|R_{CC}(a) \,\&\, CC(a)) = P(SA(a)|R_{CC}(a) \,\&\, -CC(a)).$$

Now,

$$P(SA(a)|CC(a)) = P(R_{CC}(a)|CC(a))P(SA(a)|R_{CC}(a) \,\&\, CC(a))$$
$$+ P(R_{-CC}(a)|CC(a))$$
$$\times P(SA(a)|R_{-CC}(a) \,\&\, CC(a)),$$

and

$$P(SA(a)|-CC(a)) = P(R_{CC}(a)|-CC(a))$$
$$\times P(SA(a)|R_{CC}(a) \,\&\, -CC(a))$$
$$+ P(R_{-CC}(a)|-CC(a))$$
$$\times P(SA(a)|R_{-CC}(a) \,\&\, -CC(a)).$$

So, $P(SA(a)|CC(a)) > P(SA(a)|-CC(a))$ if, and only if,

$$(\alpha + \varepsilon)(\beta + \delta) + (1 - \alpha - \varepsilon)\beta > \alpha(\beta + \delta) + (1 - \alpha)\beta.$$

By simple algebraic manipulation, this can be seen to be equivalent to $\varepsilon\delta > 0$, which is true since $\varepsilon, \delta > 0$.

So it is plausible that the agent has the type-A beliefs that (1) and (2) can be taken to characterize, i.e., the beliefs characterized by (1′) and (2′). This, however, does not justify using (1) and (2) to draw conclusions about which act – $SA(DM)$ or $-SA(DM)$ – maximizes DM's CEU, for a type-A belief is a belief about the behavior of a group of people, not of our agent. Taken as characterizations of type -A beliefs, (1) and (2) are summary descriptions of the behavior of a group of people. The important question relevant to drawing conclusions about DM's CEU of the available acts is whether (1) and (2) characterize his beliefs about *himself* as a rational agent, i.e., whether (1″) and (2″) are plausible. What is important is the probability of *his* having the common cause conditional on *his* performing the symptomatic act and not the frequency with which the common cause is present among people who perform the symptomatic act. And these two values may be quite different, for, as we shall see, the agent may know things about himself – in particular, about why he would perform the symptomatic if he would – that have implications for the first value but not for the second.

The argument that our rational agent should have the type-B beliefs characterized by (3) and (4), rather than the type-B beliefs characterized by (1″) and (2″), will involve a number of assumptions that are idealizations. However, in this primitive stage of the development of decision theory, they are not unreasonable idealizations. Indeed, I shall argue that the assumptions I shall make are little, if any, more idealistic than those commonly made in current Bayesian decision theories. (In Chapter 7, these assumptions will be weakened.)

Let Φ be the Boolean closed set of propositions that DM explicitly considers in his decision situation, i.e., Φ is the set of decision-relevant propositions. For example, in the cholesterol case, the set of decision-relevant propositions may include some or all of the following: I, L, T, 'L is outside the influence of I', $I \mathbin{\Box\!\!\rightarrow} L$, '$-T$ & L is outside the influence $-I$', $I \mathbin{\Box\!\!\rightarrow} T$ & $-L$. Now DM has degrees of belief over the set Φ and desirabilities for the maximally specific members of Φ. Let $R_\Phi(DM)$ be the (true) proposition that says what these subjective probabilities and desirabilities are at the time of decision. $R_\Phi(DM)$ attributes to DM the probabilities and desirabilities that he has at the time of decision. I assume that, near the time of decision,

$$P(R_\Phi(DM)) = 1. \tag{5}$$

That is, I assume that near the time of decision, DM knows what his degrees of belief in the members of Φ are and what his desirabilities for the maximally specific members of Φ are.

It seems to me that (5) should be unobjectionable to anyone who takes any of the competing decision theories discussed earlier seriously. At least if decision theory is to be prescriptive, then the agent must, at some time before the decision takes place, know what his probabilities and desirabilities are. And it seems to me that (5) is a good decision-theoretic explication of this. (In Chapter 7, though, the analysis of this chapter will be generalized to the case in which the agent is uncertain about what his "true," perhaps unconscious, beliefs and desires are.)

Equation (5) features the idea of the agent's assigning probabilities and desirabilities to propositions about his probabilities and desirabilities. I see nothing problematic about this, although others have. (The idea of "second-order degrees of belief" has been discussed by, e.g., Savage (1954: 57–8), Jaynes (1958), Jamison (1970), Jeffrey (1974), Mellor (1980) and Skyrms (1980a, b).) Surely people have beliefs that, decision-theoretically, could be character-ized as beliefs about their past or future probabilities and desirabilities, and those of others. They have beliefs about why they did certain things in the past and about what they will do in the future and why. Also, they are more or less certain in these beliefs and more or less desirous of their being true. Why can't the same be said about how they are currently motivated? If they don't explicitly consider propositions about how they are currently motivated – about what their current reasons, or subjective prob-abilities and desirabilities, are – then it is probably because such propositions are thought to be too obvious, irrelevant or difficult or uneconomical to formulate. But it is not because there are no such intelligible propositions. It seems that there are and that a good decision-theoretic explication of the idea that an agent knows what his current degrees of belief and desire are (even if he does not explicitly consider propositions about them) is (5).

Let '$B_{SA}(DM)$' ('$B_{-SA}(DM)$') stand for the proposition that DM (rationally) determines that $SA(DM)$ $(-SA(DM))$ is the correct act. I assume that DM will determine that one of the two acts is correct and that he believes this, so $B_{-SA}(DM)$ should be thought of, by us and him, as equivalent to $-B_{SA}(DM)$. I shall assume:

$$P(B_{SA}(DM) \leftrightarrow SA(DM)) = 1. \qquad (6)$$

That is, the agent is certain of the following: he will perform $SA(DM)$ $(-SA(DM))$ if, and only if, he determines that $SA(DM)$ $(-SA(DM))$ is the correct act. This assumption seems completely unobjectionable, especially as an idealization. Ernest Adams has suggested in discussion that (6) might be interpreted as asserting of DM that he believes he has no "weakness of will." And one may object that it would be very unrealistic to assume this of DM. However, it seems that if our agent believes that he has or might have weakness of will, then whatever utility he may attach to giving in to such weakness would enter into his deliberation about which act is best for him. And if he believes this, then it seems that (6) can accurately characterize his beliefs even if he acknowledges weakness of will.

Given (6), if the common cause is to cause an act, it must affect at least some aspects of people's deliberation as to which act is best.

But my last assumption is:

$$P(B_{SA}(DM)|R_\Phi(DM) \& CC(DM))$$
$$= P(B_{SA}(DM)|R_\Phi(DM) \& -CC(DM)). \quad (7)$$

Why is this a reasonable assumption? According to each of the decision theories discussed earlier (and according to all Bayesian decision theories), the act that a rational person determines to be best turns on just three things: his subjective probabilities over some set of decision-relevant propositions, his desirabilities for the maximally specific members of this set and a decision rule. So, if a common cause causes rational people to determine that some act is best, it must affect at least some of these things that this determination turns on. Let us assume that our agent, knowing some decision theory, believes this. But at the same time that he believes this, he believes that he is rational, that he can and will rationally assess the available courses of action. Which among these three things can the agent believe that the common cause affects *consistent with his belief that he is rational*? It is clear that the common cause could, to some extent, affect the agent's *probabilities* without rational capacity, for these are more a matter of taste than of rationality. And it is not unreasonable to suppose that the common cause could, to some extent, affect the agent's *probabilities* without affecting his rational capacity. According to the subjective interpretation of probability, two rational people with the same information can disagree in their probability assessments; perhaps the presence or absence of factors like our common causes could account for this in some cases.

But can the presence or absence of the common cause make a difference in the agent's choice of *decision rule* without affecting his rational capacity? Unlike one's subjective probabilities and desirabilities, it seems that the correctness of a decision rule – i.e., whether, given a probability and a desirability assignment, the rule gives the correct act – is not a subjective matter. Indeed, this is presupposed in all decision theories that endorse decision rules that take as input an agent's subjective probabilities and desirabilities and give as output the correct act: the rational act for a given agent is a *function* of his subjective probabilities and desirabilities. The subjective probabilities and desirabilities are allowed to vary from one agent to the next, but once these are fixed, so is the rational act. So at least the following is clear (or at least clearly presupposed by all Bayesian decision theories): Given that an agent is rational and given that he has some particular pair of probability and desirability assignments, whether a common cause is present or absent is irrelevant to which act is (rationally) determined by him to be the correct one. Of course this is consistent with the common cause having an effect on which of a number of decision rules, each of which yields the same recommendation, is used. But, while this is not essential to my argument, it seems that because of the close connection between rationality and choice of decision rule, the assumption that an agent is rational is enough to ensure that the presence or absence of a common cause will not affect which decision rule is used. Let us assume that our rational agent, knowing some decision theory, believes this.

Now I am not arguing that the agent must believe that the process of evaluating alternatives in light of beliefs and desires – which process is modeled decision-theoretically by a decision rule such as *PMCEU* and *PMKE* – is uncaused or that the agent must believe that the common cause can never have any influence on this process. But I am assuming that the agent believes that the causal influence of the common cause is sufficiently insignificant as to be irrelevant to the eventual determination of which act is correct in light of his beliefs and desires – which beliefs and desires, however, the common cause may have played a significant role in producing in the agent. This is because he believes that the causal influence of whatever is causally responsible for his rationality – his training, genetic make-up, and so on – will be overwhelming.

So I think it is reasonable to assume that the agent, knowing some decision theory, believes that the way in which the common cause causes rational people to decide on the symptomatic act is by affecting their probabilities and desirabilities in such a way that their decision rules (which the common cause plays no role in their choosing) yield the recommendation to perform the symptomatic act. He believes that the common cause can affect a rational person's probabilities and desirabilities but not the choice of decision rule. Note that since, in decision theory, subjective probabilities model beliefs, desirabilities model desires and decision rules model rational evaluation of the available acts in light of beliefs and desires, this is just a decision-theoretic formulation of the hypothesis that I have already assumed that the agent believes: the common cause causes the symptomatic act by causing such beliefs and desires that a rational evaluation of the available acts in light of them leads to the conclusion that the symptomatic act is the correct act.

Since the common cause does not affect the choice of decision rule, then, given a particular pair of probability and desirability assignments (such as those described in $R_\Phi(DM)$), there is no longer any motivation for an assumption of probabilistic relevance of the common cause to the determination of a given act to be the correct one. And (7) expresses the relevant probabilistic independence.

It follows from (6) and (7) that:

$$P(SA(DM)|R_\Phi(DM) \& CC(DM))$$
$$= P(SA(DM)|R_\Phi(DM) \& -CC(DM)). \quad (8)$$

And from (8), together with (5), it follows that:

$$P(SA(DM)|CC(DM)) = P(SA(DM)|-CC(DM)), \quad (4)$$

and

$$P(CC(DM)|SA(DM)) = P(CC(DM)|-SA(DM)). \quad (3)$$

To briefly summarize the argument: The agent's beliefs should be as characterized in (8) because he believes that the common cause can cause the symptomatic act only indirectly, by causing a person to determine that the symptomatic act is the rational act and *this* it can do only by affecting probabilities and desirabilities. The role of the common cause in producing the symptomatic act ends there. The agent believes that the symptomatic act is causally correlated with the common cause only insofar as it is causally correlated with probability and desirability assignments that are causally correlated with the presence of the common cause. Beyond affecting one's subjective probabilities and desirabilities, the common cause is completely causally inefficacious in producing the symptomatic act. Thus, given the presence of a particular pair of subjective probability and desirability assignments (such as those described in $R_\Phi(DM)$), the causal (and thus the probabilistic) correlation between the common cause and the symptomatic act should disappear. Equation (8) expresses the relevant probabilistic independence. Then, (3) and (4) follow because DM has *knowledge* that his subjective probabilities and desirabilities are as described in $R_\Phi(DM)$.

Thus, what is essential to the generation of Newcomb situation counterexamples to $PMCEU$ – that the agent should have the type-

B beliefs that $(1'')$ and $(2'')$ characterize – is false. I would like to emphasize that *this argument is completely general: it applies to all pure Newcomb situations and establishes (3) and (4) and, thus, that PMCEU gives the right answer in such situations.*

A possible objection to the argument focuses on (8). (It may also be interpreted as focusing on (7).) According to the objection, the agent might think that $R_\Phi(DM)$ & $CC(DM)$ is better evidence that $SA(DM)$ is the rational reaction to the probabilities and desirabilities described in $R_\Phi(DM)$ than $R_\Phi(DM)$ & $-CC(DM)$ is, for $R_\Phi(DM)$ & $CC(DM)$ is better evidence than $R_\Phi(DM)$ & $-CC(DM)$ for the hypotheses that the probabilities and desirabilities described in $R_\Phi(DM)$ are caused by the common cause. And of course the probability and desirability assignments caused by the common cause are those that are more likely to be such that the rational reaction to them consists in performing the symptomatic act. Therefore, goes the objection, $R_\Phi(DM)$ & $CC(DM)$ is better evidence for $SA(DM)$ than $R_\Phi(DM)$ & $-CC(DM)$ is, and this casts doubt on (8).

As we shall see, this objection raises an interesting point, but the point is not relevant to (8). The argument assumes that if the agent somehow obtained evidence to the effect that the common cause caused him to have the probabilities and desirabilities described by $R_\Phi(DM)$, he would have evidence to the effect that $SA(DM)$ is the rational response to those probabilities and desirabilities. But evidence as to the cause of those probabilities and desirabilities constitutes evidence as to what the rational response to them is only for someone who is not familiar with them. Of course if someone somehow found out that some pair of probability and desirability assignments was caused by the common cause *and knew nothing else about them*, he would have better evidence that the symptomatic act was the rational response to them than if he somehow found out that the common cause did not cause them. But for someone who, like our agent, is very familiar with the probabilities and desirabilities described by $R_\Phi(DM)$, the cause of them is irrelevant to what the rational response to them is. What is relevant is the nature of the assignments.

I believe that this objection is based on a failure to make a distinction similar to the distinction between type-A and type-B beliefs. Let 'r' be a variable that ranges over pairs of probability and desirability assignments and consider these two properties of such pairs: $Q_1(r)$ if, and only if, r is such that the symptomatic act is the rational response to r; $Q_2(r)$ if, and only if, r is caused by the common cause. Then of course the agent has the (type-A-like) belief characterized by:[1]

$$\frac{\#\{r: Q_1(r) \ \& \ Q_2(r)\}}{\#\{r: Q_2(r)\}} > \frac{\#\{r: Q_1(r) \ \& \ -Q_2(r)\}}{\#\{r: -Q_2(r)\}}.$$

That is, the agent believes that the property of being such that the symptomatic act is the rational reaction to it is more common among pairs of probability and desirability assignments caused by the common cause than among those not caused by the common cause. Now let r^* be a constant that denotes the pair of probability and desirability assignments described by $R_\Phi(DM)$, the one that the agent is certain that he has. It does not follow from the agent's having the type-A-like belief characterized above that he has the type-B-like belief characterized by:

$$P(Q_1(r^*)|Q_2(r^*)) > P(Q_1(r^*)|-Q_2(r^*)).$$

For what is relevant in assessing the rationality of different responses to r^* is the *nature* of the assignments that constitute r^*; and since the agent knows what these assignments are, he will base his probability of $Q_1(r^*)$ on the current state of his evaluation of the alternatives in light of r^*. The *cause* of r^* is irrelevant to what the rational response to r^* is, and DM can be assumed to know this.

Another objection that might be raised is that if we assume that the agent knows what decision rule he will use, then, since I am also assuming (5), all the agent's probabilities, are in effect conditional on his knowledge of his probabilities, desirabilities and decision rule. But since these determine the act, this is tantamount to taking the act to be performed as a datum so that – as Skyrms claims – "the whole decision process then threatens to become dangerously self-referential" (1980a: 131).

---

[1] As Charles Chihara has pointed out to me, for DM to have this belief, we must avoid a cardinality problem: the numerator and denominator might both be infinite. To handle this, we may let 'r' range over pairs of probability and desirability assignments actually had by people at some time when facing the decision problem at hand. Or we may assume that the set of pairs of probability and desirability assignments can be finitely partitioned in a natural way and let 'r' range over elements of the partition. (A suggestion as to how this may be done will be given in Chapter 7.) We must also assume that the agent believes that there are enough items over which 'r' ranges to ensure that the fractions mirror causal facts.

I have two responses to this objection. First, I did not assume that the agent knows what rule he will use. And second, even if he does know, there may still be some uncertainty about which act he will choose, for there may still be some calculation left to do. He may have chosen but not yet applied the rule. For instance, even if the agent knows that he will try to maximize K-expectation, he may still not know which act he will perform, for even though he knows his probabilities, desirabilities and rule, he must still *calculate* the K-expectations of the available acts.

Finally, one may object that it is not clear that an agent who held, simultaneously, the beliefs characterized by

$$P(CC(a)|SA(a)) > P(CC(a)|-SA(a)), \qquad (1')$$

$$P(SA(a)|CC(a)) > P(SA(a)|-CC(a)), \qquad (2')$$

$$P(CC(DM)|SA(DM)) = P(CC(DM)|-SA(DM)), \qquad (3)$$

and

$$P(SA(DM)|CC(DM)) = P(SA(DM)|-CC(DM)) \qquad (4)$$

is not guilty of having contradictory beliefs (or degrees of belief that are incoherent, in the sense of not obeying the probability axioms). I have already given independent arguments for the plausibility of the agent's having the beliefs characterized by $(1')$ and $(2')$ and for the plausibility of the agent's having the beliefs characterized by (3) and (4). Now I will give a new argument for the plausibility of the agent's having the type-A beliefs characterized by $(1')$ and $(2')$ and suggest a very plausible connection between a rational agent's type-A and type-B beliefs. This new argument, together with the connection I suggest between type-A and type-B beliefs, will also show that an agent having, simultaneously, the beliefs characterized by $(1')$, $(2')$, (3) and (4) will not, in virtue thereof, be guilty of having inconsistent (or incoherent) beliefs, but rather, the agent would be quite reasonable in having, simultaneously, all these beliefs.

Let H be the hypothesis that the pair of probability and desirability assignments had by DM – the pair described by $R_\Phi(DM)$ – is of the kind caused by the common cause. And let $R_\Phi(a)$ be the proposition that ascribes to (the arbitrary individual) a the assignments DM himself has and is certain that he himself has. And consider the following characterizations of type-A beliefs. (For readability, I shall here drop the '(a)' on '$CC(a)$' and '$SA(a)$' and both the '(a)' and the 'Φ' on '$R_\Phi(a)$'.)

$$P(H|CC) = P(H|-CC); \qquad (9)$$

$$P(R|H \ \& \ CC) > P(R|H \ \& \ -CC); \qquad (10)$$

$$P(SA|H \ \& \ R) > P(SA|H \ \& \ -R); \qquad (11)$$

$$P(SA|H \ \& \ -R \ \& \ CC) \geqslant P(SA|H \ \& \ -R \ \& \ -CC); \qquad (12)$$

$$P(SA|H \ \& \ R \ \& \ CC) = P(SA|H \ \& \ R \ \& \ -CC); \qquad (13)$$

$$P(R|-H \ \& \ CC) < P(R|-H \ \& \ -CC); \qquad (14)$$

$$P(SA|-H \ \& \ R) < P(SA|-H \ \& \ -R); \qquad (15)$$

$$P(SA|-H \ \& \ -R \ \& \ CC) \geqslant P(SA|-H \ \& \ -R \ \& \ -CC); \qquad (16)$$

$$P(SA|-H \ \& \ R \ \& \ CC) = P(SA|-H \ \& \ R \ \& \ -CC). \qquad (17)$$

I claim that each of (9)–(17) should be expected to hold of the agent's type-A beliefs.

Proposition (9) is plausible, for finding out merely that some arbitrary agent-like person a has the common cause should in no way affect one's degree of belief in the hypothesis H. And (10) and (11) should hold because, given H, CC causes R and, thus, R is the kind of state that brings about SA; (14) and (15) should hold for similar reasons. And (12) and (16) should hold for reasons put forth in the first objection considered previously: all of the probabilities in (12) and (16) are conditional on $-R$, and if the agent is unfamiliar with the pair of probability and desirability assignments described by some R', then $R' \ \& \ CC$ is better evidence that they are caused by the common cause (and thus better evidence for SA) than $R' \ \& \ -CC$ is. Propositions (12) and (16) have been left as weak inequalities to leave open the possibility that the agent believes that there are only two pairs of probability and desirability assignments that an agent-like person a may have in the decision problem at hand, and that the agent is familiar with both. And (13) and (17) are plausible for reasons put forth in the reply to that objection: the agent is familiar with the probability and desirability assignments described by R.

Propositions (9)–(17) imply (1′) and (2′). Here is the proof (which is tedious and which some readers may wish to skip over). Because (1′) is equivalent to (2′), it need only be shown that (9)–(17) imply

(2'), which is what I shall do. Now (2') is equivalent to:

$$P(H|CC)P(SA|H \& CC) + P(-H|CC)P(SA|-H \& CC)$$
$$> P(H|-CC)P(SA|H \& -CC)$$
$$+ P(-H|-CC)P(SA|-H \& -CC), \qquad (18)$$

which, in the presence of (9), is clearly implied by the conjunction of (19) and (20):

$$P(SA|H \& CC) > P(SA|H \& -CC), \qquad (19)$$

$$P(SA|-H \& CC) > P(SA|-H \& -CC). \qquad (20)$$

Propositions (10)–(13) imply (19), and (14)–(17) imply (20). The proofs of these two statements are parallel, so I shall only show that (10)–(13) imply (19). Now,

$$P(SA|H \& CC) = P(R|H \& CC)P(SA|H \& R \& CC)$$
$$+ P(-R|H \& CC)P(SA|H \& -R \& CC),$$

and

$$P(SA|H \& -CC) = P(R|H \& -CC)P(SA|H \& R \& -CC)$$
$$+ P(-R|H \& -CC)P(SA|H \& -R \& -CC).$$

By (10), we can let α, $\varepsilon > 0$ be such that

$$\alpha = P(R|H \& -CC),$$

and

$$\alpha + \varepsilon = P(R|H \& CC).$$

Note that $\alpha + \varepsilon \leq 1$, so that $1 - \alpha - \varepsilon \geq 0$. Now, $P(SA|H \& -R)$ is an average of $P(SA|H \& -R \& CC)$ and $P(SA|H \& -R \& -CC)$ and hence must be at least as great as the smaller of these two, which, by (12), is the latter: i.e., $P(SA|H \& -R) \geq P(SA|H \& -R \& -CC)$. Putting this together with (11), we get: $P(SA|H \& R) > P(SA|H \& -R \& -CC)$. This fact, together with (12) and (13), allows us to let β, $\delta > 0$ and $\delta' \geq 0$ be such that

$$\beta = P(SA|H \& -R \& -CC),$$

$$\beta + \delta' = P(SA|H \& -R \& CC),$$

and

$$\beta + \delta = P(SA|H \& R) = P(SA|H \& R \& CC)$$
$$= P(SA|H \& R \& -CC).$$

Thus, (18) will hold if, and only if,

$$(\alpha + \varepsilon)(\beta + \delta) + (1 - \alpha - \varepsilon)(\beta + \delta') > \alpha(\beta + \delta) + (1 - \alpha)\beta.$$

Simple algebraic manipulation shows this to be equivalent to:

$$\varepsilon\delta + \delta'(1 - \alpha - \varepsilon) > 0,$$

which is true, since ε, $\delta > 0$ and δ', $(1 - \alpha - \varepsilon) \geqslant 0$. This completes the proof of (19) from (10)–(13). Parallel reasoning establishes (20) as a consequence of (14)–(17) and thus (18) (which is equivalent to (1') and (2')) as a consequence of (9)–(17).

Now if DM believes that $R_\Phi(DM)$ is the only thing that distinguishes himself in a relevant way from the arbitrary individual in the decision situation in question, then for any proposition $X(a)$ relevant in that decision situation, $P(X(DM))$ should be equal to $P(X(a)|R_\Phi(a))$. This connection between DM's type-A and type-B beliefs together with the additional assumption that the probabilities in (13) and (17) are all equal (which is reasonable since whether or not H is true is a difference in fact and not in possessed information, the latter of which is fully recorded in R) evidently yields (3) and (4).

I have argued that it is unreasonable to assume that a rational agent would hold the type-B beliefs that (1) and (2) can be taken to characterize – the beliefs characterized by (1'') and (2'') – and that a rational agent would have the type-B beliefs characterized by (3) and (4). I have argued that an agent would be consistent and reasonable in holding the type-B beliefs characterized by (3) and (4) at the same time that he holds the type-A beliefs characterized by (1') and (2'), but that probabilistic characterizations of type-B beliefs, and not those of type-A beliefs, should figure in the calculation of an agent's conditional expected utility of an act. And (3) and (4) imply that the recommendations of $PMCEU$ agree with those of $PDOM$ and causal decision theory for pure Newcomb situations: $PMCEU$ gives the right answers.

As to diagnosing the paradox, I have the following suggestions. First, the appearance that Newcomb situations constitute counter-examples to $PMCEU$ may have arisen from a *failure to distinguish* the type-A beliefs characterized by (1') and (2') from the type-B beliefs characterized by (1'') and (2''). Second, it may have arisen from an *unwarranted inference* from the reasonableness of the beliefs characterized by (1′) and (2′) to the reasonableness of the beliefs characterized by (1″) and (2″). And third, it may have arisen from similar mistakes relative to the type-A-like and type-B-like beliefs discussed in the response to the first objection put forth previously. Recall that in the response to the objection it was pointed out that the objection would be valid if the probabilities in (8) were those of a person who, unlike DM, is not very familiar with the probabilities and desirabilities described in $R_\Phi(DM)$. This suggests that it might be easy for one to fall into the mistakes suggested in the third diagnosis if one failed to be aware of the fact that someone might recommend to DM, perhaps correctly on the basis of the information available to him, an act other than the one that DM determines, correctly on the basis of the information available to *him*, is the correct act.[2] *PMCEU* requires the use of all the relevant available information, and it appears that in some cases some of that information is not very easily accessible to persons other than DM.

[2] I owe this "inner-outer" part of the third diagnosis to discussion with Ernest Adams and Charles Chihara.

7

A general defense of PMCEU

The assumptions of the last chapter are idealizations, and they deal only with the special case of pure Newcomb situations. In this chapter, I will trade those assumptions for weaker ones relative to a more general setting with n states and m available acts. This more general setting may constitute a pure Newcomb situation, a mixed Newcomb situation or no Newcomb situation at all. After giving a probabilistic analysis of an agent's beliefs regarding the causal relations among the acts, the states and states of a special kind (like $R_\Phi(DM)$ of Chapter 6), I shall offer two theorems which indicate that *PMCEU* gives the right prescription wherever causal decision theory does. The main argument of this chapter will appeal to the plausibility of causal decision theory – in particular, *PMKE* – when its causal expectation is evaluated relative to appropriate partitions, in the sense of 'appropriate' given in Chapter 5. But before proceeding to the more general setting, I shall consider a kind of objection that might be made to the analysis of Chapter 6 to which the theory of this chapter provides an answer.

Skyrms discusses a kind of defense of *PMCEU* which has come to be known as the "tickle defense" (1980*a*: 130–2). Consider again the cholesterol case. If the way in which the lesion caused high cholesterol intake was by producing a detectable tickle of a certain kind in the taste buds and if the agent knew this and noticed whether or not he had that tickle, then obviously *PMCEU* would give the correct prescription: the man would know whether or not he had the lesion and, either way, *PMCEU* would clearly recommend the eggs benedict. This is because having the tickle (and thus the lesion) – or not having the tickle (and thus not having the lesion) – screens off the causal, and thus the probabilistic, correlation between high cholesterol intake and hardening of the arteries: given the tickle – or given its absense – the probability of atherosclerosis is the same conditional on high cholesterol intake and conditional on low to medium cholesterol intake. And if the counterpart of the tickle exists for the other Newcomb situations, then *PMCEU* will give the right answers there as well.

Skyrms counters the tickle defense as follows:

> *Why should we, in every decision situation, be in possession of knowledge of some convenient factor which screens off any probabilistic relationship which does not mirror a causal relationship?* After all, there need not *be* a tickle. The mechanism responsible for the increased intake of cholesterol might operate in any number of ways, conscious or unconscious, and the agent making the decision might not have a clue as to how it operates. For him, the example retains its force. (1980a: 131)

Perhaps one would object to the theory of the previous chapter on the grounds that it is just an elaborate "tickle theory," for it is assumed that the agent is always in possession of knowledge of his probabilities and desirabilities (by (6.5))[1] and that this factor screens off the probabilistic correlation between the common cause and the symptomatic act (by (6.6) and (6.7)). But of course there are important differences between the analysis of the previous chapter and the simple tickle defense sketched by Skyrms. First, a set of beliefs and desires – modeled by probabilities and desirabilities – can very reasonably be assumed to be present in every decision situation: indeed, each of the competing decision theories I have discussed assumes this. The defense sketched by Skyrms must assume that for each Newcomb situation one can find an analog of the tickle particularly suited to it. This seems clearly wrong. But there need to be beliefs and desires, modeled by probabilities and desirabilities, in any decision situation that is suited for rational decision making on the Bayesian model. One's beliefs and desires are indeed a convenient factor, present in every decision situation, that screens off the correlation between a common cause and a symptomatic act. A second difference is that in the defense sketched by Skyrms, knowledge of the convenient factor was assumed to be sufficient for the agent to know whether the common cause obtains or not, whereas my theory does not require that the belief and desire factor be *that* convenient.

---

[1] Displayed lines in this chapter will be numbered (1), (2), (3), and so on, as they were in the previous chapter. Thus, to refer to displayed lines of Chapter 6, I shall write '(6.1)', '(6.2)', '(6.3)', and so on.

Do these differences make the theory of the previous chapter immune to the objections Skyrms raises to the simple tickle defense he sketches? The analysis of the previous chapter does allow that the lesion may operate in any number of ways in producing high cholesterol intake and that the agent may not have a clue as to which way – as long as the agent is assumed to believe, as is reasonable, that however the lesion operates, it must ultimately affect rational people's beliefs and desires in such a way that a rational evaluation of the available acts in light of them leads to the conclusion that high cholesterol intake is the rational act. Not only is it allowed that the agent not know anything about the physical mechanism by which the lesion is able to affect his beliefs and desires, it is also allowed that the agent not know which particular sets of beliefs and desires the lesion produces (or, specifically, how the lesion moves one's beliefs and desires around).

However, the theory of the previous chapter does not allow that the agent not be certain about what his subjective probabilities and desirabilities are. And Skyrms objects that we might not have knowledge of whether the convenient factor obtains or not. He suggests, in fact, that the mechanism by which the lesion operates may be *unconscious*. One way of taking some of what Skyrms says suggests the following objection. The agent may think that the way in which the common cause causes the symptomatic act is by producing *unconscious* beliefs and desires. But then the agent does not know the relevant probabilities and desirabilities – he only knows his conscious ones – and assumption (6.5), one of the basic assumptions of Chapter 6, is false.

Recently D. H. Mellor (1980) has developed a dispositional theory of belief which incorporates the distinction between conscious and unconscious belief and which relates these two kinds of belief. Beliefs of both kinds are, on the theory, quasi-dispositions: "quasi" because, as pointed out in Chapter 2, you need desire as well as belief to be disposed to particular actions. If you want to leave the room, you may walk in a particular direction as a result of your belief that the exit is in that direction; and this belief is *unconscious* if your mind is, for example, preoccupied with your reason for leaving. If you want to get somebody else to understand that the exit is in a particular place, you might remark in conversation where you believe the exit is; this kind of behavior requires *conscious* belief that the exit is in a particular place. In a nutshell, Mellor's theory is that conscious belief, what Mellor calls 'assent', in p is belief that one believes p, and that both kinds of belief come in degrees. Degrees of assent are "second-order" probabilities, and degrees of (typically unconscious) belief are "first-order" probabilities.

Through a process which Mellor calls 'insight' we can become aware of our unconscious beliefs: we can make them conscious. Insight is an inner sense. And, just like our other senses, insight does not pick up every detail, and it is fallible. Thus, we may have imperfect knowledge of our first-order beliefs and desires. David Lewis has suggested (in correspondence with D. H. Mellor) that an agent with imperfect knowledge of his beliefs and desires cannot use the belief and desire factor to screen off the correlation between the symptomatic act and common cause in a Newcomb situation because he is not certain about what his probabilities and desirabilities are: assumption (6.5) is false for such an agent. Thus, such an agent may learn more about whether or not he has the common cause from what he *does* than from what he learns from insight.

Note that the version of "ticklism" that Skyrms discusses and that Lewis has in mind focuses on evidential relations from effect to cause, that is, on the question: "What is the probability that the common cause is present given that I do (or do not do) the symptomatic act?" The theory of the previous chapter focuses on evidential relations in the opposite direction, that is, on the question: "What is the probability that I shall do the symptomatic act given that the common cause is (or is not) present?" Due to the symmetries of probabilistic independence and probabilistic relevance, it would seem that either way of looking at the situation is equally valid. However, I find the way I looked at it in the previous chapter to be more illuminating.

In any case, the analysis of this chapter will be able to deal with the following objection. We have two kinds of beliefs and desires: conscious beliefs and desires and unconscious ("true") beliefs and desires. We know our minds imperfectly so that we are not certain about what our true beliefs and desires are. Thus, in decision making, we must rely on our conscious beliefs and desires, about whose nature we are certain but which may not reflect our true beliefs and desires. Now the common cause in a Newcomb situation may operate through our unconscious, true beliefs and desires.

Thus, the objection continues: (i) different actions may be differently probabilistically relevant to our having different sets of true beliefs and desires and (ii) different sets of true beliefs and desires may be differently probabilistically relevant to whether or not we have the common cause. In fact, the symptomatic act is strong evidence for true beliefs and desires of the kind the common cause causes, and having *these* true beliefs and desires is strong evidence for the common cause. Thus, despite our perfect knowledge of the conscious beliefs and desires, which we use in deliberation, the symptomatic act is still positively probabilistically relevant to the common cause: (6.3) and (6.4) are false.

The analysis of this chapter will allow thesis (ii) of the objection but deny thesis (i). Before describing in detail the new, more general setting and stating the new, weaker assumptions, I would like to point out in advance some important features of these. First, the agent will not be assumed to be certain about what his true degrees of belief and desire are. The theory of this chapter will show that *PMCEU* will recommend an act to such an agent which is, plausibly, the best he can self-consciously rationally do given his uncertainty about his true beliefs and desires. Second, it will be assumed that the agent has a set of conscious probabilities and desirabilities and that he knows what these are. This, of course, is necessary if the agent is to be able to apply any of the competing decision theories. Third, in addition to the usual states and acts, the analysis of this chapter introduces a new kind of proposition that the agent may consider: propositions attributing to him different pairs of true probability and desirability assignments. Fourth, in terms of the agent's conscious probabilities over the states, acts and new propositions, a variety of the agent's causal beliefs can be characterized. And finally, while the new assumptions are basically probabilistic independence assumptions, they will not claim "strict independence"; using Skyrms notion of "resiliency," I shall be able to assume only a "high degree of probabilistic independence." This, it seems to me, makes the assumptions less idealistic.

THE MORE GENERAL SETTING

Let $A_1(DM), \ldots A_m(DM)$ be the maximally specific and collectively exhaustive acts (act-propositions) which the agent considers in his decision situation. And let $S_1(DM), \ldots S_n(DM)$ be the

174

maximally specific and collectively exhaustive states (state-propositions) the agent considers. Outcomes are considered to be states of a kind. In addition to the acts and states, I shall assume that the agent also considers propositions to the effect that he has a certain pair, or kind of pair, of true, perhaps unconscious, probability and desirability assignments over the acts and states. I shall call these propositions *'reason-propositions'*, or *'reasons'*. These can be considered to be states of a special kind. Let $'P^1'$ and $'D^1'$ stand for DM's true probability and desirability assignments over the acts and states. Then the reason-propositions specify P^1 and D^1 in different ways. I shall assume that the reasons form a natural finite partition. Thus, let $R_1(DM), \ldots R_q(DM)$ be the maximally specific and collectively exhaustive reasons the agent considers. Henceforth, I shall omit the $'(DM)'$ in the names of propositions the agent considers. Unless the name of a proposition contains $'(a)'$ in the appropriate place, the act-, state- and reason-propositions should be thought of as to the effect that DM does the relevant act, stands in the relevant relation to the relevant state and has the relevant pair, or kind of pair, of true probability and desirability assignments, respectively.

I do not know how to define 'natural' in a precise way as applied to a partition of reason-propositions. Intuitively, what I want to assume is that for some q, the agent believes that there are basically q kinds of sets of beliefs and desires that he may have in the decision situation in question and that they are characterized by $R_1, \ldots R_q$. A proposition R_s does not necessarily ascribe to DM a particular pair of probability and desirability assignments; it may just say that the agent's pair is of a certain kind or in a certain set of pairs of assignments. The reason-propositions may be thought of as approximately equally descriptive. They need not be sufficiently descriptive that one of them, together with one of the competing decision rules discussed earlier, determines an act.

Here is one possibility for the form of the R_ss. There are infinitely many pairs of probability and desirability assignments. Let $\{R^*_\sigma\}_\sigma$ be the infinite set of reason-propositions describing such pairs – one R^*_σ for each pair – and assume that the desirability assignments described in the R^*_σs have been relativized to some finite interval of real numbers, so that there is an upper bound on D^1. Denote the pair of assignments described by R^*_σ by $'P_\sigma'$ and $'D_\sigma'$. Let ε_p and ε_d be small numbers, and, for each R^*_σ, consider a proposition

R'_σ to the effect that for each proposition X that is maximally specific relative to $\{A_1, \ldots A_m, S_1, \ldots S_n\}$, $P_\sigma(X) - \varepsilon_p \leqslant P^1(X) \leqslant P_\sigma(X) + \varepsilon_p$ and $D_\sigma(X) - \varepsilon_d \leqslant D^1(X) \leqslant D_\sigma(X) + \varepsilon_d$. If ε_p and ε_d are small enough, then the pairs of assignments described by any R'_σ can, for all practical decision making purposes, be identified. Clearly, finitely many R'_σs will be collectively exhaustive, say $R'_{\sigma_1}, \ldots R'_{\sigma_q}$. Then, defining R_s as

$$R'_{\sigma_s} \ \& \ \bigwedge_{s' \neq s} - R'_{\sigma_{s'}}$$

makes the set of R_ss a finite partition.

Now though I will not assume that the agent knows which of the R_ss is true (i.e., he does not necessarily know P^1 and D^1), I shall assume that he assigns probabilities and desirabilities to propositions in the Boolean closure of $\{A_1, \ldots A_m, S_1, \ldots S_n, R_1, \ldots R_q\}$ and knows what *these* probabilities and desirabilities are. These are his *conscious* degrees of belief and desirabilities and will be symbolized by 'P^2' and 'D^2'. For any proposition X in the Boolean closure of $\{A_1, \ldots A_m, S_1, \ldots S_n, R_1, \ldots R_q\}$, $P^2(X)$ and $D^2(X)$ are, respectively, the agent's best conscious estimate for decision making purposes of X's probability and desirability. For any proposition X in the Boolean closure of $\{A_1, \ldots A_m, S_1, \ldots S_n\}$, $P^1(X)$ and $D^1(X)$ are, respectively, the agent's true, perhaps unconscious, degree of belief and desirability for X, which may not be the same as $P^2(X)$ and $D^2(X)$, respectively. I am assuming that the agent knows what his conscious degrees of beliefs and desirabilities over the Boolean closure of $\{A_1, \ldots A_m, S_1, \ldots S_n, R_1, \ldots R_q\}$ are. That is, letting R^* be the proposition that says what DM's conscious probabilities and desirabilities over this set are, I assume:

$$P^2(R^*) = 1. \tag{1}$$

The agent's conscious degree of belief that his conscious degrees of belief and conscious desirabilities are as specified in R^* is 1. This is reasonable, since if decision theory is to be prescriptive, the agent must know the probabilities and desirabilities of the relevant propositions. These are his conscious degrees of belief and desirabilities. Assumption (1) will be used as part of a rationale for one of the main assumptions of this chapter, given in the next section.

I shall consider the domains of P^1 and D^1 and of P^2 and D^2 to be the Boolean closures of $\{A_1, \ldots A_m, S_1, \ldots S_n\}$ and of $\{A_1, \ldots A_m,$

$S_1, \ldots S_n, R_1, \ldots R_q, R^*\}$, respectively. But this is not to say that the agent does not have true degrees of belief and desirabilities for propositions like the R_ss and R^* that may be different from his conscious ones. If we let $\bar{P}^1$ and $\bar{D}^1$ represent the agent's true, perhaps unconscious, degrees of belief and desirabilities over all propositions for which the agent has true degrees of beliefs and desirabilities, then P^1 and D^1 are the restrictions of $\bar{P}^1$ and $\bar{D}^1$ to the Boolean closure of $\{A_1, \ldots A_m, S_1, \ldots S_n\}$, respectively. Similarly, where $\bar{P}^2$ and $\bar{D}^2$ represent the agent's conscious degrees of belief and desirabilities over all propositions for which he has conscious degrees of belief and desirabilities, P^2 and D^2 are the restrictions of $\bar{P}^2$ and $\bar{D}^2$ to the Boolean closure of $\{A_1, \ldots A_m, S_1, \ldots S_n, R_1, \ldots R_q, R^*\}$, respectively. Of course, as pointed out several times previously, for the purposes of evaluating the conditional expected utility of an act, it should not matter which propositions P^2 and D^2 assign values to.

Given this understanding, P^2 and D^2 can be thought of as second-order assignments representing second-order degrees of belief and desirabilities, since they take as arguments (among other things) propositions about what the agent's true (first-order) assignments are. I will not put any formal constraints on the relation between the second-order assignments P^2 and D^2 and the various hypotheses R_s about the nature of the first-order assignments P^1 and D^1. However, to help the intuitions, it is perhaps worth mentioning some plausible candidates.

For propositions X that P^1 can take as arguments (truth-functional combinations of acts and states), let '$P^1(X) = p$' be an abbreviation for the disjunction of all the reason-propositions that imply that the P^1-probability of X is p. Then one plausible constraint, which Skyrms (1980b) calls 'Miller's principle' (see also Miller 1966), is:

For all p between 0 and 1, inclusive, and all propositions X that P^1 can take as an argument, $P^2(X \,|\, P^1(X) = p) = p$.

Miller's principle implies, but is not implied by:

For all p between 0 and 1, inclusive, and all propositions X that P^1 can take as an argument, if $P^2(P^1(X) = p) = 1$, then $P^2(X) = p$.

It is easy to see that this latter implies that for any proposition X that P^1 can take as an argument, $P^2(X)$ is the (second-order) expectation of $P^1(X)$, that is:

$$P^2(X) = \sum_p p P^2(P^1(X) = p)$$

(Skyrms 1980a: 163–4). Thus, if the consequence of Miller's principle is true, then the P^2-probability of any proposition that P^1 can take as an argument can be calculated from the P^2-probabilities of the R_ss. Of course, for such a proposition $X, P^2(X)$ is not necessarily equal to $P^1(X)$, the agent's true probability for X.

If the R_ss just specify intervals for the possible values of the agent's true probabilities, let '$P^1(X) \in (a, b)$' be an abbreviation for the disjunction of R_ss that imply that $P^1(X) \in (a, b)$ and assume a generalized version of Miller's principle:

> For all a and b between 0 and 1, inclusive, and all propositions X that P^1 can take as an argument, $P^2(X | P^1(X) \in (a, b)) \in (a, b)$.

From this it follows that for any such a, b and X:

> $P^2(X) \in (\sum a P^2(P^1(X) \in (a, b)), \sum b P^2(P^1(X) \in (a, b)))$, where the summations are taken over the set $\{(a, b): P^1(X) \in (a, b)$ is maximally specific relative to $\{P^1(X) \in (c, d): (c, d)$ is contained in $(0, 1)\}\}$.

As to the desirabilities, for any proposition X that D^1 can take as an argument, let '$D^1(X) = d$' be an abbreviation for the disjunction of all the reason-propositions that imply that $D^1(X) = d$. Then it follows from Jeffrey's axioms and the principle:

> For any d and any X that D^1 can take as an argument, $D^2(X \& D^1(X) = d) = d$ and $P^2(D^1(X) = d | X) = P^2(D^1(X) = d)$,

that for any such proposition $X, D^2(X)$ is the (second-order) expectation of $D^1(X)$, i.e.:

$$D^2(X) = \sum_d d P^2(D^1(X) = d).$$

Again, I omit the (easy) proof of this and note that a more general principle would be needed if the reason-propositions only specify intervals for the true desirabilities of the acts and states.

Again, I do not assume these formal constraints on the relation between first- and second-order probabilities. Rather, as an aid to the intuitions, I merely present them as plausible ones that would seem to hold in a variety of circumstances. The point is just that

P^1 and D^1 represent the agent's true, perhaps unconscious, beliefs and desires and that, since the agent may not know these, the best he can do in decision making is to use his conscious beliefs and desires, which are represented by P^2 and D^2 and which may be estimates of a kind of his true ones. In a sense, P^2 and D^2 are "true" assignments. For example, it would seem that P^2 and D^2 determine the rates at which the agent would make bets. Thinking of belief and desire as dispositional, P^2 and D^2 can be thought of as representing our agent's dispositions to particular actions when the choice of action is a result of self-conscious rational deliberation; P^1 and D^1 represent his dispositions to particular actions when the choice of action is not a result of self-conscious rational deliberation, as most of our choices are not. Henceforth, I shall drop the superscript '2' on the symbols for the conscious assignments.

THE WEAKER ASSUMPTIONS

As noted earlier, the new assumptions of this chapter are basically probabilistic independence assumptions. But to make the assumptions more realistic than they would otherwise be, I shall, using Skyrms' notion of "resiliency" (1980a), assume only "high degrees of probabilistic independence." Given a probability assignment P, propositions X, $X_1, \ldots X_n$ and a number p between 0 and 1, inclusive, the *resiliency with which* $P(X)$ *has value* p *over the propositions* $X_1, \ldots X_n$ (henceforth, 'the *resiliency of* $P(X)$'s *being* p *over* $X_1, \ldots X_n$')is defined to be $1 - \max_Y |p - P(X \mid Y)|$, where '$Y$' ranges over truth-functional compounds of the X_is that are logically consistent both with X and with $-X$. Setting $p = P(X)$, the resiliency of $P(X)$'s being p over $X_1, \ldots X_n$ can naturally be thought of as a measure of the degree to which X is probabilistically independent of the X_is. In the cases which will concern us, the X_is will form a partition, so that the resiliency of $P(X)$'s being $P(X)$ over the X_is will equal $1 - \max_i |P(X) - P(X|X_i)|$, where i ranges over indices of X_is that are consistent both with X and with $-X$. (Henceforth, the consistency proviso will go understood and not explicitly mentioned.)

Given the resiliency formulation, degree of probabilistic independence has a weaker kind of symmetry than strict probabilistic independence has. Let $\{X_1, \ldots X_n\}$ and $\{Y_1, \ldots Y_m\}$ be any two partitions of propositions. Then $x = \min_i$ (resiliency of $P(X_i)$'s being $P(X_i)$ over $Y_1, \ldots Y_m$) is a measure of the degree to which the X_is are probabilistically independent of the Y_js, and $y = \min_j$ (resiliency of $P(Y_j)$'s being $P(Y_j)$ over $X_1, \ldots X_n$) is a measure of the degree to which the Y_js are probabilistically independent of the X_is. Note that

$$x = 1 - \max_{ij} |P(X_i) - P(X_i|Y_j)|,$$

and

$$y = 1 - \max_{ij} |P(Y_j) - P(Y_j|X_i)|.$$

Must y be high if x is? And must x be high if y is? (i) If it is assumed of some number $a > 0$ that for all i, $P(X_i) > a$, then it can be shown that the closer x is to 1, the closer y must be to 1, and (ii) if it is assumed of some number $b > 0$ that for all j, $P(Y_j) > b$, then it can be shown that the closer y is to 1, the closer x must be to 1. I shall show (i); the proof of (ii) is parallel. Let a be such a number. What is to be shown can be expressed as $\lim_{x \to 1} y = 1$, which is equivalent to $\lim_{(1-x) \to 0}(1 - y) = 0$. To show this, it must be shown that for every $\varepsilon > 0$, there is a δ such that for all $(1 - x) < \delta$, $(1 - y) < \varepsilon$. So, let $\varepsilon > 0$ and let $\delta = \varepsilon a$. Suppose $1 - x < \varepsilon a$. Then, for every i and j,

$$a\varepsilon > |P(X_i) - P(X_i|Y_j)|$$

$$= \left| P(X_i) - \frac{P(X_i \ \& \ Y_j)}{P(Y_j)} \right|$$

$$= \frac{P(X_i)}{P(Y_j)} \left| P(Y_j) - \frac{P(X_i \ \& \ Y_j)}{P(X_i)} \right|.$$

So,

$$\varepsilon > \frac{P(X_i)}{aP(Y_j)} \left| P(Y_j) - \frac{P(X_i \ \& \ Y_j)}{P(X_i)} \right|$$

$$> \left| P(Y_j) - \frac{P(X_i \ \& \ Y_j)}{P(X_i)} \right|$$

$$= |P(Y_j) - P(Y_j|X_i)|.$$

Since this holds for all i and j, it holds in particular for that i and j for which the last quantity is a maximum. Hence,

$$\varepsilon > \max_{ij} |P(Y_j) - P(Y_j|X_i)|$$

$$= 1 - y.$$

This establishes (i).

I shall also have use, in what follows, of the notion of the resiliency of a conditional probability: Given a probability assignment P, propositions $X, Z, X_1, \ldots X_n$ and a number p between 0 and 1, inclusive, the *resiliency of $P(X|Z)$'s being p over $X_1, \ldots X_n$* is defined to be $1 - \max_Y |p - P(X|Z \ \& \ Y)|$, where '$Y$' varies over truth-functional compounds of the X_is that are logically consistent with both $X \ \& \ Z$ and $-X \ \& \ Z$. (In what follows, the consistency proviso will go understood and not be explicitly mentioned.)

A plausible measure of the degree to which the agent is certain about his first-order assignments is the entropy of his second-order degrees of belief over the set of reason-propositions:

$$\sum_{s=1}^{q} P(R_s) \ln P(R_s).$$

This is at a minimum $(-\ln q)$ when the probabilities of all the reason-propositions are equal $(= 1/q)$ and at a maximum (0) when the probability of some R_s is 1. Thinking of $R_\Phi(DM)$ of the previous chapter as a reason-proposition in the sense given in this chapter, assumption (6.5), together with the consequence of Miller's principle noted above and the principle about desirabilities given above, implies that this entropy is at a maximum, that P and P^1 agree and that D and D^1 agree. I now want to replace (6.5) with an assumption that is consistent with any level of certainty about the reason-propositions.

The agent's degree of certainty about his reasons is one kind of familiarity he may have with them. I shall now define another kind of familiarity with reasons and assume that the agent has a high degree of familiarity of this kind with his reasons. I shall say that an agent is more or less *current* about his probabilities and desirabilities (reasons, beliefs and desires) according to whether the resiliencies of the $P(R_s)$s' being $P(R_s)$ over the act-propositions are high or low. Thus, the agent's *currency about his reasons* (*probabilities and desirabilities, beliefs and desires*) is defined to be:

$$\min_s (\text{resiliency of } P(R_s)\text{'s being } P(R_s) \text{ over } A_1, \ldots A_m).$$

This is equivalent to:

$$1 - \max_{s,k} |P(R_s) - P(R_s|A_k)|.$$

181

The agent's currency about his reasons is a measure of how much the agent's probabilities for the R_ss change upon conditionalization on the A_ks: currency is high if the probabilities change only a little, and it is low if they change a lot. The agent's currency about his reasons falls within the interval $(0, 1]$, i.e., the interval of real numbers between 0 and 1 which includes 1 but not 0. Note that maximal certainty about reasons implies maximal currency about reasons and that any other level of certainty is compatible with any level of currency; in particular, maximal currency is compatible with any level of certainty. And maximal currency is compatible with the agent's acknowledgement of any level of imperfection of what Mellor calls 'insight'.

I trade assumption (6.5) for the weaker assumption that

DM's currency about his reasons is either 1 or very close to 1.   (2)

I think the case for high currency about reasons is best made forceful by considering and disarming two natural kinds of objections to (2). An objection of the first kind would go something like this. Let R_1 be any reason-proposition to the effect that on June 30, DM's assignments are such that P^1(It is hot and sunny) = 1, $D^1(DM$ gets a tan) = 100. This reason-proposition is completed in any way consistent with the rational act's being, in light of the reason-proposition, going to the beach. And suppose that all the other reason-propositions the agent considers are such that the rational act in light of them is staying home. Then, in February, we would expect DM's beliefs to be such that $P(R_1|DM$ goes to the beach on June 30) > $P(R_1|DM$ stays home on June 30). This is because going to the beach is evidence that the agent has good reasons to (e.g., wanting a tan and its being hot and sunny) and staying home is evidence that the agent has good reason to stay away from the beach (e.g., wanting something else more than a tan, or the weather's being poor). And this inequality violates (2).

There are two responses that should be made to this objection. First, as the time of decision on June 30 closely approaches, the relation should approach equality because current *introspective* evidence about DM's reasons will then become more and more relevant for him. And because of ·this increased relevance, such evidence will become more and more weighty compared to possible evidence about what he *actually does*. And second, evidence about what he actually does is evidence about which reason proposition is true only indirectly; for the act (I am assuming throughout) is based on the agent's conscious beliefs and desires, and the agent knows this. Thus, it seems that in February, the evidential relations are really as follows. Going to the beach is evidence that the agent will have such *conscious* beliefs and desires that a rational evaluation of the available acts in light of them leads to the conclusion that going to the beach is the best act. And since conscious beliefs and desires are generally good indicators of the *true* ones (i.e., since "insight" is usually fairly reliable), having conscious beliefs and desires that lead to going to the beach is a good indication that ones true beliefs and desires are such that going to the beach would be rational in light of them, i.e., that they will be accurately described by R_1. Similarly, staying home is a good indirect evidence that R_1 is false. But while such evidential relations may hold in February, I am assuming that in the relevant decision situation – the one on June 30 – the agent knows his conscious beliefs and desires. So at the time of decision, the act is no longer evidentially relevant to what the conscious beliefs and desires will be, and the evidential chain is broken.

What this first objection shows, and what I of course concede, is that (2) can only be expected to hold at times close to the time of decision.

An objection to (2) of the second kind would go something like this. If (2) were true, then, because of the symmetry of probabilistic independence, for every k, s and s', $P(A_k|R_s)$ should be very close to $P(A_k|R_{s'})$. (As pointed out above, degree of probabilistic independence has a weaker kind of symmetry than strict independence has, but in most situations, the former can be expected to be quite symmetric, as indicated previously.) That is, the probability of any act must remain about the same, conditional on any of the reason-propositions. But the reason-propositions specify values for the probabilities of the A_ks, and it seems that if R_s says that the probability of A_k is, say, p_{ks} (or is in some interval p_{ks}), then $P(A_k|R_s)$ should be (or be in) p_{ks}. For if the agent *learned* that R_s is true, he would learn, among other things, that his degree of belief in A_k is (or is in) p_{ks}; and his revised degrees of belief – obtained by conditionalization on R_s – should reflect this by his new degree of belief in A_k being (or being in) p_{ks}. Similarly, $P(A_k|R_{s'})$ should be what $R_{s'}$ says the probability of A_k is, say, $p_{ks'}$ (or in $p_{ks'}$). But there is no reason to think that for all k, s and s',

p_{ks} should be very close to $p_{ks'}$. (Note that the basic premise employed in this objection is very similar to Miller's principle.)

I believe that there are two things wrong about this objection. First, I disagree about how the agent's degrees of belief in act-propositions should change on learning some reason-proposition to be true. And second, I think the objection involves a misapplication of the slogan "learning goes by conditionalization."

As to the first point, suppose DM is in a two-state (S and $-S$), two-act (A and $-A$) decision situation, that R_1 is a reason-proposition that implies each of the following (for maximally specific X):

$$P^1(A) = 0.7;$$

$$P^1(S|A) = 0.9;$$

$$P^1(S|-A) = 0;$$

$$D^1(X) = \begin{cases} -1000 \text{ if } X \text{ is } S \text{ \& } A \\ 0 \text{ otherwise,} \end{cases}$$

and that R_2 is a reason-proposition that implies each of the following (for maximally specific X):

$$P^1(A) = 0.7;$$

$$P^1(S|A) = 0.9;$$

$$P^1(S|-A) = 0;$$

$$D^1(X) = \begin{cases} 1000 \text{ if } X \text{ is } S \text{ \& } A \\ 0 \text{ otherwise.} \end{cases}$$

Thus, R_1 and R_2 differ only in the specification of the true desirability of S & A. It seems quite clear that, other things being equal, if DM *learned* that R_1 was true, so that he learned that his true desirability for S & A was -1000, his revised degree of belief in A would be lower than it would have been had he *learned* that R_2 was true, so that he would have learned that his true desirability for S & A was 1000. This is because it seems *clear* that if he learned R_1, he would plan to do $-A$ (and thus assign a low probability to A), and if he learned R_2, he would plan to do A (and thus assign a high probability to his doing A). This is sufficient to undermine the basic premise of the second objection, according to which the agent's revised degree of belief in A would be 0.7 whether he learned R_1 or R_2. (Note, however, that this is not sufficient to undermine Miller's principle, since, for one thing, in Miller's principle, the proposition conditionalized on is not a reason-proposition.)

At first sight, it would seem that my first reply to the second objection involves a violation of (2). Here is where my second reply comes in. Consider the following two (rough and vague) characterizations of conditional subjective probability:

CP_1: $P(X|Y)$ is equal to the degree of belief the agent would have in X *were he to learn that Y is true*, for all propositions X and Y;

CP_2: $P(X|Y)$ is equal to the degree of belief the agent has in X *under the supposition that Y is true*, for all propositions X and Y.

To help clarify the distinction (and in particular the CP_2 reading), let p_1 be $P(X|Y)$ under the CP_1 characterization of conditional subjective probability, let p_2 be $P(X|Y)$ under the CP_2 characterization, for some X and Y, and consider the following two questions: (i) "Suppose you learned Y; then what would your degree of belief in X be?" and (ii) "Suppose Y is true; what, under this supposition, is your degree of belief in X?" Now p_1 is a truthful and accurate answer to (i), and p_2 is a truthful and accurate answer to (ii). And the difference between the two questions is this: In question (ii), the agent is asked only to assume that Y is true, whereas in question (i), the agent is asked, in effect, to assume *both* that Y is true *and* that he has *learned* that it is true. The distinction can also be brought out by comparing the questions: "At what rate would you bet on X were you to learn that Y is true?" (to which the accurate answer is p_1) and "At what rate would you make a bet on X conditional on Y (i.e., a bet on X that is called off if Y turns out to be false)?" (to which the accurate answer is p_2).

Two questions come to mind. First, under what circumstances would p_1 not equal p_2? Second, which of p_1 and p_2 is $P(X|Y)$? As to the first question, I think the usual case is that $p_1 = p_2$. But there are cases where the *learning* of Y has probabilistic relevance to X beyond whatever probabilistic relevance the *truth* of Y may have to X. Clear cases of this are cases where X is an act or is probabilistically relevant to an act. Consider this case. Suppose I want to speculate in the gold market. Let X be the act-proposition 'I buy gold this morning' and let Y be the state-proposition 'The price

185

of gold will go up at least \$40 today'. Clearly p_1 is equal to, or at least very close to, 1; and clearly p_2 is not, at least not if I do not believe that I am very good at predicting gold market activity. Were I to *learn* that gold was to go up at least \$40 today, I would certainly plan on buying some this morning, and, hence, I would assign a high probability to my doing so, i.e., to X. But my merely *supposing* that gold will go up \$40 today is consistent with my also believing that it is quite unlikely. Often we suppose (as "for the sake of argument") things that we think are quite unlikely and, hence, which we are unlikely to act on. Assume, in fact, (i) I have decided that a necessary and sufficient condition for my buying gold this morning is that I somehow find out that its price will increase by at least \$40 today, (ii) my degree of belief that the price of gold will increase by at least \$40 today is 0.1, and (iii) my degree of belief that I will find out about such an increase is 0.01. (And I assume that I cannot find out about something that does not take place.) Then it would seem that on the supposition that the price of gold will go up by at least \$40, my degree of belief that I shall buy some gold this morning would be 0.1 ($=0.01/0.1$). That is, $p_2 = 0.1$, which is quite different from p_1, which, as we have seen, should be quite close to 1.

The answer to the first question, of course, points to the answer to the second. Let Z be the proposition that I somehow find out that gold will go up at least \$40 today. Then $P(Z \leftrightarrow (Z \ \& \ Y)) = 1$ and $P(Z \leftrightarrow X) = 1$. So, $P(X|Y) = P(X \ \& \ Y)/P(Y) = P(Z \ \& \ Y)/P(Y) = P(Z)/P(Y) = 0.01/0.1 = 0.1 = p_2$. Note also that $P(X|Y \ \& \ Z) = P(X|Z) = 1 = p_1$. I believe that in general CP_2 is the correct characterization of $P(X|Y)$ and that CP_1 characterizes $P(X|Y \ \& \ Z)$ in general, where Z is the proposition that the agent learns Y. This is not to say that CP_1 is a *poor* characterization of $P(X|Y)$, for it is most commonly the case that X and Y are such that X is probabilistically independent of learning that Y is true, given Y. The slogan "conditionalization models learning" applies only in such cases (unless we construe 'learning' as 'learning with detachment', i.e., where learning Y takes place in such a way that one does not also learn that one has learned Y).

Thus, my second response to the second objection to (2) (which also answers those who may think that my first response involves a violation of (2)) is that the objection takes CP_1 to be an accurate characterization of conditional subjective probability in a case

186

where it makes a difference, in a case where the relevant propositions are such that CP_2, but not CP_1, accurately characterizes the relevant conditional probabilities. I am assuming throughout that the agent *does not know* which of the R_ss is true and that the agent *knows that he does not know* which is true. He may *suppose* that a particular R_s is true, but at the same time as he does this, he believes with degree 1 that R^* – which specifies his conscious degrees of belief in, among other things, the R_ss – is true. This is analogous to my *supposing*, in the gold market example, that gold will go up at the same time that I *know that I believe it just to degree* 0.1. R^* summarizes all the information the agent has about which R_s is true and specifies his conscious probabilities for all the acts, states and reasons; it specifies all the data on which the decision will be based. Thus, since the agent's act will be based on information he has on hand, which R_s is true should be irrelevant to which act is performed, given R^*: for all k, s and s', $P(A_k|R^* \& R_s) = P(A_k|R^* \& R_{s'})$. This, together with the agent's certainty about his conscious beliefs and desires, implies that for all s, k and k', $P(R_s|A_k) = P(R_s|A_{k'})$, and, indeed, that (2) is true.

That the agent should be very current about his beliefs and desires has been seen to be plausible from two directions: the probabilities of the reason-propositions should be relatively invariant conditional on the various act-propositions, and the probabilities of the act-propositions should be relatively invariant conditional on the various reason-propositions. In each case, the agent's knowledge of his conscious probabilities and desirabilities and his knowledge that his act will be based on his conscious probabilities and desirabilities interrupts evidential relations connecting the acts and reasons. And, indeed, such knowledge should also interrupt evidential relations which would otherwise connect an act-proposition and a reason-proposition because the agent may believe that there is a common cause of the act and reason.

Note that it does not follow from (2) that the agent is very current about the $R_s(a)$s. That is, probabilities $P(R_s(a)|A_k(a))$s may be quite different from probabilities $P(R_s(a)|A_{k'}(a))$s. That is because $A_k(a)$ may be good evidence that "the arbitrary individual" a has conscious degrees of belief and desire of some particular kind. For one thing, $A_k(a)$ is good evidence that a has conscious beliefs and desires of the kind that rationally lead to the act $A_k(a)$. And since one's conscious beliefs and desires are generally good indicators of true beliefs and desires, $A_k(a)$ may indirectly be good evidence for particular $R_s(a)$s. For similar reasons, we would expect some $P(A_k(a)|R_s(a))$s to be quite different from some $P(A_k(a)|R_{s'}(a))$s.

Assumptions (6.6) and (6.7) – the other two main assumptions of Chapter 6 – will be replaced here with one assumption that is weaker than their conjunction and which applies to the more general setting of this chapter. First, I shall present a consequence of (6.6) and (6.7). Second, I shall extend that consequence to the more general setting of this chapter. And third, I will present a weaker version of the extension. This will be the final version.

Proposition (6.8) is a consequence of (6.6) and (6.7). By symmetry of (strict, conditional) probabilistic independence, it follows from (6.8) that

$$P(CC(DM)|R_\Phi(DM) \& SA(DM)) = P(CC(DM)|R_\Phi(DM)).$$
$$(3)$$

In the setting of Chapter 6, the agent considered only the states $CC(DM)$ and $-CC(DM)$. These are states which, in Skyrms' terminology, are outside the influence of the agent's acts. We would not expect (3) to hold if $CC(DM)$ and $-CC(DM)$ were replaced with states that DM believes to be within the influence of his acts. Hence, to extend (3) to the new setting, where we have states $S_1, \ldots S_n$, we must identify those states that are believed to be outside the influence of DM's actions. In fact, let us assume that a certain pair of partitions $\{K_1, \ldots K_{n_1}\}$ and $\{C_1, \ldots C_{n_2}\}$ satisfy the appropriateness conditions AC_1, AC_2^* and AC_3^* of Chapter 5. Let '$\mathcal{K}$' denote the set of K_is, and let '$\mathcal{C}$' denote the set of C_js. The S_is will be assumed to be sufficiently specific that each K_i is the disjunction of some S_is, as are the C_js.

Before proceeding with the extension of (3) to the more general setting, it is worth noting two things. First, as pointed out in Chapter 5, the really important thing relative to K-expectation is the partition of K_is and its satisfaction of AC_1 and AC_4^*. The reason I wanted to have a partition of C_js around is that in the next section I will give a probabilistic characterization of some of the agent's causal beliefs, including those about propositions like the C_js. The second thing worth noting is that it has not been forgotten that, as pointed out in Chapter 5, constructing appropriate partitions of

188

K_is cannot be assumed always to be a routine matter. This problem will be dealt with later.

Clearly, we want the extension of (3) to be something like allowing any K_i to substitute for $CC(DM)$ in (3) and allowing any of the m available acts to substitute for $SA(DM)$ in (3). But recall that in Chapter 6, the agent's knowledge of his beliefs and desires screened off the correlation between $SA(DM)$ and $CC(DM)$. In this chapter, we are allowing that the agent may not have knowledge of his true beliefs and desires, though he does have knowledge of his conscious ones. And of course it is possible that different sets of true beliefs and desires may be differently subjectively prob-abilistically relevant to different K_is.

As a concrete example of this, consider again the Fisher smoking hypothesis Newcomb situation. Assume the agent believes that smoking and lung cancer are effects of a common cause: a certain genetic make-up. This genetic make-up causes smoking by causing certain beliefs and desires, and the agent, having imperfect "insight," is not certain about what his true beliefs and desires are. Suppose R_1 and R_2 are two reason-propositions that favor smoking, but in different ways. Roughly, R_1 says that calm nerves is very desirable and that smoking calms the nerves, and R_2 says that appearing sophisticated in some particular way is very desirable and that smoking makes one appear sophisticated in that way. More definitely, calling the kind of sophistication which, according to R_2, smoking makes one appear to have 'sophistication*', R_1 says, among other things:

$D(DM$ has calm nerves$) = 100$;

$P(DM$ has calm nerves$|DM$ smokes$) = 0.9$;

$P(DM$ has calm nerves$|-DM$ smokes$) = 0.3$;

$D(DM$ appears sophisticated*$) = 0$;

$P(DM$ appears sophisticated*$|DM$ smokes$)$

$\quad = P(DM$ appears sophisticated*$|-DM$ smokes$) = 0.4$;

and R_2 says, among other things:

$D(DM$ appears sophisticated*$) = 200$;

$P(DM$ appears sophisticated*$|DM$ smokes$) = 0.9$;

189

$P(DM$ appears sophisticated$^*|-DM$ smokes$) = 0.2$;

$D(DM$ has calm nerves$) = 100$;

$P(DM$ has calm nerves$|DM$ smokes$)$

$\quad = P(DM$ has calm nerves$|-DM$ smokes$) = 0.9$.

Now, between R_1 and R_2, it seems that R_1 is more likely to be caused by genetic-make-up; R_2 is more likely to be caused by learning rather than by genetic make-up. This is because the reason for smoking, inherent in R_2, is to appear sophisticated in some particular way, and it would seem that the desire to appear sophisticated in some particular way would be a result of learning rather than of genetic make-up. In any case, let us assume that DM believes that R_1 is more likely than R_2 to be caused by genetic make-up, while R_2 is more likely to be a result of learning rather than of genetic make-up. Thus, where G is the proposition that DM has the genetic predisposition to smoking and lung cancer and S is the act-proposition to the effect that the agent smokes, we should expect the agent's conscious beliefs to be such that $P(G|R_1 \, \& \, S) > P(G|R_2 \, \& \, S)$ and $P(G|R_1 \, \& \, -S) > P(G|R_2 \, \& \, -S)$.

The extension of (3) to the more general setting of this chapter will explicitly allow for the possibility that different reason-propositions can be differently probabilistically relevant to the K_is. It is:

$$\text{for all } i, s \text{ and } k, \; P(K_i|R_s \, \& \, A_k) = P(K_i|R_s). \tag{4}$$

This says that given the truth of some reason-proposition, which act is performed is probabilistically irrelevant to which K_i obtains. Note that it does not follow from (4) together with high or unit currency about reasons (the other main assumption of this chapter) that:

$$\text{For all } i, s, s', k \text{ and } k', \; P(K_i|R_s \, \& \, A_k) = P(K_i|R_{s'} \, \& \, A_{k'});$$

nor does it follow that:

$$\text{For all } i, s \text{ and } s', \; P(K_i|R_s) = P(K_i|R_{s'}).$$

Thus, (4) allows that what DM's true, perhaps unconscious, beliefs and desires are may be probabilistically relevant to some K_is.

It is interesting to note that it does follow from (4) together with unit currency about reasons that:

For all k, s, s', i and i',

$$P(A_k|R_s \ \& \ K_i) = P(A_k|R_{s'} \ \& \ K_{i'}),$$

so that both:

For all k, s and s',

$$P(A_k|R_s) = P(A_k|R_{s'})$$

(which follows from unit currency alone), and:

For all k, i and i',

$$P(A_k|K_i) = P(A_k|K_{i'}).$$

And it is reasonable to think that all these relations should hold if the agent is going to base his decision on his conscious beliefs and desires and he believes this. However, it does not follow that:

For all k, s, s', i and i',

$$P(A_k(a)|R_s(a) \ \& \ K_i(a)) = P(A_k(a)|R_{s'}(a) \ \& \ K_{i'}(a)),$$

or that:

For all k, s and s',

$$P(A_k(a)|R_s(a)) = P(A_k(a)|R_{s'}(a)),$$

or that:

For all k, i and i',

$$P(A_k(a)|K_i(a)) = P(A_k(a)|K_{i'}(a)).$$

In fact, it is likely that corresponding *inequalities* would hold. This is because evidence like $R_s(a) \ \& \ K_i(a)$ or $R_s(a)$ or $K_i(a)$ may be good evidence to the effect that a has P^2- and D^2-assignments of a certain kind (perhaps a pair close to the true P^1- and D^1-assignments described in $R_s(a)$ or, if the agent thinks $K_i(a)$ causes acts, a pair that he thinks $K_i(a)$ tends to bring about – perhaps indirectly by causing some pair of first-order assignments). And evidence to the effect that a has P^2- and D^2-assignments of a certain kind is relevant to which act a performs, if DM believes that a will base his decision on his conscious beliefs and desires.

Of course (4) is an idealization in that it claims strict probabilistic independence of the K_is from the A_ks given an R_s. Using the notion of the resiliency of a conditional probability, (4) can be weakened to a version that claims only a high degree of conditional probabilistic independence. Where S is any state, I define the agent's R_s-*conditional currency about S* to be the resiliency of $P(S|R_s)$s being $P(S|R_s)$ over the set of act-propositions. Thus, (4) says that for each i and s, the agent is of unit R_s-conditional currency about K_i. Where $\mathcal{S}$ is any set of states, I define the agent's R_s-*conditional currency about $\mathcal{S}$* to be $\min_{S \in \mathcal{S}}$ (DM's R_s-conditional currency about S). Thus, (4) says that for each s, the agent is of unit R_s-conditional currency about $\mathcal{K}$. I define the agent's R-*conditional currency about $\mathcal{S}$* as $\min_s$ (DM's R_s-conditional currency about $\mathcal{S}$). DM's R-conditional currency about $\mathcal{K}$ is equal to:

$$1 - \max_{i,s,k} |P(K_i|R_s) - P(K_i|R_s \ \& \ A_k)|.$$

Thus, (4) says that the agent is of unit R-conditional currency about $\mathcal{K}$. It will be useful later to have this definition: The agent's R-*conditional currency about a state S* in his R-conditional currency about $\{S\}$. The final version of the assumption replacing (6.6) and (6.7) is:

DM's R-conditional currency about $\mathcal{K}$ is either
1 or very close to 1. $\qquad\qquad(5)$

The main assumptions of this chapter are (2) and, where $\mathcal{K}$ is an appropriate partition in the sense of satisfying AC_1 and AC_4^*, (5). These assumptions, and their plausibility, have important implications for the relation between *PMCEU* and causal decision theory; these will be investigated in the last section of this chapter. Of course we shall there have to address the problem of whether or not an appropriate partition $\mathcal{K}$ always exists. Before that, though, I shall take a section to stress the meaning and importance of the notion of R-conditional currency and some other conditional currency notions.

CAUSES, REASONS AND PROBABILITY

In this section, I shall show how, using various conditional currency notions, a variety of an agent's causal beliefs can be characterized.

Let us make the following reasonable assumptions about *DM*'s causal beliefs:

CB_1: The agent believes that a state cannot have direct causal influence on acts; i.e., it must intermediately have causal influence on reasons;

CB_2: The agent believes that an act can have direct causal influence on states, i.e., it need not intermediately have causal influence on reasons;

CB_3: The agent believes that a reason cannot have direct causal influence on states, i.e., it must intermediately have causal influence on acts;

CB_4: The agent believes that a state can have direct causal influence on reasons, i.e., it need not intermediately have causal influence on acts;

CB_5: The agent believes that an act cannot have direct causal influence on reasons, i.e., it must intermediately have causal influence on states;

CB_6: The agent believes that a reason can have direct causal influence on acts, i.e., it need not intermediately have causal influence on states.

If 'A_k', 'S' and 'R_s' stand for an arbitrary act, state and reason, respectively, and an arrow indicates the possibility of direct causal influence, and a slashed arrow indicates the impossibility of direct causal influence, CB_1–CB_6 can be summarized by Figure 3.

Thus, according to the diagram, a state can indirectly cause an act by causing the agent to have reasons for performing the act. A

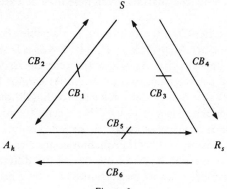

Figure 3.

reason can indirectly cause a state by causing the agent to perform an act that brings about the state. And an act can indirectly affect one's beliefs and desires by causing a state that directly affects them: e.g., if one desires to drink, one may perform an act – drinking – that brings about a state – hangover – that causes one to desire not to drink.

Of course the reasons referred to here are the possible *true, perhaps unconscious*, beliefs and desires. Conscious beliefs and desires have been left completely out of the picture. Thus, the assumptions about the agent's causal beliefs can be expected to hold only if either (i) the acts referred to in the assumptions are conceived by the agent to be not a result of self-conscious rational deliberation invoking conscious beliefs and desires *or* (ii) the agent believes that the only way in which a state can cause conscious beliefs and desires (which are invoked in self-conscious rational deliberation) is *by way of causing true beliefs and desires*, fairly good estimates of which become conscious *via* the fairly reliable inner sense of insight. Of course we can imagine other ways in which a state may affect one's conscious beliefs and desires: the state may, for example, affect one's insight, thus distorting in particular ways one's perception of one's true beliefs and desires. If conscious beliefs and desires must, for such a reason, be brought into the picture, then the second part of CB_1 and the first part of CB_6 may not hold: the agent may believe that a state could have direct causal influence on one's conscious reasons, bypassing the true ones, and he may believe that, *via* insight, the true beliefs and desires must affect the conscious ones, thus only indirectly causing the act. At the end of this section, I will indicate how the analysis given here may be extended to such cases.

Assuming CB_1–CB_6, the following is plausible: For every state S, reason R_s and act A_k, $|P(S|R_s) - P(S|R_s \ \& \ A_k)|$ is large if, and only if, the agent believes that A_k is causally relevant to S. The size of the difference between the two probabilities cannot be accounted for by a belief that S is causally relevant to A_k (although the agent may have this belief) because, by CB_1, a state (in particular, S or $-S$) can cause an act (in particular, A_k or $-A_k$) only indirectly, i.e., by causing a reason; and both probabilities are already conditional on a particular reason: R_s. Also, the size of the difference between the two probabilities cannot be accounted for by a belief that there is a common cause of A_k and S, for our assumptions guarantee that

194

the agent believes that anything that causes an act must intermediately cause a reason, and both probabilities are already conditional on a reason. So, given the subjective common cause principle stated in Chapter 5, the only way to account for the difference is the one allowed by CB_2: the agent believes that A_k is causally relevant to S.

It is also plausible that the magnitude of the difference between $P(S|R_s)$ and $P(S|R_s \& A_k)$ measures the degree of causal efficacy one of A_k and $-A_k$ has on one of S and $-S$, according to the agent's beliefs. And since it is irrelevant which reason-proposition R_s was used above, it seems that a plausible, though crude, measure of the degree to which A_k is causally *irrelevant* to S, according to the agent's beliefs, is:

$$1 - \max_s |P(S|R_s) - P(S|R_s \& A_k)|.$$

And a plausible measure of the degree to which *all* of the available acts are causally irrelevant to S, according to the agent's beliefs, is:

$$1 - \max_{s,k} |P(S|R_s) - P(S|R_s \& A_k)|.$$

But this is just the agent's R-conditional currency about S. Thus, *a plausible measure of the degree to which the state S is outside the influence of the agent's acts, according to the agent's beliefs, is his R-conditional currency about S.* If $\mathscr{S}$ is a set of states that the agent considers to be outside the influence of all the available acts, then we would expect

$$1 - \max_{S \in \mathscr{S}, s, k} |P(S|R_s) - P(S|R_s \& A_k)|$$

to be high, i.e., we would expect the agent's R-conditional currency about $\mathscr{S}$ to be high. In particular, we would expect (5) to hold. *High R-conditional currency about $\mathscr{K}$ is, plausibly, roughly equivalent to condition AC_1 for the appropriateness of a partition $\mathscr{K}$.*

Satisfaction of AC_2^* and AC_3^* (and thus AC_4^*) can also be characterized in terms of high conditional currency of a kind. Before defining this kind of conditional currency, which I call '$\mathscr{T}$-A-conditional currency', I shall, as a first step, define 'A-conditional currency'. Let S be any state. Then the agent's A_k-*conditional currency about S* is defined to be the resiliency of $P(S|A_k)$'s being $P(S|A_k)$ over the reason-propositions. This is a measure of how much $P(S|A_k)$ changes on further conditionalization on the reason-propositions. Where $\mathscr{S}$ is any set of states, the agent's A_k-*conditional currency about $\mathscr{S}$* is defined to be $\min_{S \in \mathscr{S}} (DM$'s A_k-conditional

195

currency about S). The agent's *A-conditional currency about $\mathscr{S}$* is defined to be $\min_k$ (DM's A_k-conditional currency about $\mathscr{S}$). This is equal to:

$$1 - \max_{S \in \mathscr{S}, s, k} |P(S|A_k) - P(S|A_k \ \& \ R_s)|,$$

and thus is a measure of how much the various $P(S|A_k)$s change on conditionalization on the R_ss. Finally, the agent's *A-conditional currency about S* is defined to be his A-conditional currency about $\{S\}$, which is equal to:

$$1 - \max_{sk} |P(S|A_k) - P(S|A_k \ \& \ R_s)|.$$

What kind of causal belief would a large difference, $P(S|A_k) - P(S|A_k \ \& \ R_s)$, indicate, for some particular S, A_k and R_s? Assuming that the agent has the causal beliefs indicated by CB_1–CB_6 and assuming the common cause principle, it can only indicate a belief that S or causes of S are causally relevant to R_s. The difference cannot be accounted for by a belief that R_s is causally relevant to S, for, by CB_3, for a reason to have causal influence on a state, it must intermediately have causal influence on an act, and both probabilities are already conditional on a particular act. Thus, by the common cause principle, the difference can only be accounted for by a belief that S is causally relevant to R_s or by a belief that there is some factor that is commonly causally relevant to both S and R_s or by the agent's having both beliefs. Of course if the agent believes there is a direct common cause of both S and R_s, this common cause can only be a state.

As a concrete example illustrating this, consider again the Fisher smoking hypothesis Newcomb situation, as described a few pages before the end of the last section. (Recall that here G is the state-proposition asserting the presence of the genetic predisposition to smoking and lung cancer, S is the *act*-proposition asserting that the agent smokes and R_1 and R_2 are the reason-propositions described.) The agent in this situation believes that G causes R_1 more strongly than he believes that G causes R_2, and that accounts for why $P(G|S \ \& \ R_1) > P(G|S \ \& \ R_2)$ and $P(G|-S \ \& \ R_1) > P(G|-S \ \& \ R_2)$. If the agent believes quite strongly that G causes R_1, then we would expect $P(G|S \ \& \ R_1)$ and $P(G|-S \ \& \ R_1)$ to be quite large, so that the differences between $P(G|S \ \& \ R_1)$ and $P(G|S)$ and between $P(G|-S \ \& \ R_1)$ and $P(G|-S)$ would also be large. Also, assuming that the agent believes that G is the primary cause of lung cancer (C), we would expect the differences between $P(C|S \ \& \ R_1)$ and $P(C|S)$ and between $P(C|-S \ \& \ R_1)$ and $P(C|-S)$ to be large: the more strongly he believes that R_1 is the reason caused by G, the larger would be the difference. In this case, of course, the differences between the probabilities reflects the agent's belief that there is a common cause (G) of both C and R_1.

Considering again the general case and the difference between $P(S|A_k)$ and $P(S|A_k \ \& \ R_s)$, it seems that the difference between these two probabilities would be about the same no matter which act A_k figures in the two probabilities. This is because the causal beliefs that the difference indicates are about causal relations just among the state S, its causes and R_s, in which the act does not figure. This may be checked in connection with the Fisher example just discussed. Thus, a plausible, though crude, measure of the degree to which S and its causes are causally irrelevant to R_s is:

$$1 - \max_k |P(S|A_k) - P(S|A_k \ \& \ R_s)|.$$

And a plausible, though crude, measure of the degree to which S and its causes are causally irrelevant to *all* the reasons is:

$$1 - \max_{sk} |P(S|A_k) - P(S|A_k \ \& \ R_s)|,$$

i.e., the agent's A-conditional currency about S. Also, for any set of states $\mathscr{S}$, the agent's A-conditional currency about $\mathscr{S}$ is a plausible, though crude, measure of the degree to which the states in $\mathscr{S}$ and their causes are causally irrelevant to the reasons.

Now if the agent believes that a state is causally inefficacious in the production of reasons, then, by CB_1, he must believe that it is causally inefficacious in the production of acts. Thus, *the agent's A-conditional currency about a state S is a measure of the degree to which he believes that S or its causes can causally affect which act is performed.* This involves, roughly, two claims: (i) if his A-conditional currency about S is low, then he believes that S or its causes can affect which act is performed, and (ii) if his A-conditional currency about S is high, then he believes that S and its causes cannot affect which act is performed. Thinking of 'high' as the negation of 'low', each of these two claims is roughly equivalent to the other's converse. Claim (ii), and thus the converse of (i), depends on the assumption, set forth previously, that *either* the agent conceives of the acts as not resulting from self-conscious rational deliberation *or* he believes that the only way a state can affect behavior that *is* a result of self-conscious rational deliberation is by affecting the conscious beliefs and desires *by way of affecting the true ones*. Claim (i) and the converse of (ii) do not depend on this assumption.

Recall that the appropriateness conditions AC_2^* and AC_3^* say that once some K_i is fixed, the C_js are causally irrelevant to the A_ks, as are the causes of the C_js, according to the agent's beliefs. This suggests that these two appropriateness conditions will be satisfied by just those pairs of partitions $\mathcal{K}$ and $\mathcal{C}$ which are such that the agent has high A conditional currency about $\mathcal{C}$ relative to each of the probability assignments gotten from his subjective assignment P by conditionalization on any member of $\mathcal{K}$. Given any two partitions, $\mathcal{T}$ and $\mathcal{S}$ of states, I define the agent's $\mathcal{T}$-A-*conditional currency about $\mathcal{S}$* to be $\min_{T \in \mathcal{T}}$ (DM's A-conditional currency about $\mathcal{S}$ relative to the probability assignment gotten from P by conditionalization on T). This is equal to:

$$1 - \max_{T \in \mathcal{T}, S \in \mathcal{S}, s, k} |P(S|T \ \& \ A_k) - P(S|T \ \& \ A_k \ \& \ R_s)|.$$

Where $\mathcal{T}$ is any partition of states and S is any state, the agent's $\mathcal{T}$-A-*conditional currency about S* may be defined as his $\mathcal{T}$-A-conditional currency about $\{S\}$. Thus, given our assumption that CB_1–CB_6 hold, it is plausible that a pair of partitions, $\mathcal{K}$ and $\mathcal{C}$, satisfies the appropriateness conditions AC_1, AC_2^* and AC_3^* if, and only if, (5) holds (for AC_1) and

> DM's $\mathcal{K}$-A-conditional currency about $\mathcal{C}$ is either 1 or close to 1. (6)

Note that the claim that appropriate partitions satisfy (5) and (6) does not depend on the assumption that either the agent conceives of the acts as not being a result of self-conscious rational deliberation or he believes that a state cannot directly affect conscious beliefs and desires. But the claim that pairs of partitions that satisfy (5) and (6) are appropriate – specifically, the claim that if (6) is satisfied then so are AC_2^* and AC_3^* – does depend on that assumption. The main result of this chapter, given in the next section, does not depend on (6).

Thus, a variety of the agent's causal beliefs can be characterized by the nature of his subjective probabilities over the acts, states and reasons. Assuming that CB_1–CB_6 are all true, then (i) DM's R-conditional currency about a state S is a measure of the extent to which he believes he can or cannot affect S by his actions,

(ii) DM's A-conditional currency about a state S is a measure of the extent to which he believes that S or its causes can or cannot affect his actions, and (iii) the extent to which the agent believes that factors in some partition $\mathcal{T}$ screen off causal relevance of a state S and its causes to his actions is measured by his $\mathcal{T}$-A-conditional currency about S. In fact, we have seen that pairs of partitions, $\mathcal{T}$ and $\mathcal{S}$, that satisfy the appropriateness conditions AC_1, AC_2^* and AC_3^* can plausibly be *identified* as those for which the agent has high R-conditional currency about $\mathcal{T}$ and high $\mathcal{T}$-A-conditional currency about $\mathcal{S}$. I do not claim that the various conditional currency notions are very precise and fine tools for measuring the extent of the agent's causal beliefs, but only plausible, crude tools. Perhaps finer measurements could be made if the conditional currency notions were defined in terms of a finer notion of resiliency, e.g., where resiliency is defined not in terms of absolute differences but rather in terms of the statistical notion of variance. But I shall not explore such possibilities here.

What about the case in which the second part of CB_1 and the first part of CB_6 do not hold, i.e., the case in which the agent believes that a state can affect conscious beliefs and desires directly, without operating through the true ones? Since all of DM's probabilities are, in effect, conditional on R^*, the proposition that ascribes to DM his conscious beliefs and desires, the various conditional currency notions only measure the potential that a state may have to affect action that is not a result of self-conscious rational deliberation and the extent to which a state may have affected the conscious beliefs and desires by way of affecting the true ones, according to the agent's beliefs. Of course in the case of an individual agent who knows his conscious beliefs and desires, this is all we can hope for in the way of detecting such causal beliefs that pertain to himself and his actions: the agent's knowledge of his conscious beliefs and desires screens off any direct causal correlation that may exist between a state and conscious beliefs and desires. If the agent believes that there is direct causal relevance of states to conscious beliefs and desires (without intermediate causal relevance to true beliefs and desires), then I suggest (though I will not develop this proposal in detail) that (i) "type-A" (in the sense of Chapter 6) correlates of the conditional currency notions developed here be used – i.e., use $A_k(a)$ instead of A_k, $S(a)$ instead of S, and so on, in conditional currency – and (ii) use reason-propositions of the form $R_t^*(a)$ & $R_s(a)$, instead of those of the form $R_s(a)$, in conditional currency, where the $R_t^*(a)$s attribute conscious degrees of belief and desire to the arbitrary individual a. Thus, for example, the agent's "type-A" A-conditional currency about $S(a)$ would be equal to:

$$1 - \max_{stk} |P(S(a)|A_k(a)) - P(S(a)|A_k(a) \text{ \& } R_t^*(a) \text{ \& } R_s(a))|.$$

This quantity will, of course, measure the extent to which the agent believes that $S(a)$ and its causes are causally relevant both to the true beliefs and desires of a – i.e., to which $R_s(a)$ is true – *and* to the conscious beliefs and desires of a – i.e., to which $R_t^*(a)$ is true – whether the causal influence of the state on the conscious beliefs and desires is indirect *via* the true ones or direct, bypassing influence on the true ones. Thus, this kind of conditional currency measures the extent of influence of a state and its causes on action whether or not the agent conceives the acts as resulting from self-conscious rational deliberation and whether the agent believes the state may operate directly on conscious beliefs and desires or only indirectly on them *via* operating on the true ones.

Whether we must use type-A conditional currency notions or the type-B notions will suffice, it is significant, if the foregoing analysis is correct, that *this way of measuring and characterizing an agent's causal beliefs does not involve introducing decision-relevant propositions that contain counterfactual conditionals or involve causal notions.* That is, all the factors involved in conditional currency – acts, states and reasons – may be factors under the *narrow* construal of 'factor', discussed in Chapter 5. That an agent's subjective probabilities over factors, narrowly construed, are sensitive to the difference between a state's being under the influence of an act and an act's being under the influence of a state is *prima facie* evidence that *PMCEU* decision theory is sensitive in the right way to the causal distinctions to which causal decision theories were designed – by way of introducing factors, broadly construed – to be sensitive. And this is what I shall argue in the next section.

THE GENERAL DEFENSE

In this section, I shall state, prove and discuss two theorems. The first theorem relies on the existence of an appropriate pair of

200

partitions, $\mathcal{K}$ and $\mathcal{C}$, in the sense of satisfaction of AC_1, AC_2^* and AC_3^* of Chapter 5, and their satisfaction, therefore, of (5) and (6) of this chapter. The result is that as the agent's currency about his reasons, R-conditional currency about $\mathcal{K}$, and $\mathcal{K}$-A-conditional currency about $\mathcal{C}$ all approach 1 (as they should, by (2), (5) and (6)), $CEU(A_k)$ approaches $U_K(A_k)$, for all acts A_k. The second theorem relies on a plausible suggestion about the partition $\mathcal{K}$ and shows that as the agent's currency about his reasons and R-conditional currency about $\mathcal{K}$ approach 1 (as they should, by (2) and (5)), $CEU(A_k)$ approaches $U_K(A_k)$, for all acts A_k. Finally, I address the problem of finding an appropriate partition $\mathcal{K}$ of factors narrowly construed and offer a suggestion.

Theorem 1

Let $\mathcal{K} = \{K_1, \ldots K_{n_1}\}$ and $\mathcal{C} = \{C_1, \ldots C_{n_2}\}$ be any two partitions of states. Let $\mathcal{R} = \{R_1, \ldots R_q\}$ be the agent's partition of reason-propositions. Let x be DM's currency about $\mathcal{R}$. Let y be DM's R-conditional currency about $\mathcal{K}$. And let z be DM's $\mathcal{K}$-A-conditional currency about $\mathcal{C}$. Assume that for all i, j, k and s.

$$D(K_i \,\&\, C_j \,\&\, A_k \,\&\, R_s) = D(K_i \,\&\, C_j \,\&\, A_k).$$

Then for all acts A_k,

$$\lim_{x,y,z \to 1} CEU(A_k) = U_K(A_k),$$

where $U_K(A_k)$ is evaluated relative to the K_is being the maximally specific specifications of factors outside DM's influence and the C_js being factors within his influence.

Proof

Let $\varepsilon > 0$.

Let $u_{sk} = P(R_s | A_k) - P(R_s)$, for all s and k.
Let $v_{isk} = P(K_i | R_s \,\&\, A_k) - P(K_i | R_s)$, for all i, s and k.
Let $w_{jiks} = P(C_j | K_i \,\&\, A_k \,\&\, R_s) - P(C_j | K_i \,\&\, A_k)$, for all j, i, k and s.
Let $d_{ijk} = D(K_i \,\&\, C_j \,\&\, A_k) = D(K_i \,\&\, C_j \,\&\, A_k \,\&\, R_s)$, for i, j, k and s.

Then for any act A_k,

$$CEU(A_k) = \sum_{sij} (P(R_s) + u_{sk})(P(K_i|R_s) + v_{isk})(P(C_j|K_i \ \& \ A_k) + w_{jiks})d_{ijk}$$

$$= U_K(A_k) + \sum_{sij} (P(R_s)P(K_i|R_s)w_{jiks}$$

$$+ P(R_s)v_{isk}P(C_j|K_i \ \& \ A_k) + P(R_s)v_{isk}w_{jiks}$$

$$+ u_{sk}P(K_i|R_s)P(C_j|K_i \ \& \ A_k) + u_{sk}P(K_i|R_s)w_{jiks}$$

$$+ u_{sk}v_{isk}P(C_j|K_i \ \& \ A_k) + u_{sk}v_{isk}w_{jiks})d_{ijk}.$$

Now let

$$p_1 = \max_s P(R_s), \quad p_2 = \max_{is} P(K_i|R_s),$$

$$p_3 = \max_{jik} P(C_j|K_i \ \& \ A_k), \quad d = \max_{ijk} |d_{ijk}|, \quad u = \max_{sk} |u_{sk}|,$$

$$v = \max_{isk} |v_{isk}| \quad \text{and} \quad w = \max_{jiks} |w_{jiks}|.$$

Then

$$|CEU(A_k) - U_K(A_k)| \leq qn_1n_2d(p_1p_2w + p_1vp_3 + p_1vw + up_2p_3 + up_2w$$

$$+ uvp_3 + uvw) < 7qn_1n_2d(\max(u, v, w)).$$

Note that $x = 1 - u$, $y = 1 - v$ and $z = 1 - w$. So,

$$|CEU(A_k) - U_K(A_k)| < 7qn_1n_2d \max(1-x, 1-y, 1-z).$$

Thus, if $x, y, z > 1 - (\varepsilon/7qn_1n_2d)$, then $\max(1-x, 1-y, 1-z) < (\varepsilon/7qn_1n_2d)$, so that $|CEU(A_k) - U_K(A_k)| < \varepsilon$. $\square$

Theorem 2

Let $\{K_1, \ldots K_{n_1}\}$ and $\{C_1, \ldots C_{n_2}\}$ be any two partitions of states, and let $\mathscr{R} = \{R_1, \ldots R_q\}$ be the agent's partition of reason-propositions. Let $\mathscr{K} = \{K_i \ \& \ R_s\}_{i,s}$. Let x be DM's currency about $\mathscr{R}$, and let y be DM's R-conditional currency about $\mathscr{K}$. Then for any act A_k,

$$\lim_{x, y \to 1} CEU(A_k) = U_K(A_k),$$

where $U_K(A_k)$ is evaluated relative to $\mathscr{K}$ being the partition of maximally specific specification of factors outside the agent's influence and the C_js being factors within his influence.

202

Proof

Just note that all the conditions of Theorem 1 are satisfied. In particular, $D(K_{is'} \& C_j \& A_k \& R_s) = D(K_{is'} \& C_j \& A_k)$ (where $K_{is'} = K_i \& R_{s'}$) if $s = s'$ and is undefined otherwise; and DM is automatically of unit $\mathscr{K}$-A-conditional currency about the set of C_js. $\square$

Part of the conditions of Theorem 2 is that $\mathscr{K}$ is maximally specific with respect to the reason-propositions. Obviously, $\mathscr{K}$ in the theorems is to be interpreted as the set of maximally specific specifications of factors that the agent thinks are outside the influence of his actions at the time of decision. I think it is very reasonable for the agent to believe that the reasons are factors outside his influence at the time of decision. While we surely have the power to choose and perform acts, it is not so much within our influence to choose or affect the reasons for which we perform the act we perform. This point is very much like a point that Leibniz made about opinions:

> It does not depend on man to have this or that opinion in the present state, but it depends on him to prepare himself to have it eventually, ... thus opinions are voluntary only in an indirect manner. (1765: 528)

Similarly, it does not depend on the agent to have such and such true beliefs and desires in the decision situation at hand, but to bring about some state that will affect his true beliefs and desires for some future decision situation. (Recall CB_5 and the discussion following Figure 3.)

Thus, Theorem 2 trades the rather implausible assumption of Theorem 1 about desirabilities for the more plausible condition that the agent believes his present true beliefs and desires to be outside the influence of his present action. Note, incidentally, that for any set of factors $\{F_i\}_i$, the agent's R-conditional currency about $\{F_i\}_i$ is equal to his R-conditional currency about $\{F_i \& R_s\}_{i,s}$.

The significance of the theorems depends on the existence of an appropriate partition $\mathscr{K}$ – i.e., a partition $\mathscr{K}$ which, together with some other, and thus any other, partition, satisfies AC_1, AC_2^* and AC_3^*, i.e., a partition $\mathscr{K}$ that satisfies AC_1 and AC_4^*. There must exist a partition $\mathscr{K}$ whose members are outside the influence of the available acts and screen off any causal relevance of any factor to the acts. Note that the significance of the theorems does *not* depend on the agent's being able to *find* such a partition, for the *CEU* of any act is the same no matter which partitions are used to calculate it. But how do we know that an appropriate partition $\mathcal{K}$ will always exist?

I suggest that at least for most decision situations, we may let $\mathcal{K} = \mathcal{R} =$ the set of reason-propositions. As urged previously, it seems that the nature of one's true beliefs and desires is outside the influence of the agent at the time of decision, though he may act in certain ways to change them for the future. Also, fixing an R_s (so that both the conscious beliefs and desires – of which the agent has knowledge – and the true ones are fixed), no factor can influence the agent's act whether the act will be based on self-conscious rational deliberation or not. Thus, $\mathcal{R}$ satisfies AC_1 and AC_4^*, and, indeed, the agent automatically has unit R-conditional currency about $\mathcal{R}$ and unit $\mathcal{R}$-A-conditional currency about any partition of factors. Thus, the theorems tell us that as the agent's currency about $\mathcal{R}$ approaches 1, as, by (2), it should, the conditional expected utility of any act approaches its K-expectation.

There is one more possibility that must be covered in the argument for the general applicability of *PMCEU*. The R_ss are factors under the narrow construal of 'factor': they are the kind of thing that we think of as a cause or an effect. The argument for high currency about the R_ss proceeded on the assumption that the agent was going to base his act on his conscious beliefs and desires, of which he has knowledge. Given this assumption, the agent's knowledge of his true beliefs and desires screens off any causal relevance of the R_ss to the acts. But what about agents – like Lewis' agent with eccentric beliefs – who believe that *everything* is within the influence of his actions, but only a little. Such an agent may believe that the R_ss are within his influence, in which case $\mathcal{R}$ would not be appropriate: though $\mathcal{R}$ would satisfy AC_4^*, it would not satisfy AC_1, and, for that reason, we could not expect arbitrarily high currency about $\mathcal{R}$.

My response to this is, of course, that indeed we should not expect arbitrarily high currency about reasons, but *only* due to the failure of $\mathcal{R}$'s satisfaction of AC_1. That is, the agent's currency about his reasons should fall short of 1 just to the (small) extent that he believes that his acts *can* (via, for example, backwards causality) affect the R_ss. The difference between a $P(R_s)$ and a $P(R_s | A_k)$ should not reflect a belief that R_s is causally relevant to

A_k or a belief that there is a common cause of R_s and A_k, because these probabilities are, in effect, conditional on R^*, which ascribes to the agent his true beliefs and desires on which his action will be based, knowledge of which screens off such causal correlations. Thus, the R_s should be expected to satisfy the condition:

$AC_1^{(*)}$: For all k and s, the difference between $P(R_s/A_k)$ and $P(R_s)$ reflects the extent to which the agent believes that A_k is causally relevant to R_s, and not the extent to which he may believe that R_s is causally relevant to A_k, and not the extent to which he may believe that some factor is commonly causally relevant to both R_s and A_k.

Note that this condition stands in the same relation to AC_1 as AC_2, AC_3 and AC_4 stand to AC_2^*, AC_3^* and AC_4^*, respectively. And just as AC_2, AC_3 and AC_4 justify taking the probabilities $P(C_j|K_i)$ conditional on an act in the evaluation of expected utility for *PMKE*, so $AC_1^{(*)}$ justifies taking the probabilities $P(R_s)$ conditional on the act in the evaluation of expected utility for *PMCEU*. Of course this is relevant only for those bizarre cases in which the agent thinks that his present actions are causally relevant to what his present true, perhaps unconscious beliefs and desires are, but it does indicate the generality of *PMCEU*.

8

Newcomb's paradox

In the Newcomb situations described in Chapter 4, the principle of dominance and our intuitions agreed that one act was correct while it seemed that *PMCEU* prescribed the other act. Newcomb's paradox, presented in the introduction, involves a decision situation which is, as we shall see, essentially identical in structure to the Newcomb situations of Chapter 4. However, people's intuitions seem not to be as committed to the correctness of the prescription of the principle of dominance in the decision situation of Newcomb's paradox (i.e., taking both boxes) as they are in the other, less fantastic, Newcomb situations. Indeed, there is much controversy as to which act is correct in Newcomb's paradox. As I indicated in the introduction, I believe that the correct act is to take the contents of both boxes. However, my goal in this chapter is not to convince the reader of this. I shall do three things in this chapter, the third of which is the most important. First, I shall summarize some of the main existing arguments for the correctness of one act or the other in Newcomb's paradox. My main reason for presenting these arguments – with minimal evaluation – is to help the reader gain a deeper understanding of the controversy and the kinds of considerations brought to bear on each side. Second, I shall suggest a way of making one of the arguments in favor of taking the contents of both boxes more persuasive. And third, I shall show how the analysis of Newcomb situations developed in the previous chapters can be applied to Newcomb's paradox. This will show that, contrary to what has generally been thought, one can consistently be both a *CEU*-maximizer and a "two-boxer": the choice between being a one-boxer and being a two-boxer is not a choice between being and not being a *CEU*-maximizer.

I shall present three one-box arguments and three two-box arguments. The first one-box argument is the best known and was already presented in the introduction: Given that I take only the contents of the opaque box, the probability is almost 1 that the predictor predicted this, so that I would get the $1,000,000; given that I take the contents of both boxes, the probability is almost 1 that the predictor predicted *this*, so that I would get only $1,000; therefore I should take only the contents of the opaque box. My reply to this argument consists in showing, below, how the analysis of Chapters 6 and 7 applies to Newcomb's paradox, thus casting doubt on the subjective probabilistic inequality relations assumed in the argument. The assumed relations are to be diagnosed in the way suggested at the end of Chapter 6.

The first two-box argument relies on the principle of dominance and was sketched in the introduction; it goes as follows. The predictor has already made his prediction, and he has already put either the $1,000,000 or nothing in the opaque box. He has already made his move, and the contents of the opaque box will not, cannot, be changed either by your act or by anything the predictor can now do. Now, no matter which act you perform, you will possess the contents of the opaque box. But if you take the contents of both boxes, you will possess, in addition to the contents of the opaque box, another $1,000; and no matter what is in the opaque box, you are better off with that plus the $1,000 than with that without the $1,000. Therefore, you should take the contents of both boxes.

James H. Fetzer has suggested (in correspondence of March 1, 1980 and in discussion) a one-box argument to the effect that dominance reasoning is not applicable in Newcomb's paradox. (Schlesinger (1974) considers a similar argument, and Bar-Hillel & Margalit (1972) argue that the usual application of the dominance principle is injudicious in a different way.) According to his argument, if the agent takes seriously the premise that the predictor will make the correct prediction in every case, then the agent should not list among the possible outcomes of his action his getting $1,001,000 or his getting $0. To get $1,001,000, the agent would have to take both boxes and the predictor would have to have predicted (wrongly) his taking just the opaque box, thus violating the premise in question. To get $0, the agent would have to take just the opaque box and the predictor would have to have predicted (wrongly) his taking both boxes, thus again violating the premise in question. Dominance reasoning in Newcomb's paradox involves, of course, the premises that the outcome of getting $1,001,000 is preferred to the outcome of getting $1,000 000 and that the outcome of getting $1,000 is preferred to the outcome of getting $0. Thus, since the agent should not list getting $1,001,000 or getting $0 among the possible outcomes of his action, then, clearly, dominance reasoning is not applicable. Furthermore, the only possible outcomes are, therefore, getting $1,000,000 and getting $1,000, the former arising from the act of taking just the opaque box and the latter arising from taking both. Hence, one should take just the opaque box.

I have two responses of Fetzer's argument. First, it clearly does not apply to the agent whose degree of confidence in the proposition that the predictor will predict correctly is just short of 1, whose degree of confidence in that proposition is, say, 0.999999. Surely, such an agent should count getting $1,001,000 and getting $0 as possible outcomes of his action. And if dominance reasoning applies in this case and if taking the contents of both boxes is correct for this agent, then it is hard to see why it would not also be correct for an agent whose degree of belief in the proposition that the predictor will predict correctly is higher by a mere 0.000001.

But second, it seems to me that an agent who thought that getting $1,001,000 or getting $0 was impossible – even one who assigned probability 0 to getting $1,001,000 and to getting $0 – would, in virtue thereof, be irrational. I agree that if the agent assigned probability 0 to some relevant outcome-proposition, then the principle of dominance may not apply. Indeed, in Jeffrey's theory, agents do not rank such propositions in their preferences or assign desirabilities to them: their conditional expected utility would involve probabilities conditional on them, and thus ratios with denominator 0. But, as David Lewis argues, assigning probability 0 to a proposition

is tantamount to a firm resolve never to change your mind, and that is objectionable. However much reason you may get to think that option A will not be realized if K holds, you will not if you are rational lower $[P(K \ \& \ A)]$ quite to zero. Let it by all means get very, very small; but very, very small denominators do not make utilities go undefined. (1981)

The agent in the decision situation of Newcomb's paradox would have to take the relevant premise very seriously indeed for him to be willing to bet his life on his not getting $1,001,000 or $0, which it would seem he should be willing to do if he thinks the probabilities of getting $1,001,000 or $0 are 0; and this would indeed require a very special kind of irrationality. In any case, at least one interesting version of Newcomb's paradox, the version with which I shall be concerned, is the one in which the agent is merely enormously confident in the predictor's ability and believes it to be just possible that the predictor will err.

The second two-box argument is found in a paper by G. Schlesinger (1974): Suppose the opposite side of the opaque box is transparent and that Smith, your intelligent friend who always wishes you well, is sitting behind the boxes. Smith understands the situation, and, since he can see the contents of both boxes, he is sufficiently informed to know which act it is in your best interest to perform. And, of course, *whatever* is in the opaque box, you know that Smith knows that it is in your best interest to take both boxes. Smith is not allowed to communicate with you, but, of course, you know that he would, if allowed, advise you to take both boxes. Thus, if you accept the following proposition:

A given act is in your best interest to perform if, and only if, a person who is sufficiently informed to know whether it is in your best interest and who wishes you well would advise you to perform that act if he could communicate advice to you and if he existed;

then you should conclude that taking the contents of both boxes is in your best interest. Furthermore, it does not matter that Smith may not be there or may not exist, for you know what he would secretly advise if he existed and were there.

The third one-box argument is succinctly summarized by Gibbard and Harper (1978) as: "If you're so smart, why ain't you rich?" Both one-boxers and two-boxers want to be millionaires, but, almost invariably, the one-boxers leave the decision situation of Newcomb's paradox as millionaires, and, almost invariably, the two-boxers do not; therefore, taking just the opaque box must be the rational act. (My reply to this argument consists in pointing out that the argument is based on the agent's having certain type-A beliefs and that what is relevant in assessing the alternatives is type-B beliefs, and not type-A beliefs.)

The third two-box argument was presented by Nozick in his classic paper on Newcomb's paradox (1969: 135), and something like it can be found in Gibbard and Harper's paper (1978: 156). Essentially, it is a challenge to the one-boxers. Clearly, in the cholesterol case and in the charisma case and in other Newcomb situations, the correct act is the analog of the two-box act of Newcomb's paradox: the dominant act. But these situations are identical to the situation of Newcomb's paradox with respect to the structure of the agent's causal and probabilistic beliefs and his desirabilities. So, if you think that taking just the opaque box is the correct act in Newcomb's paradox, then what is the difference between the decision situation of Newcomb's paradox and those of the other Newcomb situations that accounts for the one-box act being correct in the former and the analogs of the two-box act being correct in the latter?

In what follows, I shall look into this last two-box argument in more detail and try to make it more forceful. At first sight, it seems that there may be important differences between the decision situation of Newcomb's paradox and those of the other, less fantastic, Newcomb situations I have discussed. First, the other Newcomb situations do not involve a being with fantastic powers of prediction. And second, no common cause is mentioned in setting up Newcomb's paradox. I do not think that these are really important differences. And I think that once this is clearly seen, and when some decision situations "intermediate between" that of Newcomb's paradox and those of the other Newcomb situations are considered, then the last two-box argument gains force.

The relevant features of the causal structure of the previously considered Newcomb situations is represented by the diagram at the beginning of Chapter 6; it does not really matter whether the propositions in the diagram are of the form $X(DM)$ or $X(a)$, in the notation of Chapter 6. What is the causal structure of the decision situation of Newcomb's paradox? For convenience, let '$A_1(a)$' and '$A_2(a)$' stand for the act-propositions to the effect that a takes just the opaque box and that a takes two boxes, respectively. And let '$P_1(a)$' and '$P_2(a)$' stand for the state-propositions to the effect that the predictor predicts '$A_1(a)$' and '$A_2(a)$', respectively.

It seems that if the agent is rationally to have enormous confidence in the accuracy of the predictor – i.e., if there is to be a high subjective probabilistic correlation between $A_i(a)$ and $P_i(a)$, for each i – then the agent must believe that there is a causal explanation for his success, though he may not know what that explanation is, and neither may the predictor. Indeed, it seems presupposed by much of our inductive reasoning that a high statistical correlation has a causal explanation. The only *kind* of causal explanation of the predictor's success that I can think of that is consistent with the set-up of Newcomb's paradox is one that invokes a common cause: for $i = 1, 2$, there is a common cause of *predictions* of $A_i(a)$ and *acts* $A_i(a)$. Indeed, by the subjective common cause principle, stated in Chapter 5, that is the only possibility, since the predictions do not cause the acts and the acts do not cause the predictions. (If you think that the prediction may somehow cause the act in a version of Newcomb's paradox, then think of $P_i(a)$ as a common cause of $A_i(a)$ and, in a degenerate sense, of itself.) Also, it seems that on any plausible account of any kind of successful prediction, the causal structure must be of this form. A successful predictor must have – consciously or unconsciously – a method, in the sense that the predictions are based on observations, conscious or unconscious. And if we look far enough back in the causal chain culminating in the relevant observations, we must be able to find factors that are causally relevant to the event predicted. It is easy to see that this is the causal structure involved in weather prediction, for example.

For $i = 1, 2$, let '$Q_i(a)$' stand for the state-proposition that the common cause of $P_i(a)$ and $A_i(a)$, whatever it may be, obtains. Let '$M_1(a)$' stand for the proposition that, in the case of a, the \$1,000,000 is in the opaque box, and let '$M_2(a)$' stand for the proposition that, in the case of a, the opaque box is empty. Then, where $\mathcal{R}$ is the set of propositions describing the possible pairs of probability and desirability assignments an agent may have in the decision situation of Newcomb's paradox, the causal structure of the decision situation of Newcomb's paradox can be diagrammatically represented as follows:

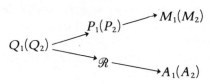

This diagram is to be interpreted in the same way as the one at the beginning of Chapter 6, and the propositions involved may be thought of either as of the form $X(a)$ or as of the form $X(DM)$.

This diagram is very similar to the one at the beginning of Chapter 6. The only structural difference is that there are two propositions after the common cause in the top causal chain instead of just one. If we think of the M_is as symtomatic outcomes (which is reasonable since the M_is are more directly related to an agent's happiness than the P_is are), then, in the diagram above, there is a factor between the common cause and the symptomatic outcome. None is in the diagram at the beginning of Chapter 6. However, this does not mark an important difference between the decision situation of Newcomb's paradox and those of the less fantastic Newcomb situations discussed previously. It should not matter to the man in the cholesterol case that there may be intermediate factors that are outside his influence in the causal chain between the lesion and hardening of the arteries. Nor should it matter to Solomon that uncharisma may cause revolts indirectly by causing some intermediate factor that is outside Solomon's influence – such as a sneaky and ignoble bearing. In fact, the world is so complex that one can almost always be certain that, given a cause and an effect, there are intermediate factors between them in the causal chain.

And it is not important that the intermediate factor in the second diagram has to do with prediction. Consider this modification of the charisma case. In it, Solomon believes that uncharisma does not directly cause revolts. Instead, he believes that an evil genius (or perhaps a just genius) who is blind to kings' actions, but can detect whether or not they have charisma, has the (true) theory that whether or not a king acts justly is reliably predictable on the basis of whether or not the king has charisma. This evil genius wants to reward kings who act justly and punish those that act unjustly, and he is able to cause revolts. Since he cannot *observe* kings' actions, he causes revolts against kings who he *predicts* (on the basis of whether or not they have charisma) will act unjustly. Letting $P_J(P_{-J})$ be the proposition that the evil genius predicts that Solomon will act justly (unjustly), the causal structure of the decision situation can be represented as follows:

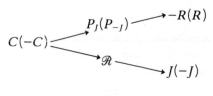

So the causal structure is the same as that of the decision situation of Newcomb's paradox. And it seems that the rational act is still $-J$ – the analog of A_2.

Thus, neither the presence of a very accurate predictor in Newcomb's paradox nor the fact that no common cause is mentioned in setting up Newcomb's paradox constitutes an important difference between the decision situation of Newcomb's paradox and those of the less fantastic Newcomb situations, a difference which should affect which act is correct. Also, the decision situation described just above is so similar in structure to that of Newcomb's paradox that it is hard to see how anybody could justify thinking both that $-J$ is correct in the former and that A_1 is correct in the latter.

I think that giving examples of decision situations that are similar with respect to some of the details both to that of Newcomb's paradox and to, for example, the cholesterol case can make the last two-box argument more persuasive. One could construct a long sequence of decision situations, $(ds_1, \ldots ds_n)$, whose first member is that of the cholesterol case, whose last member is that of Newcomb's paradox and such that for any member ds_i, the next member ds_{i+1} is only slightly more different from the decision situation of the cholesterol case than ds_i is and only slightly more similar than ds_i is to that of Newcomb's paradox. The purpose of constructing such a sequence is to gradually force one who has eggs-benedict intuitions to have two-box intuitions. In the first decision situation in the sequence, I is clearly the correct act, and I of the cholesterol case is the analog of A_2 of Newcomb's paradox. The next decision situation in the sequence should be so similar to the one of the cholesterol case that one would be forced to agree that, in it, the analog of I and A_2 is correct, and so on. One member of the sequence might be one in which the agent believes that an evil genius who can detect the lesion but not high cholesterol intake wants, for some reason, to punish people who have high cholesterol intake; so he causes atherosclerosis in those who he predicts (on the basis of the presence of the lesion) will have high cholesterol intake. Another member might be the situation exactly like that of Newcomb's paradox except that the agent knows that the predictor makes his prediction on the basis of the presence or absence of a lesion-like object in the brain. Yet another member might be the decision situation, exactly like that of the cholesterol case except that those who have the lesion tend to develop hardening of the arteries and all of its bad symptoms immediately after making the policy decision about the level of one's cholesterol intake: some have thought that one-box intuitions result from an illusion of causal relevance of A_1 to M_1; the immediacy of the payoff may partially account for such an illusion.

How does the analysis of the previous chapters apply to Newcomb's paradox? (Henceforth, I shall drop the '(DM)' on the names of the propositions the agent considers: in what follows, all names 'X' of propositions will be abbreviations for names '$X(DM)$'.) As before, it seems appropriate to simplify and treat the decision situation of Newcomb's paradox as a two-state $(Q_1$ and $Q_2)$, two-act $(A_1$ and $A_2)$ decision situation: all the utility or disutility of the states and outcomes not explicitly considered attaches appropriately – given the agent's causal and probabilistic beliefs – to the states explicitly considered.

Turning first to the analysis of Chapter 6, the relevant assumptions are:

(5′) The agent knows what his beliefs and desires are, i.e., he has degree of belief 1 in the proposition R_Φ, which says what his probabilities over the decision-relevant propositions are and what his desirabilities for the maximally specific decision-relevant propositions are;

(6′) For each i, the agent believes with probability 1 that he will perform A_i if, and only if, he determines that A_i is the correct act; and

(7′) For each i, the proposition that the agent determines that A_i is correct is probabilistically independent of Q_i, given R_Φ.

As before, (5′)–(7′) imply:

$$P(Q_1|A_1) = P(Q_1|A_2),$$

and

$$P(Q_2|A_1) = P(Q_2|A_2).$$

Now, assuming that the agent believes that his action does not interfere with the predictors' prediction process or with the predictor's filling the opaque box correctly, given his prediction, then we should expect the following to hold:

For each $i, j = 1, 2, P(P_i | Q_j \ \& \ A_1) = P(P_i | Q_j \ \& \ A_2),$

and

For each $i, j, k = 1, 2, P(M_i | P_j \ \& \ Q_k \ \& \ A_1) = P(M_i | P_j \ \& \ Q_k \ \& \ A_2).$

From this, together with the consequences of $(5')$–$(7')$ noted above, it follows that:

$$P(M_1 | A_1) = P(M_1 | A_2),$$

and

$$P(M_2 | A_1) = P(M_2 | A_2).$$

Thus, *PMCEU* will agree with *PMKE* (taking M_1 and M_2 to be the factors outside the influence of the agent's actions) and with *PMUE* (assuming, with Gibbard and Harper, that $P(A_1 \square\!\!\rightarrow M_1) = P(A_2 \square\!\!\rightarrow M_1)$ and that $P(A_1 \square\!\!\rightarrow M_2) = P(A_2 \square\!\!\rightarrow M_2)$). Thus, since, as everyone agrees, A_2 dominates A_1 in the agent's preferences relative to the partition $\{M_1, M_2\}$, all the rules recommend act A_2: the act of taking both boxes.

Assumption $(5')$ is uncontroversial relative to the controversy about which act is correct in Newcomb's paradox. That is, people who argue for one act or the other do so on grounds other than what they believe about $(5')$. And $(6')$ is also uncontroversial relative to the controversy about which act is correct in Newcomb's paradox. Hence, I shall assume $(5')$ and $(6')$ for the remainder of this chapter. Just as in Chapter 6, $(5')$ and $(6')$ are reasonable idealizations.

But what about $(7')$? A one-boxer who believes that *PMCEU* gives the right recommendation – or a two-boxer who believes that *PMCEU* gives the wrong recommendation – may still argue that the predictor can, on the basis of Q_1 and Q_2, predict how the agent will *evaluate* the available acts in light of the probabilities described in R_Φ: the antecedent factors described in Q_1 and Q_2 are causally relevant to, and cause prediction-relevant clues for, not only what *DM*'s beliefs and desires are, but also how *DM* evaluates the acts in light of them. If *DM* believes that Q_1 and Q_2 are causally relevant to (and cause prediction-relevant clues for) how he will rationally evaluate the acts in light of his known beliefs and desires, then his knowledge of his beliefs and desires will not screen off the probabilistic correlation between the Q_is and the propositions to the effect that he determines A_i to be the correct act, $i = 1, 2$.

Let us consider this possibility in more detail. In this case, the agent believes both that he is rational – that he will rationally determine which act is correct in light of his beliefs and desires – *and* that Q_1 and Q_2 can affect which act he determines is correct in light of his known probabilities and desirabilities. Now it seems clear that a given assessment of the available acts in light of his beliefs and desires is a rational assessment given that Q_1 is true if, and only if, it is a rational assessment given that Q_2 is true: since the agent does not know which of Q_1 and Q_2 is true, which of Q_1 and Q_2 is actually true is irrelevant to the rationality of a given assessment of the available acts in light of his beliefs and desires. But the agent believes that Q_1 can cause his assessment, which he believes will be rational, to favor A_1 and that Q_2 can cause his assessment, which he believes will be rational, to favor A_2. But this means that he must believe that *both* acts could be rational in light of his beliefs and desires. The agent believes that there is not necessarily a unique rational act for him. It is important to understand that 'there is no unique correct act' has, here, a more radical sense than 'on rational evaluation, one should be indifferent' and a more radical sense than 'it is beyond my powers of rational evaluation to determine which act is correct'. This sense of nonuniqueness of the correct act implies that one's degrees of belief and desirabilities together with rational evaluation of the available acts in light of them do not determine a unique ranking of the available acts.

I will not attempt to make sense of this radical sense of non-uniqueness of the correct act. Instead, I shall assume that the notion is unintelligible. (It is worth pointing out that all of the competing decision theories I have discussed imply that, given probabilities and desirabilities over the decision-relevant propositions, there is a unique rational ranking of the available acts.) Thus, if one is rational (and does not hold beliefs that involve unintelligible notions), one will not fully believe both that he will rationally evaluate the alternatives in light of his beliefs and desires *and* that Q_1 and Q_2 can affect which act he determines is correct in light of his beliefs and desires. Thus, the more strongly the agent believes that he can rationally come up with the correct assessment, the less strongly he believes that Q_1 and Q_2 can affect his rational deliberation – and, thus, the higher will be the degree of probabilistic independence of Q_1 and Q_2 from the propositions that he will determine A_1 or A_2 to be the correct act in light of his beliefs and desires.

Thus, one reason why $(7')$ may not strictly hold is that the agent has less than complete faith in his powers of rational evaluation. Another reason is that he may be, consciously or unconsciously, under the illusion that A_1 and A_2 are causally relevant to Q_1 and Q_2. We have already seen in Chapter 7 how this may affect the degrees to which Q_1 and Q_2 are probabilistically independent of A_1 and A_2. Given $(6')$, these are the same degrees as those to which Q_1 and Q_2 are probabilistically independent of propositions to the effect that the agent determines that A_1 or A_2 are correct in light of his beliefs and desires. There may be other reasons why $(7')$ may not strictly hold, but it seems to me that these are at least the main reasons; I shall not consider others.

Given $(6')$, the degrees to which Q_1 and Q_2 are probabilistically independent of propositions to the effect that the agent determines that A_1 or A_2 is the correct act are equal to the degrees to which Q_1 and Q_2 are probabilistically independent of A_1 and A_2. And the latter, in the terminology of Chapter 7, is the agent's R-conditional currency about $\{Q_1, Q_2\}$, since, by $(5')$, $P(R_\Phi) = 1$. Thus, we can conclude that the more faith the agent has in his ability to rationally evaluate the alternatives in Newcomb's paradox and the less he is under the illusion that A_1 and A_2 are causally relevant to Q_1 and Q_2, the greater is the agent's R-conditional currency about $\{Q_1, Q_2\}$. Assuming $(5')$, the agent is of unit currency about his reasons. Thus, by the theorems of Chapter 7, the more faith the agent has in his ability to rationally evaluate and the less he is under the illusion that A_1 and A_2 are causally relevant to Q_1 and Q_2, the closer is $CEU(A_i)$ to $U_K(A_i)$, for $i = 1, 2$. Of course, $U_K(A_2) > U_K(A_1)$.

To what extent can we expect a rational agent to have faith in his ability to rationally evaluate the alternatives and to be free of the illusion that the A_is are causally relevant to the O_is in Newcomb's paradox? I shall not pursue the second part of the question. Most discussions of Newcomb's paradox assume that the agent has the belief that the act will not causally affect the contents of the opaque box. This may be an idealization, but it seems to me that this is not a central issue for Newcomb's paradox. (However, see Bar-

Hillel & Margalit 1972.) Let us assume that the agent is thoroughly convinced that the contents of the box, and thus Q_1 and Q_2, are not affected by the acts.

I think some very interesting things can be said with regard to the extent to which the agent has faith in his ability to rationally evaluate the alternatives. Suppose the agent is thoroughly convinced that *PMCEU* should always be used as the tool for rationally evaluating the available acts in a decision situation and that he is completely convinced that he is competent to do the computations necessary to apply the rule. In this case, he has complete faith in his ability to rationally evaluate his alternatives in light of his known probabilities and desirabilities. Thus, in this case, $(7')$ should hold, so that $CEU(A_2) = U_K(A_2) > U_K(A_1) = CEU(A_1)$. Now suppose the agent is thoroughly convinced that *PMKE* should always be used as the tool for rationally evaluating alternatives and that he is completely convinced that he is competent to apply the rule. Again, he has complete faith in his ability to rationally evaluate his alternatives in light of his beliefs and desires, and we get the same result. More generally, if the agent knows what rule he is going to use – even if that rule happens to sometimes lead to the wrong act and even if the agent is aware of that – *PMCEU* will recommend what I take to be the correct act: A_2. For if he knows that he will use such and such a rule, he knows that he will use it whether Q_1 is true or Q_2 is true. But then, the only things which Q_1 or Q_2 can affect which determine the act are *DM*'s probabilities and desirabilities. But *DM* already knows what these are. Given R_Φ and the agent's knowledge of R_Φ, Q_1 and Q_2 should be causally and probabilistically independent of A_1 and A_2. Thus, $(7')$ should be expected to hold.

And, in particular, even a not thoroughly convinced, though completely faithful, *CEU*-maximizer who believes that taking both boxes is the correct act should not regard Newcomb's paradox as a counterexample to *PMCEU*.

Appendix 1   Logic

The only logic used in this book is a small part of propositional, or sentential, logic. Here, I review the relevant part and clarify some notation and terminology.

The basic entities of propositional logic are *propositions* and the propositional *connectives*. One way of thinking of propositions is as subsets of the class of all possible worlds, so that a proposition is true in a given world if, and only if, the world is an element of the proposition. Of course, one need not think of propositions in this way: they may be left as primitive, undefined objects, or they may be thought of as linguistic entities of a certain kind, e.g., as "meanings."

The connectives of propositional logic – sometimes called 'sentential connectives' or 'truth-functional connectives' or 'Boolean connectives' – are used to construct "new" propositions from "old" ones. The "new" propositions are sometimes called 'truth-functional compounds (or combinations)' or 'Boolean compounds' (or 'combinations') of the "old" ones. The usual connectives are: '$-$', '$\&$', '$\vee$', '$\rightarrow$' and '$\leftrightarrow$'. If X and Y are any propositions, then: (i) $-X$ (the *negation* of X) is the proposition that is true just in case X is false; (ii) $X \& Y$ (the *conjunction* of X and Y) is true just in case both X and Y are true; (iii) $X \vee Y$ (the *disjunction* of X and Y) is true just in case at least one of X and Y is true; (iv) $X \rightarrow Y$ (the *conditional* of X and Y) is equivalent to $-X \vee Y$; and (v) $X \leftrightarrow Y$ (the *biconditional* of X and Y) is equivalent to $(X \rightarrow Y) \& (Y \rightarrow X)$. X and Y are said to be the *conjuncts* of $X \& Y$ and the *disjuncts* of $X \vee Y$; X is the *antecedent* and Y the *consequent* of $X \rightarrow Y$. A set of propositions is said to be *closed* under the Boolean connectives if it contains all Boolean compounds of propositions it contains; the *closure* of a set of propositions is the union of that set with the set of all Boolean compounds of its members. Thinking of propositions as subsets of the set of all possible worlds, $-X$ is the complement of X (the set of possible worlds not in X), $X \& Y$ is the intersection of X and Y (the set of worlds in both of X and Y), $X \lor Y$ is the union of X and Y (the set of worlds in at least one of X and Y), and so on. In the same way as '$\sum_{i=1}^{n} a_i$' is used to denote the numerical sum of $a_1, \ldots a_n$, so the expressions

$$\bigwedge_{i=1}^{n} X_i$$

and

$$\bigvee_{i=1}^{n} X_i$$

are used, respectively, to symbolize the conjunction of the propositions $X_1, \ldots X_n$ (which is true just in case all the X_is are true) and the disjunction of $X_1, \ldots X_n$ (which is true just in case at least one of the X_is is true).

A proposition X is a *tautology* (*contradiction*) if it is true (false) no matter what the truth values are of the basic propositions from which X is constructed using the Boolean connectives. Some examples of tautologies are: $X \lor -X$, $X \leftrightarrow X$ and $(X \to Y) \lor (Y \to X)$; some examples of contradictions are: $X \& -X$ and $-(X \lor -X)$. The negation of any tautology (contradiction) is a contradiction (tautology).

Three important relations (to be distinguished from the connectives) between propositions are those of logical implication, logical equivalence and logical independence. A proposition X *implies* a proposition Y if, and only if, $X \to Y$ is necessarily true. Thinking of propositions as sets of possible worlds, X implies Y just in case Y is true in all possible worlds in which X is true (i.e., $X \to Y$ is the set of all possible worlds, i.e., X is a subset of Y). X is *equivalent* to Y if, and only if, X and Y imply each other. And two propositions are *logically independent* if, and only if, neither implies the other.

Propositions in a given set of propositions are said to be *mutually exclusive* if at most one of them can be true (i.e., if each implies the negations of all the others, i.e., if the conjunction of any two of them is necessarily false); they are said to be *collectively exhaustive* if at least one of them must be true (i.e., if, in any given world, at least one of them is true, i.e., if their disjunction is necessarily true). A *partition* is a set of mutually exclusive and collectively exhaustive propositions. Exactly one element of any partition is true (in any given world).

Relative to a set $\mathscr{S}$ of propositions that is closed under the usual sentential connectives, a proposition X is *maximally specific* if X is a member of $\mathscr{S}$ and there is no proposition Y in $\mathscr{S}$ such that both (i) Y implies X and (ii) Y is not equivalent to X. Relative to any set $\mathscr{S}$ of propositions, a proposition is *maximally specific* if it is maximally specific relative to the closure of the set under the usual connectives. Thus, any element in a set of propositions is equivalent to a disjunction of propositions that are maximally specific relative to the set. A maximally specific proposition relative to a set is always equivalent to a conjunction of members and negations of members of the set. The set of propositions maximally specific relative to a set (modulo equivalence) is always a partition. If $\mathscr{S}_1, \ldots \mathscr{S}_n$ are partitions, then a proposition is maximally specific relative to the union of the $\mathscr{S}_i$s if, and only if, it is equivalent to a conjunction $X_1 \& \cdots \& X_n$ where each X_i is an element of $\mathscr{S}_i$.

Not every set of propositions is such that, relative to it, there exist maximally specific propositions. A set of propositions that is closed under the usual connectives, together with the relation of implication, is one kind of *Boolean algebra*. A Boolean algebra is said to be *atomless* if, for every element of it, there is another element of it that is strictly less than the first. In the case of an algebra of propositions, this means that for every proposition X, there is another proposition Y that is not equivalent to X but which implies X. Of course an atomless Boolean algebra must be infinite. But every finite Boolean algebra of propositions has maximally specific elements, "atoms." A Boolean algebra is said to be *complete* (or σ-*additive*) if it contains all infinite conjunctions and disjunctions of its members as well as the finite ones.

Appendix 2   Probability

A probability P on a Boolean algebra (see Appendix 1) is a rule
or function P which assigns to each proposition X in the Boolean
algebra a real number, $P(X)$, and which satisfies the following three
simple conditions:

$$P(X) \geqslant 0, \text{ for every } X; \tag{1}$$

$$P(T) = 1, \text{ if } T \text{ is a tautology;} \tag{2}$$

$$P(X \vee Y) = P(X) + P(Y), \text{ if } X \text{ and } Y \text{ are mutually exclusive.} \tag{3}$$

These three conditions are the probability axioms, also known as
'the Kolmogorov axioms'. The following are some easy consequences of the probability axioms.

$$P(-X) = 1 - P(X), \text{ for every } X. \tag{4}$$

Proof: By (1), $P(X \vee -X) = 1$; by (3), $P(X \vee -X) = P(X) + P(-X)$; so, $1 = P(X) + P(-X)$, and $P(-X) = 1 - P(X)$.

$$P(C) = 0, \text{ if } C \text{ is a contradiction.} \tag{5}$$

Proof: $-C$ is a tautology; so, by (2), $P(-C) = 1$; by (4), $P(-C) = 1 - P(C)$. So, $1 = 1 - P(C)$, and $P(C) = 0$.

$$P(X) = P(Y), \text{ if } X \text{ and } Y \text{ are logically equivalent.} \tag{6}$$

Proof: X and $-Y$ are mutually exclusive, and $X \vee -Y$ is a tautology; so, by (2), (3) and (4), $1 = P(X \vee -Y) = P(X) + P(-Y) = P(X) + 1 - P(Y)$; hence, $0 = P(X) - P(Y)$, and $P(X) = P(Y)$.

$$P(X) \leqslant P(Y), \text{ if } X \text{ logically implies } Y. \tag{7}$$

$$P(X \vee Y) = P(X) + P(Y) - P(X \& Y), \text{ for all } X \text{ and } Y. \tag{8}$$

222

The probability of X *conditional on* (or *given*) Y, $P(X|Y)$, is defined to be equal to $P(X \& Y)/P(Y)$. Note that $P(X|Y)$ is defined only if $P(Y) \neq 0$. Since, for any X and Y, $P(X \& Y) = P(Y \& X)$, an immediate consequence of the definition of conditional probability is the *multiplication rule*:

$$P(X \& Y) = P(X)P(Y|X) = P(Y)P(X|Y), \text{ for all } X \text{ and } Y. \quad (9)$$

From (9) follows this simple version of Bayes' theorem:

$$P(X|Y) = \frac{P(Y|X)P(X)}{P(Y)}, \text{ for all } X \text{ and } Y.$$

A proposition X is said to be *probabilistically* (or *statistically*) *independent* of a proposition Y if $P(X|Y) = P(X)$. Alternatively, and equivalently, X's being probabilistically independent of Y can be defined as $P(X \& Y) = P(X)P(Y)$. Thus, probabilistic independence is symmetric, i.e., if X is probabilistically independent of Y, then Y is probabilistically independent of X, for all X and Y.

If X and Y are not probabilistically independent, then there is said to be a *probabilistic* (or *statistical*) *correlation* between X and Y. The correlation is said to be *positive* or *negative* according to whether $P(X|Y)$ is greater or less than $P(X)$. The situation is sometimes characterized by saying that Y is positively or negatively probabilistically *relevant* to Y. Note that the following six probabilistic statements are equivalent:

$$P(X) < P(X|Y);$$
$$P(Y) < P(Y|X);$$
$$P(X|-Y) < P(X);$$
$$P(Y|-X) < P(Y);$$
$$P(X|-Y) < P(X|Y);$$
$$P(Y|-X) < P(Y|X).$$

Also, they would remain equivalent if all the '<'s were replaced with '>'s or with '='s. Thus, the two kinds of probabilistic correlation, as well as probabilistic independence, are symmetric. If $P(X|Z \& Y) = P(X|Z)$, then the proposition Z is said to *screen off* any probabilistic correlation between X and Y.

Probabilistic independence is to be distinguished from logical independence. And probabilistic independence and relevance are to be distinguished from causal independence and relevance. We may say that X is *causally independent* of Y if neither of Y and $-Y$ causes either of X and $-X$. ('X causes Y' is to be understood as 'the state of affairs under which X is true causes the state of affairs under which Y is true'.) Y is *positively causally relevant to* X if either Y causes X or $-Y$ causes $-X$; Y is *negatively causally relevant to* X if either Y causes $-X$ or $-Y$ causes X. Note that the notions of causal independence and relevance are not symmetric.

A generalization of the common notion of an average is the statistical notion of expectation, or expected value. Given a parameter (or "random variable") N (e.g., the amount of money that you win when you play blackjack for a weekend) which can take on the possible values, say, $n_1, \ldots n_r$, and a probability P on propositions of the form '$N = n_i$' (i.e., 'N takes on value n_i'), the *expectation* – or *expected value* – of N (calculated in terms of the probability P) is:

$$\sum_{i=1}^{r} P(N = n_i)n_i.$$

If the probabilities in terms of which an expectation is calculated are conditional probabilities, then the expectation is a *conditional expectation* – or *conditional expected value*. For example, if 'R' symbolizes the proposition that the play will take place in Reno, then

$$\sum_{i=1}^{r} P(N = n_i/R)n_i$$

is a conditional expectation.

Bibliography

Adams, E. W. & Rosenkrantz, R. D. (1980). Applying the Jeffrey decision model to rational betting and information acquisition. *Theory and Decision*, **12**, 1–20.

Alexander, H. G. (1958). The paradoxes of confirmation. *The British Journal for the Philosophy of Science*, **9**, 227–33.

Allais, M. (1953). Le comportement de l'homme rationnel devant le risque: critique des postulats et axiomes de l'école americaine. *Econometrica*, **21**, 503–46.

Bar-Hillel, M. (1973). On the subjective probability of compound events. *Organizational Behavior and Human Performance*, **9**, 396–406.

Bar-Hillel, M. & Margalit, A. (1972). Newcomb's paradox revisited. *The British Journal for the Philosophy of Science*, **23**, 295–304.

Becker, G. M. & McClintock, C. G. (1967). Value: behavioral decision theory. *Annual Review of Psychology*, **18**, 239–86.

Black, M. (1966). Notes on the "paradoxes of confirmation". In *Aspects of Inductive Logic*, ed. J. Hintikka and P. Suppes, pp. 175–97. Amsterdam: North Holland Publishing Company.

Bogdan, R. J. (1976). (ed.) *Local Induction*. Dordrecht: D. Reidel Publishing Company.

Bolker, E. D. (1967). A simultaneous axiomatization of utility and subjective probability. *Philosophy of Science*, **34**, 333–40.

Borch, K. (1968). The Allais paradox: a comment. *Behavioral Science*, **13**, 488–9.

Braithwaite, R. B. (1933). The nature of believing. In *Knowledge and Belief*, ed. A. P. Griffiths, pp. 28–40. (1973). London: Oxford University Press.

Braithwaite, R. B. (1953). *Scientific Explanation*. (1960). New York: Harper & Brothers.

Brown, P. M. (1976). Conditionalization and expected utility. *Philosophy of Science*, **43**, 415–19.

Carnap, R. (1950). *Logical Foundations of Probability*, 2nd edn. (1962). Chicago: University of Chicago Press.

Cartwright, N. (1979). Causal laws and effective strategies. *Nous*, **13**, 419–37.

Chihara, C. (1981). Quine and the confirmational paradoxes. In *Midwest Studies in Philosophy 6: Foundations of Analytic Philosophy*, ed. P. French, H. Wettstein & T. Uehling, pp. 425–52. University of Minnesota Press.

Churchman, C. W. (1948). *Theory of Experimental Inference*. New York: The Macmillan Company.

225

Churchman, C. W. (1956). Science and decision making. *Philosophy of Science*, **23**, 247–9.

Cohen, L. J. (1981). Can human irrationality be experimentally demonstrated? *Behavioral and Brain Sciences*, **4**, 317–31.

Coombs, C. H., Bezembinder, T. G. & Goode, F. M. (1967). Testing expectation theories of decision making without measuring utility or subjective probability. *Journal of Mathematical Psychology*, **4**, 72–103.

DeFinetti, B. (1937). Foresight: its logical laws, its subjective sources. Trans. H. E. Kyburg in *Studies in Subjective Probability*, ed. H. E. Kyburg & H. E. Smokler, pp. 93–158. (1964). New York: John Wiley & Sons, Inc.

DeFinetti, B. (1970). *Theory of Probability: A Critical Introductory Treatment*, trans. A. Machí & A. Smith, vol. 1. (1973). New York: John Wiley & Sons, Inc.

Domotor, Z. (1978). Axiomatization of Jeffrey utilities. *Synthese*, **39**, 165–210.

Dorling, J. (1979). Bayesian personalism, the methodology of scientific research programmes, and Duhem's problem. *Studies in History and Philosophy of Science*, **10**, 177–87.

Edwards, W. (1961). Behavioral decision theory. *Annual Review of Psychology*, **12**, 473–98.

Ellsberg, D. (1961). Risk, ambiguity and the Savage axioms. *The Quarterly Journal of Economics*, **75**, 643–69.

Fellner, W. (1961). Distortion of subjective probabilities as a reaction to uncertainty. *The Quarterly Journal of Economics*, **75**, 670–89.

Gibbard, A. & Harper, W. L. (1978). Counterfactuals and two kinds of expected utility. In *Foundations and Applications of Decision Theory*, ed. C. A. Hooker, J. J. Leach & E. F. McClennen, vol. 1, pp. 125–62. Dordrecht: D. Reidel Publishing Company.

Glymour, C. (1980). *Theory and Evidence*. Princeton: Princeton University Press.

Good, I. J. (1967). The white shoe is a red herring. *The British Journal for the Philosophy of Science*, **17**, 322.

Goodman, N. (1955). *Fact, Fiction and Forecast*, 3rd edn. (1973). Indianapolis: The Bobbs–Merrill Company, Inc.

Hacking, I. (1967). Slightly more realistic personal probability. *Philosophy of Science*, **34**, 311–25.

Hempel, C. G. (1945). Studies in the logic of confirmation. In his *Aspects of Scientific Explanation and other Essays in the Philosophy of Science*, pp. 3–46. (1965). New York: The Free Press.

Hempel, C. G. (1960). Inductive inconsistencies. In his *Aspects of Scientific Explanation and other Essays in the Philosophy of Science*, pp. 53–79. (1965). New York: The Free Press.

Hesse, M. (1974). *The Structure of Scientific Inference*. Berkeley: University of California Press.

Hosiasson-Lindenbaum, J. (1940). On confirmation. *Journal of Symbolic Logic*, **5**, 133–48.

Jackson, F. & Pargetter, R. (1976). A modified Dutch book argument. *Philosophical Studies*, **29**, 403–7.

Jamison, D. (1970). Bayesian information usage. In *Information and Inference*, ed. J. Hintikka & P. Suppes, pp. 28–57. Dordrecht: D. Reidel Publishing Company.

Jaynes, E. T. (1958). *Probability Theory in Science and Engineering*, Colloquium Lectures in Pure and Applied Science, no. 4, Field Research Laboratory, Socony Mobil Oil, Dallas. (Lecture 5, The A_p distribution, pp. 152–87.)

Jeffrey, R. C. (1956). Valuation and acceptance of scientific hypotheses. *Philosophy of Science*, **23**, 237–46.

Jeffrey, R. C. (1965a). Ethics and the logic of decision. *The Journal of Philosophy*, **62**, 528–39.

Jeffrey, R. C. (1965b). *The Logic of Decision*. New York: McGraw-Hill Book Company.

Jeffrey, R. C. (1974). Preferences among preferences. *The Journal of Philosophy*, **71**, 377–91.

Jeffrey, R. C. (1977). Savage's omelet. In *PSA 1976*, ed. F. Suppe & P. D. Asquith, vol. 2, pp. 361–71. East Lansing. Philosophy of Science Association.

Jeffrey, R. C. (1978). Axiomatizing the logic of decision. In *Foundations and Applications of Decision Theory*, vol. 1, ed. C. A. Hooker, J. J. Leach and E. F. McClennen, pp. 227–31. Dordrecht: D. Reidel Publishing Company.

Jeffrey, R. C. (1981a). Choice, chance and credence. In *Philosophy of Language/Philosophical Logic*, ed. G. H. von Wright & F. Fløustad, pp. 367–86. The Hague: Nijhoff.

Jeffrey, R. C. (1981b). The logic of decision defended. *Synthese*, **48**, 473–92.

Kahneman, D. & Tversky, A. (1972). Subjective probability: a judgment of representativeness. *Cognitive Psychology*, **3**, 430–54.

Kahneman, D. & Tversky, A. (1973). On the psychology of prediction, *The Psychological Review*, **80**, 237–51.

Kennedy, R. & Chihara, C. (1979). The Dutch book argument: its logical flaws, its subjective sources. *Philosophical Studies*, **36**, 19–33.

Krantz, D. H., Luce, R. D., Suppes, P. & Tversky, A. (1971). *Foundations of Measurement*, vol. 1. New York: Academic Press.

Kyburg, H. (1978). Subjective probability: criticisms, reflections, and problems. *Journal of Philosophical Logic*, **7**, 157–80.

Leibniz, G. W. (1765). *New Essays Concerning Human Understanding*, trans. A. G. Langley, 3rd. edn. (1949). La Salle, Illinois: The Open Court Publishing Company.

Levi, I. (1961). Decision theory and confirmation. *The Journal of Philosophy*, **58**, 614–25.

Lewis, D. (1979). Prisoners' Dilemma is a Newcomb problem. *Philosophy & Public Affairs*, **8**, 235–40.

Lewis, D. (1981). Causal decision theory. *Australasian Journal of Philosophy*, **59**, 5–30.

Luce, R. D. & Krantz, D. H. (1971). Conditional expected utility. *Econometrica*, **39**, 253–71.

MacCrimmon, K. R. (1968). Descriptive and normative implications of the decision-theory postulates. In *Risk and Uncertainty*, ed. K. Borch & J. Mossin, pp. 3–23. New York: Saint Martin's Press.

Mackie, J. L. (1963). The paradox of confirmation. *The British Journal for the Philosophy of Science*, **13**, 265–77.

Mellor, D. H. (1971). *The Matter of Chance*. Cambridge University Press.

Mellor, D. H. (1978). Conscious belief. *Proceedings of the Aristotelian Society*, **78**, 87–101.

Mellor, D. H. (1980). Consciousness and degrees of belief. In *Prospects for Pragmatism: Essays in Honor of F. P. Ramsey*, ed. D. H. Mellor, pp. 139–73. Cambridge: Cambridge University Press.

Miller, D. (1966). A paradox of information. *The British Journal for the Philosophy of Science*, **17**, 59–61.

Morrison, D. G. (1967). On the consistency of preferences in Allais' paradox. *Behavioral Science*, **12**, 373–83.

Nozick, R. (1969). Newcomb's problem and two principles of choice. In *Essays in Honor of Carl G. Hempel*, ed. N. Rescher, *et al*, pp. 114–46. Dordrecht: D. Reidel Publishing Company.

Pears, D. (1950). Hypotheticals. *Analysis*, **10**, 49–63.

Pfanzagl, J. (1968). *Theory of Measurement*. New York: John Wiley & Sons, Inc.

Quine, W. V. (1969). Natural kinds. In his *Ontological Relativity and Other Essays*, pp. 114–38. New York: Columbia University Press.

Raiffa, H. (1961). Risk, ambiguity and the Savage axioms: comment. *The Quarterly Journal of Economics*, **75**, 690–4.

Ramsey, F. P. (1926). Truth and probability. In his *The Foundations of Mathematics and other Logical Essays*, ed. R. B. Braithwaite, pp. 156–98. (1931). London: Routledge and Kegan Paul. Republished in his *Foundations*, ed. D. H. Mellor, pp. 58–100. (1978). London: Routledge and Kegan Paul. Also in *Studies in Subjective Probability*, ed. H. E. Kyburg & H. E. Smokler, pp. 61–92. (1964). New York: John Wiley & Sons, Inc.

Rapoport, A. & Wallsten, T. S. (1972). Individual decision behavior. *Annual Review of Psychology*, **23**, 131–76.

Rawls, J. (1971). *A Theory of Justice*. Cambridge, Massachusetts: The Belknap Press of Harvard University Press.

Rosenkrantz, R. D. (1976). Simplicity. In *Foundations of Probability Theory, Statistical Inference, and Statistical Theories of Science*, ed. W. L. Harper & C. A. Hooker, vol. 1, pp. 167–203. Dordrecht: D. Reidel Publishing Company.

Rudner, R. (1953). The scientist *qua* scientist makes value judgments. *Philosophy of Science*, **20**, 1–6.

Savage, L. J. (1954). *The Foundations of Statistics*, 2nd edn., 1972, New York: Dover Publications, Inc.

Savage, L. J. (1967). Difficulties in the theory of personal probability. *Philosophy of Science*, **34**, 305–10.

Scheffler, I. (1963). *The Anatomy of Inquiry*, Indianapolis: The Bobbs–Merrill Company, Inc.

Schlesinger, G. (1974). The unpredictability of free choices. *The British Journal for the Philosophy of Science*, **25**, 209–21.

Skyrms, B. (1980a). *Causal Necessity: A Pragmatic Investigation of the Necessity of Laws.* New Haven: Yale University Press.

Skyrms, B. (1980b). Higher order degrees of belief. In *Prospects for Pragmatism: Essays in Honor of F. P. Ramsey*, ed. D. H. Mellor, pp. 109–37. Cambridge: Cambridge University Press.

Slovic, P., Fischhoff, B. & Lichtenstein, S. (1977). Behavioral decision theory. *Annual Review of Psychology*, **28**, 1–39.

Slovic, P. & Lichtenstein, S. (1971). Comparison of Bayesian and regression approaches to the study of information processing in judgment. *Organizational Behavior and Human Performance*, **6**, 649–744.

Slovic, P. & Tversky, A. (1974). Who accepts Savage's axiom? *Behavioral Science*, **19**, 368–73.

Suppes, P. (1956). The role of subjective probability and utility in decision-making. In *Proceedings of the Third Berkeley Symposium on Mathematical Statistics and Probability*, vol. 5, ed. J. Neyman, pp. 61–73. Berkeley: University of California Press.

Suppes, P. (1960). Some open problems in the foundations of subjective probability. In *Information and Decision Processes*, ed. R. E. Machol, pp. 162–9. New York: McGraw-Hill Book Company.

Suppes, P. (1961). The philosophical relevance of decision theory. *The Journal of Philosophy*, **58**, 605–14.

Suppes, P. (1966). A Bayesian approach to the paradoxes of confirmation. In *Aspects of Inductive Logic*, ed. J. Hintikka & P. Suppes, pp. 198–207. Amsterdam: North Holland Publishing Company.

Swinburne, R. (1973). *An Introduction to Confirmation Theory.* London:Methuen.

Teller, P. (1976). Conditionalization, observation and change of preference. In *Foundations of Probability Theory, Statistical Inference, and Statistical Theories of Science*, vol. 1, ed. W. L. Harper and C. A. Hooker, 205–59. Dordrecht: D. Reidel Publishing Company.

Tversky, A. (1967a). Additivity, utility and subjective probability. *Journal of Mathematical Psychology*, **4**, 75–201.

Tversky, A. (1967b). Utility theory and additivity analysis of risky choices. *Journal of Experimental Psychology*, **75**, 27–36.

Tversky, A. (1969). Intransitivity of preferences. *The Psychological Review*, **76**, 31–48.

Tversky, A. & Kahneman, D. (1971). Belief in the law of small numbers. *Psychological Bulletin*, **76**, 105–10.

Tversky, A. & Kahneman, D. (1973). Availability: a heuristic for judging frequency and probability. *Cognitive Psychology*, **5**, 207–32.

Tversky, A. & Kahneman, D. (1974). Judgment under uncertainty: heuristics and biases. *Science*, **185**, 1124–31.

Tversky, A. & Kahneman, D. (1981). The framing of decisions and the psychology of choice. *Science*, **211**, 453–8.

Von Neumann, J. & Morgenstern, O. (1947). *Theory of Games and Economic Behavior*, 2nd edn., Princeton: Princeton University Press.

Index

representation theorems, 9–11, 25, 41, 81–2, 106, 134, 148
representativeness, heuristic of, 22
resiliency, 174, 199
  defined, 179
  of a conditional probability, 192; defined, 181
  see also currency
risk, *vs* uncertainty, 35, 39
ROC, see conditionalization, rule of
Rosenkrantz, R. D., 5, 7, 49, 60, 64, 74, 82
Rubin, J., 39
Rudner, R., 27ff

SA, see act, symptomatic
Savage, L. J., 9–11, 31–2, 34–5, 37–8, 51–2, 65, 71ff, 82ff, 95–7, 107, 111, 117, 144, 146, 159
Scheffler, I., 61
Schlesinger, G., 207, 209
screen off, explained, 223
sentential connective, explained, 219
SEU, see subjective expected utility
SEV, 31
Skyrms, B., 21, 32, 46, 64, 89–92, 94–5, 100, 103, 105ff, 134ff, 146ff, 159, 164, 170–4, 177–9, 188
Slovic, P., 21, 34–5, 37
SO, see outcome, symptomatic
Sobel, J. H., 95
special consequence condition, 55–8, 60
state, 6–8, 71ff, 79, 84–5, 175, 193ff
  -proposition, 79, 175
  see also factor
statistical correlation (relevance), explained, 223
statistical independence, explained, 223
structural axioms, *see* nonnecessary axioms

subjective common cause principle, 122, 128, 195–6, 211
subjective expected utility (*and* maximization theory (*SEU* theory))
  and acceptance, 25ff
  and moral deliberation, 29ff
  SEU and theory explained, 6–10, 65–86
  theory as descriptive, 14–15, 24, 33ff
  theory as explanatory, 24–5, 41ff
  theory as normative, prescriptive, 24ff, 36ff
Suppes, P., 31, 36, 53, 61, 77, 83, 85
sure-thing principle, 10, 34ff
swamp, 93–4
Swinburne, R., 61

tautology, explained, 220
Teller, P., 15–21
transivity paradox, 56–8
truth-functional combination (compound), explained, 219
truth-functional connective, explained, 219
Tversky, A., 21–3, 34–7, 39–40, 77, 85

U-expectation (and the principle of maximizing (*PMUE*)), 95ff, 108–9, 134, 142ff, 146ff, 155–6, 215
  defined, 95
  principle stated, 96
uncertainty, *vs* risk, 35, 39
utility, 6; *see also* desirability

Von Neumann, J., 78, 85

Wallsten, T. S., 21